GUY HARVEY'S UNDERWATER WORLD

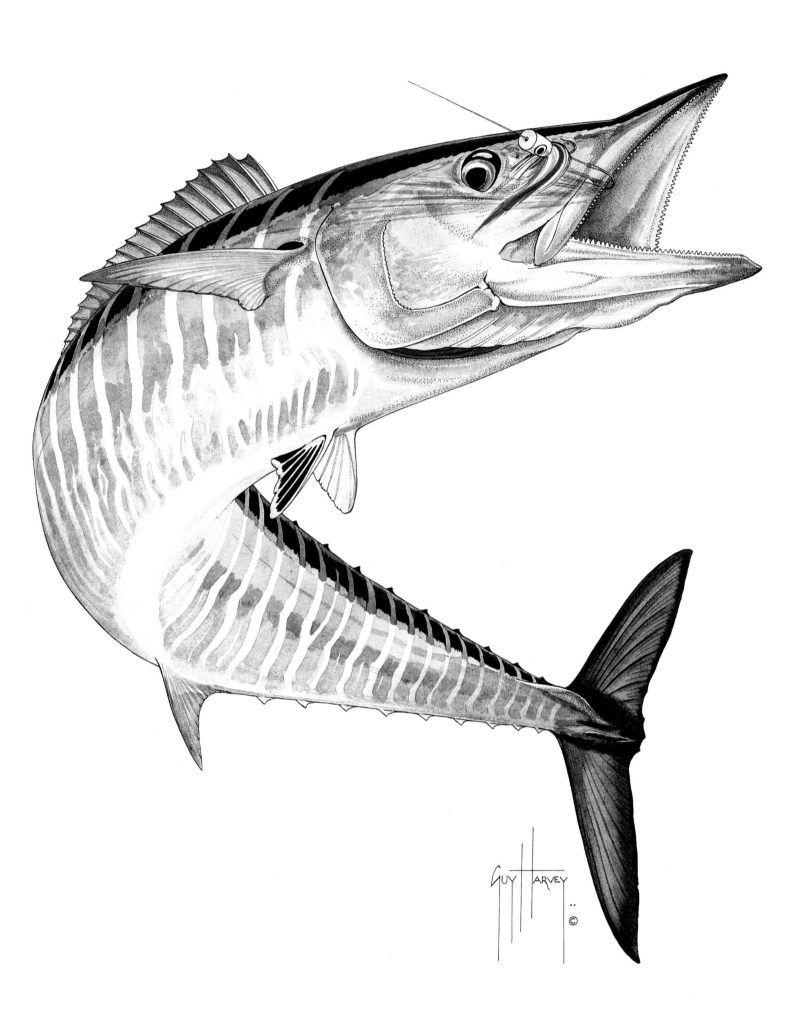

GUY HARVEY'S UNDERWATER WORLD

By Guy Harvey

Stackpole
Books

Guilford, Connecticut

Published by Stackpole Books
An imprint of The Rowman & Littlefield Publishing Group Inc.
4501 Forbes Blvd., Ste. 200
Lanham, MD 20706
www.rowman.com

Distributed by NATIONAL BOOK NETWORK

Edited by Shawn Bean and Sam White
Design by David Weaver
Art by Guy Harvey
All photos by Guy Harvey unless otherwise credited

British Library Cataloguing-in-Publication information available

Library of Congress Cataloging in Publication data available

ISBN 978-0-8117-6990-7 (cloth : alk. paper)
ISBN 978-0-8117-6991-4 (electronic)

♾™ The paper used in this publication meets the minimum requirements of American National Standard for Information Sciences—Permanence of Paper for Printed Library Materials, ANSI/ NISO Z39.48-1992.

"We can restore the life and habitats of the sea because it is in everyone's interest that we do so. The large-scale networks of marine reserves, complemented by other measures of fish and habitat protection, best serve interests of both commerce and conservation. You can have exploitation with protection, because reserves help sustain catches in surrounding fishing grounds. But you cannot have exploitation without protection, not in the long term."

—Callum Roberts

My life and work are dedicated to Gillian, Jessica and Alexander, who have tolerated my infatuation with the sea and its creatures, and have withstood the ordeals of long periods of separation.

ACKNOWLEDGMENTS

MANY PEOPLE HAVE BEEN influential, helpful, and supportive over my many years of business, art shows, research, and expeditions. The greatest support has come from my family, Gillian, Jessica, Alexander, and now Julia and granddaughter Harper. This book is dedicated to them.

Gillian has been the rock on which I have been able to keep the brand going through good times and bad over the past 35 years. Jessica has been project manager with the Guy Harvey Ocean Foundation, working tirelessly, particularly in the arena of education, and is now hosting documentaries and short lectures under the banner of Jessica Harvey's Expedition Notebook. Alexander has, in the past four years, climbed the ladder at Guy Harvey Incorporated, with a focus on marketing and social media.

My younger brother, Piers, and his wife, Connie, have been supportive through the decades, particularly during the recent transition period in changing licensees and with personnel changes in the parent company, GHI. They also left Jamaica in 2005 and now live in Kentucky.

The expeditions, research, education and conservation could not be done without having a successful business backing these projects. In my case, that business model is based on licensing my original art, which has worked well, particularly in apparel. The administration of all this takes a team, which is currently led by CEO Steve Roden, with Jane Tebbe-Shemelya and Harvey Taulien working on licensees and personnel. Michele Grey has administered art sales for nearly 30 years. Dave Chafin, the road warrior, over many years has covered hundreds of events with the Guy Harvey mobile store at NASCAR races, concerts, tournaments, boat shows and seafood festivals in many states. Fred Garth has been the editor of *Guy Harvey Magazine* for eight years and is also working on our educational projects these days.

Several graphic artists have come and gone, all of whom have had a positive influence, particularly Todd Dawes and Alexandra Lytle. Currently in the stable we have Michele Dammyer and Lea Vizzone, under Alexander Harvey's artistic eye. Debbie Childers has been our bookkeeper for several years, and Mireya Villegas handles customer service and our showroom. Greg Jacoski has been the executive director for the GHOF for five years. Jay Perez and Patrick Bailey were with the company for a long time and had a positive impact on growing licenses and art sales, as well as mentoring Alex as he started his career at GHI four years ago. Anthony (Tony) Fins brought a refreshing journalistic perspective to the GHOF for a year, and I wish he had stayed longer.

The AFTCO Bluewater apparel license was a major part of our business for nearly two decades. Bill Shedd and his family did a wonderful job over many years, particularly from 2004 to 2014. His children, sons Cody and Casey and daughter Christie, also worked in the family business as they came of age. Beginning with Anne Holms in the creative section, the art department grew as business grew. Simon Purll and Dino Sakelliou became the graphic designers, with whom we worked closely. Over this time there were several managers for the brand, including Dick Nagle, Jim Knapp and Casey Shedd. They were backed up by a solid reps group, including Jim Whitten and his wife, Sue, with whom we worked going back to the T-Shirts of Florida days. The AFTCO fishing hardware division was run by Greg Stotesbury, an angler extraordinaire in his own right, with whom I swapped many fishing stories.

We did countless appearances and visited many independent accounts as well as big-box stores from the Gulf Coast all the way through the mid-Atlantic states over the decades. Texas and the Carolinas were and still are big supporters of the brand. Stack Bell was another superb rep in the Carolinas. One of the best accounts we have is the Palmetto Moon group of stores located throughout South Carolina, owned then by Bob and Karen Webster, with Eric Holzer, husband to their daughter, Whitney, running the show. They run a very good operation and embraced the brand; I went to all of their stores on many occasions throughout the state. Nowadays they have expanded into North Carolina and Georgia.

Moving farther north, Dick and Bobby Weber invited us to participate in the annual MidAtlantic $500,000 fishing tournament. This is held in mid-August in beautiful Cape May, New Jersey, each year from its inception, for 20 consecutive years, 1992-2012. We hosted an art show in the tournament tent and provided the event art for shirts and limited-edition prints, which were collected by anglers and participants. During that time, we built an extensive clientele in the Northeast through the generosity of Dick and his son, Rick. When the tournament expanded to also include Ocean City, Maryland, we set up art shows there as well.

During the AFTCO era, Bill Shedd was very supportive of the GHOF's work as well as the TV series, *Portraits from the Deep*, filmed and produced by the *Sport Fishing* magazine TV crew, with producer Ken "Kendog" Kavanaugh and two very capable camera guys, Ricky Westphal and Dee Gele. There were lots of laughs and very few screw-ups in the 58 episodes we filmed together, many of which are described in this book.

Over all this time, we have worked with a number of conservation organizations, all of whom do great work in many countries. Some of these include the Bahamas National Trust (Eric Carey), The Billfish Foundation (Ellen Peel), the Nature Conservancy, Pew Charitable Trust (Matt Rand), the Center for Sportfishing Policy (Jeff Angers), the Ocean Conservancy, the Coastal Conservation Association, United Anglers of Southern California, Oceana, the Sandals Foundation, Mission Resolve, Shark Allies (Stefanie Brendl) and Reef Environmental Education Foundation.

The next chapter on the business front started recently in 2019, with Miami-based company Intradeco taking on the apparel license, under Felix Siman's firm hand. We expect to make rapid progress following the delayed start caused by the 2020 coronavirus pandemic. Intradeco is a vertically integrated company with great production capability.

The Guy Harvey Research Institute team, led by Dr. Mahmood Shivji, has been operating for 21 years, has published 135 peer-reviewed papers and is going strong. Many of the chapters of the book recount the fieldwork undertaken by Brad Wetherbee, Jeremy Vaudo, Derek Burkholder and numerous postgraduate students who have

been through our doors. Dean Richard Dodge has been at the helm of the Oceanographic Center ever since we started working with Nova Southeastern University, then under President Ray Ferraro. Currently, President George Hanbury II continues to support the work of the GHRI, and NSU is a co-sponsor of the Eastern Pacific Seascape Research Project based out of Tropic Star Lodge in Panama.

We have had a capable board for the GHOF for many years. Leading the pack are Rich Andrews and Rich Davies, who are keen anglers and have been extremely supportive of various research projects, including the Panama Project. Jeff Harkavy, Paul Castronovo, Chris Peterson, Dean Klevan, Rick Murphy, Jim Jacoby, Bob Osborne and our late co-chairman, Jim Harvey, have all been major players over a long time. Steve Roden is the new co-chairman, joined by additional board members Rob Kornahrens, George Schellenger and Jessica Harvey.

We have been ably assisted by our lobbyist, Fred Dickinson, and his team at Poole McKinley in Tallahassee, Florida. We required his input with a number of projects, including working with the Florida Lottery, the state's specialty license plates, marine-education courses for schools and new legislation to ban the trade in shark fins in the state of Florida.

Other major supporters of the GHOF have been extremely generous in their long-term support, particularly Dave and Cheryl Copham, who support the Panama Project, and Nancy Binz, who is supporting our work in the Cayman Islands and the shark genomic work being conducted by Dr. Mahmood Shivji. Jim and Connie Elek, from New Jersey, have been big supporters of the GHOF and collect my artwork; we have had the pleasure of fishing in Panama and Costa Rica together. Ron Bergeron and his family in Florida have been supportive of the GHOF, and Ron has hosted us several times at his beautiful ranch in the Everglades.

The Cayman GHOF "branch" has accomplished a lot in a short time under Jessica Harvey and Louisa Sax. Living in the Cayman Islands, we have conducted a number of research and education projects that are relevant to the conservation of marine resources, as you will read in the chapters on the Cayman Islands. The Grouper Moon Project is one of the most gratifying projects with which we have been involved. Dr. Brice Semmens and his wife, Dr. Christie Semmens, as well as a host of volunteers listed in the Little Cayman chapter, have embraced our participation in this project, for which we are grateful. My thanks go to the Cayman Islands' Department of Environment and director Gina Ebanks-Petrie and her staff for the leadership shown in driving marine conservation in these small, delicate islands.

My special thanks go out to all the dozens of volunteers who have assisted with fishing, shark tagging, diving and stingray surveys, particularly Dr. Ioana Popescu and Pete Foster-Smith of Epic Divers. A number of people and companies have supported the research and education projects in the Cayman Islands. These include the Cayman Islands Brewery (James Mansfield), Kirk Freeport (Chris and Daniel Kirkconnell, Tom Guyton), the Kenneth B. Dart Foundation (Chris Duggan), HSBC, Sunset Divers (Adrien Briggs), Cayman Aggressor (Wayne Hasson), George Town Yacht Club (Neville Scott), Cayman Islands Angling Club (Frank Thompson), Harbour House Marina (Chris Briggs, Mark Rickman, Jonathan Cuff), Hurley's Media (Randy Merrin), Luca restaurant (Andi and Tash Marcher), Captain Asley's Watersports (Capt. Derrin Ebanks), and several generous individuals: Martin and Penny Lancaster, Bart and Julia Hedges, Paula and Andrew McCartney, Attlee and Patti Bodden, David and Andie Likrish, David and Karen Towriss, Charlie and Lori Adams, and particular thanks to Mark and Jacqueline Hennings and their daughter, Samantha, who always made time and their boat available to assist.

Our first documentary on stingrays, *The Stingray Chronicles*, was filmed and produced by Diana Udel's company, Broadcast Quality, in Coral Gables, Florida. Our next production in 2000 was the documentary *Billfish: Nomads of the Ocean*. This was followed by a miniseries, *Guy Harvey's Underwater Realm*, featuring episodes on striped marlin, sailfish, sharks, bluefin tuna and whale sharks that were filmed in Mexico, the Bahamas, Guatemala, Panama, Spain, Costa Rica, Puerto Rico and the US.

George Schellenger, of Status Productions, has been part of the team since shooting our first documentary together in 2010, *This Is Your Ocean: Sharks*. George has become an expert angler after being on so many tagging expeditions in the Caribbean and Central America. George has done great work for both GHI and GHOF, having filmed and

Bill Boyce

produced 20 long-form documentaries, many short-form pieces, PSAs, advertisements, time lapses and photos that have documented the brand for the past 10 years. An excellent script writer, narrator and producer, George has increased the visibility of the brand through compelling content and made relevant the research efforts by the GHRI and through the GHOF's marine education and conservation projects.

Wyland

Bill Boyce has accompanied me on many expeditions since the late 1990s. Several expeditions since 2002 are included in this book. Bill is an amazing diver, photographer, angler and journalist. We are always glad to have Bill out with us fishing and diving. One of our best expeditions was filming striped marlin at Magdalena Bay, Mexico, in 1998 with Kent Ullberg, where we were covered up in the water with schools of striped marlin feeding on sardines for four consecutive days. That same year we covered the Cape Verde islands, the Azores, Venezuela and Panama, and I never heard him tell the same joke twice. Many of Bill's great photos are included in this book. Bill also very kindly wrote the foreword.

Diving with sharks guided by Jim Abernethy is one of the greatest underwater experiences any diver can have. Jim's knowledge of the species is unmatched, and he is one of the best of many great underwater photographers. His leadership in marine conservation, particularly of sharks, is exemplary.

Kent Ullberg is America's most famous wildlife sculptor and has been a mentor since we first met in 1987. He was in Fort Lauderdale when he installed his largest public sculpture at the Broward County Convention Center. Kent then did the 24-foot-high swordfish in stainless steel at the International Game Fish Association's headquarters in Dania, Florida, followed by the large mako shark in bronze at NSU's University Center in Davie, Florida. Since then we have held many joint exhibitions at shows and tournaments, as well as annual traveling exhibitions hosted by the Society of Animal Artists, including "The Art of the Dive" at Miami Metro Zoo and the South Texas Museum of Art. We had a joint show at the Blauvelt Museum of Wildlife Art in Oradell, New Jersey, in March 2014. Kent has been on many research, filming, and diving expeditions with us to Australia, Panama, Mexico, Cocos Island in Costa Rica, and to Tiger Beach in the Bahamas.

Jeff Whiting is the president and CEO of Canada-based wildlife artists group Artists For Conservation. Many AFC members are also members of the SAA. There are some 500 international artists from around the world who participate in the AFC's annual shows. In 2011 we showed *This Is Your Ocean: Sharks* to Canadian audiences through the AFC annual event at Grouse Mountain in North Vancouver. We have participated in traveling exhibitions for many years and have hosted two of the AFC field trips to the Cayman Islands, with several members participating.

I have painted five large murals with Wyland, all of them in Florida. Whenever Wyland needs help with mural, he will call me. His large public murals are very beautiful and effective messaging tools for marine conservation. But my largest piece of public art is on the hull of Norwegian Cruise Lines' *Norwegian Escape*, built in 2015. I was deeply honored when I was asked to be the hull artist for such a reputable cruise-ship company. The people who made this happen were President Frank del Rio, CEO Andy Stuart, SVP Bob Becker and Simon Murray, VP Guest Experiences and Innovation. We worked closely with other senior staff—Karina Parreno, director of brand partnerships, Sarah Brown of environmental operations, and Morgan McCall of compliance and sustainability—during the annual Conservation Cruises. In 2017, Wyland was asked to be the hull artist for *Norwegian Bliss,* which featured his iconic whales and other marine mammals. Thanks, NCL, for keeping it in the family.

As a consequence of having the art on the hull of a Norwegian ship, there was an opportunity through Park West to have my art available in the art gallery on *Norwegian Escape* and on other cruise ships around the world. Albert Scaglione is the owner of Park West and turned his father's framing business into the world's largest art dealership. I am appreciative of the opportunity and for their continued support of the conservation efforts of the GHOF.

I was sitting on the patio at Tropic Star Lodge in January 1993 after a day of fishing when I was advised that I had been elected to the board of trustees of the International Game Fish Association. I had been a representative of the IGFA for Jamaica since 1986, and had been active in gamefish conservation from long before that. Over the past 28 years, I have served on the board under several chairmen. One of the best was George Matthews, who was actually chairman twice. I worked closely with President Mike Leech for many years, and then with Rob Kramer. Mike was keen to promote my art through the IGFA catalogs and gave me a great start in my art career. I was asked many years ago to design a new logo for the IGFA. The first logo by Lynn Bogue Hunt featured a swordfish and baitfish. Mike and the board wanted more species included to better represent the worldly nature of our constituents, so I made a blue marlin, mako shark, yellowfin tuna, tarpon, bass and rainbow trout collage; I considered these six cosmopolitan species did that job well.

I've met many famous anglers from all over the world through the IGFA, which was a great honor. Jack Anderson (vice chairman) was one of the early big-game pioneers who became a good friend and source of vintage fishing stories.

Acknowledgments

I maintained good relationships with many other trustees, including Maumus Claverie from New Orleans, Curt Gowdy from Florida, Peter Fithian from Hawaii, Ruben Jaen from Venezuela, Carlos Pellas from Nicaragua, Jose "Pepe" Anton from Ecuador, Jonno Johnston and Neil Patrick from Australia, and Jose Luis Beistegui from Spain.

Of all of these, Pierre Clostermann from France was the greatest. As a teenager, I read two books frequently: *The Old Man and the Sea* by Ernest Hemingway (a founding VP of the IGFA) and *The Big Show* by Clostermann. Pierre flew Spitfires for the Royal Air Force in World War II and quickly became an ace. He wrote the best war story ever. He was my hero. After the war he came a politician, a statesman and an author, as well as being an accomplished artist. Then many years later, I discovered he loved fishing and was on the IGFA board of trustees. I first met Pierre in 1986 at an IGFA auction event, and then we spent time together at the International Billfish Symposium in Hawaii in 1988. He asked me to do some artwork for his next books on fishing, which I was so proud to do. We fished with Stewart Campbell in Madeira in 1995 and kept in contact after that, until he passed away in 2006. I still have his photo on my "fish wall" just a few feet from where I paint.

Some of the other influential people I met through the IGFA include Johnny Morris of Bass Pro Shops, the late Paxson Offield, and the late Don Tyson, who sponsored the IGFA headquarters building in Dania. Eventually the IGFA Fishing Hall of Fame was relocated from Dania to Springfield, Missouri, by Morris. However, the IGFA's administrative personnel and the wonderful Elwood K. Harry Library remain in Dania. The library is one of the greatest treasures that the IGFA holds. I was fortunate to have access to this while Gail Morchower was the curator as I conducted research about the history of Tropic Star Lodge for *Panama Paradise* in 2009.

Tim Choate was one of the original founders of The Billfish Foundation in 1986 and has sponsored many billfish-conservation organizations since then, such as the National Coalition for Marine Conservation, now called Wild Oceans, and the Central American Billfish Association. In addition, Tim worked with Dr. Nelson Ehrhardt at the University of Miami for many years, sponsoring billfish research and socioeconomic studies in Central America. Tim had worked for years with many governments in Central America to curb the export of billfish, but none would agree to take this action. He then approached the problem from the consumption end, to ban importation into the US. In 2010, the act was first introduced to Congress, and was passed by both the House and the Senate in September 2012. Tim is on the IGFA board of trustees and was the main sponsor of the Billfish Conservation Act that was signed into law in 2018. This law prevents the importation of billfish into the US, reducing the incentive for billfish to be harvested in many developing countries.

Just as important as the trustees and staff are the captains and mates who have put their anglers on many great fish over many decades. Many of these people are now recognized as Legendary Captains and Mates in the IGFA Fishing Hall of Fame, organized by Frank "Skip" Smith and his team in 2011. We have fished with many of these, all listed in *Portraits from the Deep* in 2002. Since then we have fished with fewer captains, but more often, usually in one location. My most sincere appreciation and thanks go to the following captains: the late Vernon "OB" O'Bryan and Anthony Mendillo in Isla Mujeres, Mexico; in Costa Rica, Frank "Skip" Smith; in Australia, Laurie Wright and Dennis "Brazakka" Wallace; in Alaska, Travis Peterson; in British Columbia, Gill McKean; in Nova Scotia, Eric Jacquard, Brad Simmons and Anthony Mendillo; in Bermuda, James Robinson and Allen De Silva. In Panama, with Tropic Star Lodge, we fished the last 20 of my 29 years there with captains Alberto Alvarez, Epifanio Candelo, Yunier "Flaco" Palacios, Gilberto "Pucaro" Seciada and Dagoberto Arango, and I have spent a lot of time recently with Jose Mosquera and Obdulio "Gavilan" Cordoba. All the captains and mates are just awesome fishermen, and we get a chance to fish with them all during the annual *torneo*.

On the subject of Panama, I thank Terri and Mike Andrews and their son, Zane, for all the years of amazing experiences we have had fishing out of Tropic Star Lodge. Many of the great experiences from 1991 to 2009 are told in *Panama Paradise*. Since then we have returned with film crews, with other friends and guests, and best of all, with family. The staff at TSL is just as awesome as the crews. Albert Battoo was the fishing director from 2008 to 2016 and was followed by Richard White, who is there now as resident manager of the lodge with his wife, Mallory, and their young son, Logan. The guest-relations team has included stars such as Catherine "Queena" Wilder, Adrienne Reeve and, more recently, Kyla Lunt. Many of the bar staff and kitchen staff at the lodge have been there for 30 or more years. Edgardo Patterson is still the maître d' and continues to do an amazing job, but he has yet to beat me at pingpong. Keishmer Hermoso, the superb resident photojournalist, has become an integral part of the Tropic Star team.

Ursula Marais is the general manager for the Tropic Star group of companies, with new owner Carlos de Obaldia. They are supportive of the GHOF-NSU partnership in its five-year research project.

As you will discover, many of the expeditions were focused on research work. We have collaborated with a number of prominent scientists over a long period of time, most of whom played an important role in our collective understanding of many species. Recently we have had the pleasure of working with Rafael de la Parra in the Yucatan. Rafael has assisted us with all the permits necessary to tag sailfish, mako sharks and white marlin, and now Rafael is leading the tracking study on whale sharks. Michael Domeier has been working on white sharks for many years, as well as striped marlin and black marlin. We have been fortunate to accompany Michael on several of his expeditions. We have worked with Dr. Molly Lutcavage and Barbara Block on bluefin tuna in Nova Scotia and in North Carolina.

Dr. John Graves of the Virginia Institute of Marine Science and I go as far back as the Jamaican tournaments in 1988, collecting blue marlin data. We have worked with Julian Pepperell and Eric Prince (now retired) on billfish tracking, and collaborated with a number of shark researchers, including Neil Hammerschlag (University of Miami) and Robert Hueter (Mote Marine). On the Dolphin (dorado, mahimahi) Research Project, we are working with Wessley Merten in the Caribbean, as well as out of Tropic Star Lodge on Pacific dorado migrations. We have worked with the veterinarian team from the Georgia Aquarium for several years on the stingray population in Grand Cayman. The scientists and film crews at SeaWorld have been great partners in our mako shark research project, as well as with the ongoing stingray surveys in Grand Cayman, where veterinarian Dr. Dominique Keller gave us much-needed assistance.

There are a number of friends who have organized diving and fishing expeditions in various locations about which you will read. The three amigos are brothers Jimmy and Steve Valletta along with Bill Watts, all of whom have fished and dived with us in the Galapagos Islands, Cocos Island, Guadalupe (Mexico), Turks and Caicos, Venezuela, Panama, the Bahamas and the Cayman Islands. They are great anglers, divers, photographers and friends, and are good to have on your team anywhere; they contributed some of the photographs in this book.

A big thank you to Shawn Bean and Sam White for taking on the task of editing this manuscript, and the production team of Dave Weaver (design), Cindy Elavsky (copy editing) and Don Hill (imaging).

Tight lines.

CONTENTS

FOREWORD

By Bill Boyce

IN THE WORLD OF WILDLIFE art, many forms are used to pursue and present inspirational pieces to the imagination of the viewer. The goal of these works is not only to capture the hearts and minds of those who admire, but to compel the spectator to leave their seats and mentally immerse themselves into the field of action. No matter the art format—be it high-quality video and photography, the brilliant colors of a painting, or the fine lines of a detailed sketch—few artists in the world can convey such imagery more intimately than Guy Harvey.

Above and beyond his amazing ability to capture artistic subject matter in any variety of these mediums, it's Guy's ability to walk the walk and talk the talk in all economic, scientific and political circles that places Guy Harvey in a league of his own. He is a gifted communicator who leverages his influence to make measurable differences in a world where such progress happens slowly, in increments that often appear insignificant. Without powerful visions and voices such as Guy's, progress in fisheries conservation might never be attained at all.

In every form of Guy's art comes a level of passion that can be invoked only from infancy, in a family upbringing that promotes its germination. Guy was raised in such a family in Jamaica, where fishing, diving and exploring the ocean around them was prioritized in unity. From this childhood, the Harvey tradition has been righteously passed to his own prodigy, and as a longtime friend, I've been honored to witness these seeds of his children, Jessica and Alex, grow from sprouts to blooming foliage.

I met Guy in Kona, Hawaii, as featured artists in the prestigious HIBT tournament back in 1994. From the moment of introduction, our intense interest in the marine-science world took us from mutual respect to, now, a moment of mutual reflect. We traveled the world for the next many years as brethren—filming, photographing and sharing the most amazing oceanic experiences a human could seek. And with these adventures, our friendship transformed into kinship. I felt more as family than mere friend, and I grew to understand what truly makes Guy Harvey the institution he has become.

In this book, Guy captures nearly 20 years' worth of memories, scientific exploits and accomplishments—a lifetime of achievement. But more than that, he captures the magic that ties them all together. People. Friends. Colleagues. Family. From the vast international locations he has explored, to the characters he worked with, to the epic results his art has achieved in sharing these moments with his admirers, Guy gives us all the most intimate accounts of these travels, and within them, hope to inspire others to follow in his footsteps. To have played a small part in these stories gives me great pleasure to relive them for the rest of my life through Guy's words, images and my own innermost thoughts. For this I am forever indebted; and for those who take the time to enjoy this book, may you all walk away with a deeper sense of appreciation for a life well-served.

Cheers, Guy.

Working on a watercolor in
my first Cayman studio.

INTRODUCTION

SO MUCH HAS TRANSPIRED since 2002 when I wrote *Portraits from the Deep*, a deeply personal and auto-biographical account of my early professional endeavors, which were rooted in a childhood spent in Jamaica under the guiding hands of loving parents who gave me an appreciation for nature and encouraged my artistic interests. Those parents provided a balanced childhood, challenging educational opportunities, experiences that influenced my decision to become a marine scientist and later an artist, and prepared me well for what I do today. More important, they gave me life lessons that I hope I have been able to pass on to Gillian's and my children, Jessica and Alexander.

In 2008, I considered continuing the underwater saga in a follow-up book but chose instead to tell the history of Tropic Star Lodge in Panama, a place I love to visit that has some of the best fishing in the Western Hemisphere. That book, *Panama Paradise,* was a wonderful challenge and lots of fun to prepare—sitting every day and telling fishing stories, looking through vast archives of action shots, and spending time on paintings inspired by what we were lucky enough to encounter.

Another 10 years have gone by since *Panama Paradise*, and still there was no follow-up to *Portraits*. That time came in early March 2020, when the airport in Grand Cayman was closed, and all of a sudden, my travel calendar for March to June was vaporized as we saw the shelter-in-place requirements take effect. It was not just for us on this small Caribbean island; it was for everyone on the planet.

COVID-19 was as welcome as a hand grenade coming through the letter box.

Our conditions on Cayman Island were strict, with curfews every night, and all day on Sunday. We were allowed out every other day for a supermarket run, but the tough part was no boating, no fishing, no diving, no swimming at public beaches...no fun. For a family who is all about fishing and diving, that was a bit much. But it worked, and we largely kept the coronavirus out of our islands.

So, with time suddenly on my hands, I decided to take a break from painting and instead embarked on this project—a look back at the expeditions since 2002, the work being done by the GHRI for the past 21 years, the invaluable alignment with Nova Southeastern University, the formation of the GHRI and the GHOF, the corporate relationships built, and the expanding nature of the brand from just licensing art to one that supports research, education, outreach and marine conservation.

The pages to follow are stories of adventure. The expeditions are multidisciplinary in design and execution—where science meets art, where discovery initiates authenticity, and where inspiration is the driving force to more and improved knowledge, providing better education about marine ecosystems.

Before we dive in, a few tributes are in order.

I have been fortunate to make many good friends while on this journey. Unfortunately they passed before their time, and we remember them fondly. They all loved fishing, and in different ways, made a positive impact in the world of fishing, diving and marine conservation. This is a brief tribute to our friends, anglers, divers and co-workers, with whom we have shared so many good experiences:

SCOTT BOYD

Scott "discovered" me in Jamaica in 1984 at the Port Antonio tournament, during which I was holding an art exhibition. He brought my art to Florida and, along with Charlie

Forman, helped me set up Florida corporations in 1986. Scott ran a popular tackle store in Fort Lauderdale and knew everybody in the sport-fishing industry. He was most instrumental in building the brand in the early years, before passing away in 2005. The 90-foot-high mural I painted in Terminal 1 at the Fort Lauderdale International Airport is dedicated to Scott.

RALEIGH WERKING

Through an introduction from Scott Boyd, I signed my first license in 1987 with Raleigh Werking, owner of T-Shirts of Florida in Fort Lauderdale. Raleigh was a dedicated light-

tackle angler and holder of dozens of IGFA world records, many of which still stand. He took a personal interest in building my apparel line in the beginning. After selling T-Shirts of Florida to his partner, Raleigh and I maintained a good business relationship through Guy Harvey Publishing. More important for the long term, he took me to Tropic Star Lodge in 1991, in Panama. Raleigh introduced me to the Kittredge

family and the best place in the Western Hemisphere for big-game fishing. At Tropic Star, Raleigh loved teaching people to become good anglers, and coached Jessica and Alex to catch their own billfish. He coached me on hosting TV shows and assisted with the marketing of the brand.

KAYE PEARSON

I met Kaye through Scott Boyd in 1986, and he immediately took me under his wing as a starving artist. Kaye owned Show Management, which ran the Fort Lauderdale International Boat Show as well as several other major boat shows and

concerts. For 17 consecutive years, Kaye and Cheri Pearson asked me to do the art for the program cover and posters for the Fort Lauderdale Boat Show. They collected my art, and that of my best friend and legendary American sculptor, Kent Ullberg. Kaye was a keen angler and was able to fish with us on a couple of expeditions. They resurrected and ran the famous Bertram-Hatteras Shootout in Marsh Harbour for many years and loved fishing in the Bahamas. Kaye's businesses linked all aspects of the boating and marine manufacturing industry, which made a vast impact on the socioeconomic well-being of the South Florida community. He was generous with his time and efforts in supporting many charitable causes.

PAXSON OFFIELD

Packy, as he was known to his friends, was more supportive of billfish conservation than any other person on the planet. He was the only person to serve as chairman of

both The Billfish Foundation and the International Game Fish Association. Packy was a keen angler and often fished by the rules of the Avalon Tuna Club in Catalina, the oldest big-game fishing club in the world. Packy sponsored a great deal of research work on billfish through the Offield Foundation for Billfish Studies, hosted the International Billfish Symposium in Catalina in 2005, and was one of the most generous sponsors of the work done by the GHOF. In Panama and Central America, he worked on preserving birds of prey, in particular the rare harpy eagle, through the Peregrine Fund. He received the Gran Orden de la Maestre Vasco Nunez de Balboa, the highest honor a non-Panamanian can receive from that country.

NEIL BURNIE

Neil was unique; everyone who ever met him would agree. He spread his knowledge, energy and joie de vivre, brim-ming with optimism, generosity and lots of music wherever he went. He invited us to participate in the tagging of tiger sharks where he lived in Bermuda, and we began an exciting scientific collaboration as well as a marvelous friendship, cut short for everyone around him by his untimely passing. Neil remains an inspiration and a hero for everyone he touched. "Oh the whales and sharks of the ocean they seem to call to me, though my body is here on the dry land, my soul is deep in the sea...."

G. RAYMOND CHANG

Ray was one of Jamaica's most successful businessmen ever. He migrated to Canada in 1967 to go to the University of Toronto. He made a successful career as a chartered financial analyst, culminating in becoming chairman of one of the largest publicly traded fund companies in the country. Ray was consistent with his philanthropy, giving back to a wide variety of Jamaican schools, colleges and charities. He received the Order of Jamaica in 2010 and the Order of Canada in 2014. Ray was part of Team Canada, which fished every year at the torneo at Tropic Star Lodge, with boatloads of friends from Jamaica and Canada. He loved fishing and was a successful angler, catching many marlin, and supported billfish research and conservation. Through his hard work and generosity, Ray improved the lives of thousands of people, never forgetting his roots.

WAYNE HASSON

I first met Wayne at the marlin tournament in Port Antonio, Jamaica, in 1982. Shortly afterward Wayne started the liveaboard dive concept in the Cayman Islands, called *Cayman Aggressor*, where he lived. Wayne built a luxury dive fleet worldwide, becoming one of the most innovative pioneers in the four decades he worked in the dive industry. As you will read in this book, we were fortunate enough to go diving with Wayne on many expeditions on Aggressor fleet liveaboards in places such as the Galapagos, Cocos Island, Cayman Islands, Turks and Caicos, and Cuba. Wayne was a scuba diver and photographer extraordinaire. He was a family man, a Marine, an instructor, a pilot, a world traveler and a pioneer. Wayne formed philanthropic organizations, including Sea of Change and Oceans for Youth. He received many prestigious awards, including the Beneath the Sea Legend Award, and was inducted into the International Scuba Diving Hall of Fame. CEO of Aggressor Adventures Wayne Brown said: "His passion for the scuba diving world was clearly evident to everyone who met him. In his 36 years with Aggressor, his dedication to his company and staff was unwavering. We are all blessed to have crossed paths with him. May his memory and accomplishments be remembered forever."

And with that, let's get started.

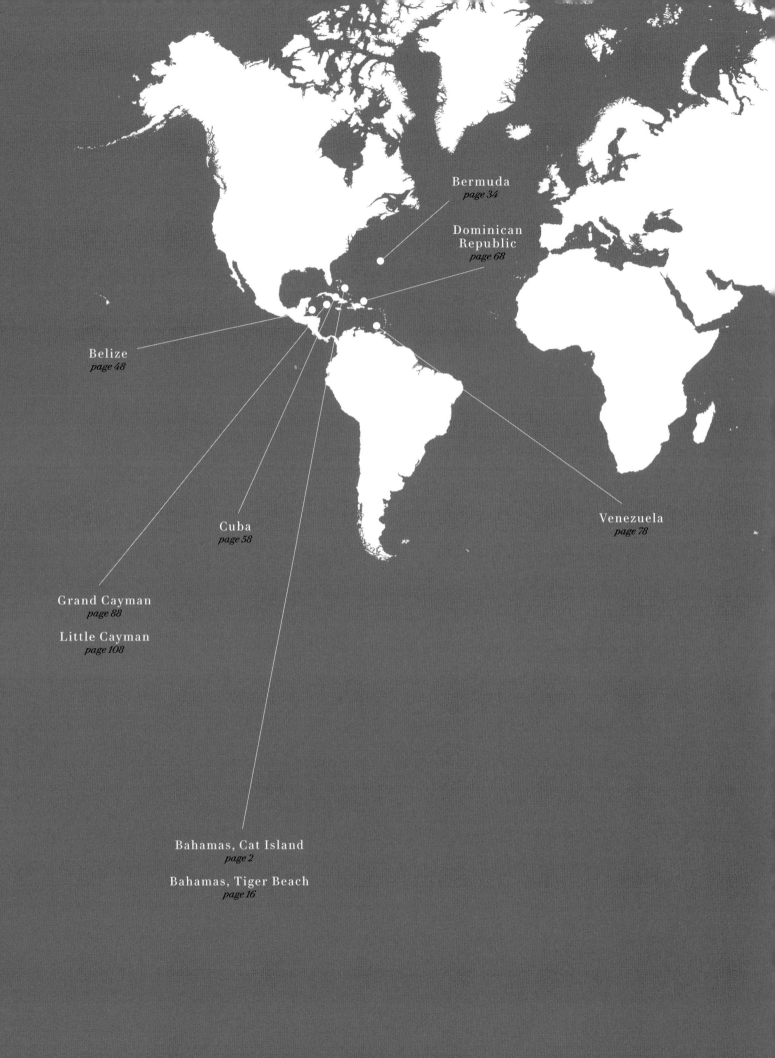

01

Neon reef fish and turquoise water, sharks of every make and model, curious saltwater crocodiles, blue marlin leaping against bluebird skies, chaotic spawning seasons, tornadic baitballs, tagging, research and conservation—it doesn't get better than this.

THE ISLE OF WHITETIP SHARKS

THE GUY HARVEY RESEARCH Institute's fishing, diving and shark-tagging expedition had taken several months to plan—the goal was to make a new documentary under the auspices of the Guy Harvey Ocean Foundation, with direction from award-winning producer George Schellenger. The target species was the oceanic whitetip shark; a new tracking study was being conducted by a team from Stony Brook University in New York and the Cape Eleuthera Institute in the Bahamas. It was May 2013, which is a good month to see oceanic whitetips in the outer islands of the Bahamas. We would be aboard Jim Abernethy's *Shear Water* for this trip.

Little is known about the life history of the oceanic whitetip shark, which is found in all of the world's warm oceans. Growing up in Jamaica, we would encounter them offshore while fishing, close to flotsam or trailing a school of pilot or beaked whales. They used to be the most abundant large animal on the planet, but whitetip populations have been annihilated in the past 50 years by longline commercial fishing. Because of the large size of their fins, this species is preferred

In the open ocean, a whitetip will check out all things floating at the surface—wood, weed, turtles, trash and dead animals—to see what is edible. They always have an entourage, which might include rainbow runners, bar jacks and pilotfish. Acrylic on canvas.

in the shark-fin trade. According to Dr. Shelley Clarke, between 400,000 and 1.5 million oceanic whitetips were killed for their fins in 2000 alone. Further research and analysis showed that this species had been reduced to 10 percent of its population in the South Pacific and down to just 1 percent in the Gulf of Mexico.

The local abundance of oceanic whitetips was "discovered" in Cat Island, Bahamas, by Jim and his Ultimate Shark Diving Expedition team. He had heard stories about gamefishermen visiting this productive area who were losing their hooked tuna, dolphin and marlin to the aggressive whitetips. His interest piqued, Jim organized expeditions to this remote location, which was a two-day cruise from West Palm Beach, Florida.

One reason for the local abundance of this species is because the Bahamas has banned longline fishing since 1993. Then in 2011, the government protected all species of sharks from commercial exploitation throughout the archipelago. The research opportunity here was initiated by Dr. Edd Brooks of the Cape Eleuthera Institute, also known as the Island School, and by Dr. Demian Chapman, who was the assistant director of science at the Institute for Ocean Conservation Science at Stony Brook University at the time. Demian was

ably assisted by Lucy Howey and Dr. Lance Jordan from Microwave Telemetry, the company that makes the satellite tags used in this study. We also met Brenda Anderson, who was using ultrasound to test for pregnancy in female whitetips.

Accompanied by Dr. Mahmood Shivji, director of the GHRI, plus Brad Wetherbee and graduate student Shara Teter, we set off with the crew of *Shear Water* from West Palm Beach. Our gentle itinerary included a stop near Staniel Cay to experience the novelty of the swimming pigs; we also had our checkout dive in the famous Thunderball Cave, which was used in the James Bond movie *Thunderball*. The last leg of the transit to Columbus Point, Cat Island, was made in choppy conditions and gray skies, but we were amped up about diving with the whitetips the following day.

Jim's pre-dive briefing was thorough. He emphasized how inquisitive this species can be and how close they like to come on the first and subsequent passes. We had to wear a black hood, black gloves and black socks, covering up all of our skin. We also had to stay in a group at the same depth and constantly keep swiveling to check all around. We trolled out about 4 miles south of Columbus Point and dropped a dozen buoyed milk crates loaded with fish scraps into the water.

I had brought some softhead lures, so while we waited for the sharks to appear in the chum, we put out a spread of four lures and teasers. We did catch a couple of nice 25-pound dolphin for dinner that night before the sharks showed up and we went into dive mode. The two research boats from the Island School joined us, catching oceanic whitetips and deploying SPOT tags on them.

The next day saw better weather, and again we worked with the research crew. We did find that the sharks left the area once they were tagged and released, and the number of sharks

Back to trolling, heading in at 6p.m., a blue marlin jumped on the black-and-purple Mold Craft on the right long, and I was hooked up to an active blue marlin. The giant fish unzipped the calm water with its jumps. As the marlin got closer, I said to Jim that he should get his gear on and go in. He had never dived with a blue marlin before and needed no further encouragement.

I WAS AMAZED *at how quickly they swam off once the hook was removed and the tail rope loosened.* THEY ARE TOUGH ANIMALS.

we encountered dropped as the days went by. I was amazed at how resilient these whitetips really were, and how quickly they swam off once the hook was removed and the tail rope loosened. Demian said the survival rate was 100 percent last year. They are tough animals.

More important, Demian, Edd and Lucy's work showed that some sharks stayed within the Bahamas' exclusive economic zone all year. Additionally there were three areas outside the Bahamas that were visited by the oceanic whitetips on a regular basis in the western Atlantic, but all sharks returned to the area around Cat Island year after year. They show a similar cyclical migratory behavior that we have seen in tiger sharks migrating between Bermuda and the Bahamas. The whitetips spent a lot of their time within the 200-mile EEZ of the Bahamas, therefore enjoying the protection those boundaries afford them. According to Demian: "Perhaps this is why we can still find them there, in contrast to so many other regions where the species has been depleted. In any event, this research helped inspire the Bahamian government to press for stricter international controls on trade in oceanic whitetips."

Back to trolling, heading in at around 6 p.m., a blue marlin jumped on the black-and-purple Moldcraft Wide Range on the right long, and I was hooked up to an active blue marlin.

The giant fish unzipped the calm water with its jumps. As the marlin got closer, I said to Jim that he should get his gear on and go in. He had never dived with a blue marlin before and needed no further encouragement. He came up beaming, then we took the hook out of the marlin's mouth and let it go. It swam off strongly. It was the first blue marlin, about 175 pounds, ever caught aboard *Shear Water*.

I put the spread back out, and not three minutes later, another blue marlin came up on the right short lure, a black and green Moldcraft Super Chugger. After three bites it failed to hook up, then it went across to the left long and then committed on the right long—we were hooked up again. At one point the marlin turned and came jumping toward the boat, head shaking, pectoral fins spread wide, its tail churning and leaving a foamy wake on the surface. I got the marlin to the boat a few minutes later only to find that it was rapidly losing weight: A whitetip had taken three 20-pound chunks out of the marlin.

ABOVE LEFT

Mahmood examines the bite marks inflicted on a blue marlin by a large whitetip shark. We kept the carcass to use as chum the following day.

ABOVE RIGHT

Jim: our guide, photographer and shark conservationist, as well as owner of Shear Water, *our home for the expedition.*

FACING PAGE

With large schools of blackfin tuna around the Bahamian islands, blue marlin are frequently encountered. We caught three during the expedition. Acrylic on canvas.

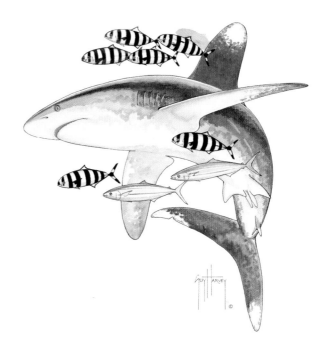

We decided to boat the carcass and use it as chum the following day. Mahmood, Brad, and the crew had never seen a dead marlin before and spent a while examining the great fish. It looked like the scene from Ernest Hemingway's *The Old Man and the Sea,* when Santiago tied the huge marlin to his skiff and the sharks took it apart on his way home. Oceanic whitetips had to be part of that story.

We decided to move to another location the following day near Tartar Bank, south of Hawk's Nest. Here we caught a suitable whitetip and secured it in the water but still on *Shear Water*'s dive platform. Mahmood and Brad took measurements, tissue samples and attached the SPOT tag to the dorsal fin. When the dorsal fin and tag breaks the surface, the tag sends its location to the satellites above with much greater accuracy than a PAT tag.

Just after lunchtime, I saw a blue marlin inhale the red-and-black Moldcraft on the left short rod. Matt Heath had his hands full with the rampaging 150-pound blue. It was flat-calm, and the marlin tail-walked all over the ocean. When Matt reeled the marlin closer to the boat, Jim and crew got ready to go in and dive on the marlin. It was a bright, sunny day and calm—ideal conditions. We got four divers in the water with the marlin that was paddling contentedly below the boat, upright and clean.

Suddenly Jim popped to surface yelling: "Mako! Mako! Mako!" and went down again. I expected the mako to pounce on the tired marlin, but nothing happened. The only clue I had about the big shark in the area was that the marlin suddenly lit up with vivid neon blue stripes. The fish was definitely excited. We waited a bit longer, then I removed the hook and released the marlin. It swam off through the divers, out of sight into the blue. I could only imagine what would happen if the reception committee was still lingering below.

As Jim got in the boat, out came a flood of garbled words describing how close the big mako came, moving rapidly through the scene and then departing just as quickly. Jim and Mike both said that the mako was over 10 feet long, which put it around 600 pounds. A good trip had become a great one. Jim had never seen a big mako before, and one so close was a dream encounter.

We took another 40 hours to get back to West Palm Beach. As we hit the dock, Brad checked his email and found that the oceanic whitetip we had tagged and named Lucy was reporting on a regular basis; we had some 30 hits in just a few days. The shark had already gone halfway up the west side of Eleuthera and was heading south again toward Cat Island—great stuff. The tracking instruments were working well. Oceanic whitetips, blue marlin, several other shark species including a big mako, lots of great dives, research efforts, conservation—it doesn't get better than this.

DIVING IN THE SHARK TANK

JIM ABERNETHY IS ONE OF those unique human beings who has been able to bring sharks—particularly tiger sharks—into people's lives. Luckily, I am one of those people. My diving family are those people. And many of my friends became those people.

There are several reasons why the Bahamas has more sharks than any other jurisdiction in the Western Hemisphere. Sharks were protected in many respects in 1993 by a ban on longline fishing initially aimed at conserving reef fish; in 2011, sharks were protected from commercial exploitation because the Bahamas had been receiving a lot of interest from potentially invasive Asian commercial shark-fishing operations.

The Bahamas National Trust, under the capable leadership of Eric Carey, has been a vigilant protector of fish sanctuaries, marine parks, and sharks in particular. The BNT was created in 1959 as an independent statutory organization charged with conservation and preservation of the natural heritage of the Bahamas. Now there are 32 land and sea parks in the archipelago.

The first time I dived with tiger sharks on purpose was with a group of friends on the liveaboard dive boat *Gulf Stream Eagle*, on the Little Bahama Bank in May 2008. I had a memorable close encounter with a female tiger: As she passed above me, something made her bend down and check out my Nikonos RS camera. She pushed her nose down on it and in doing so, forced me into the sand. Quite alarming. I was just glad she did not open her mouth because the camera would have disappeared in her wide jaws.

On the next expedition in May 2009, and as part of the exercise collaborating with Dr. Sonny Gruber, we caught and tagged a 10-foot female tiger shark with a sonic transducer. Doc Gruber had a network of receiver beacons on the bank to track the movement of tiger sharks in the northern Bahamas. With Dr. Mahmood Shivji, director of the Guy Harvey Research Institute, and Dr. Michael Domeier on the trip, we were investigating the option of tagging and tracking more tiger sharks in the Bahamas. Sue Cocking, legendary outdoor reporter for the *Miami Herald*, was on board for the

week as well. However, an opportunity in Bermuda quickly evolved, where we tagged many tigers with SPOT trackers. From that data, we discovered the sharks were overwintering in the Bahamas after spending the summer months roaming the open ocean of the northwestern Atlantic Ocean.

We were lucky enough to have Doc Gruber participate in the documentary we were making about tiger sharks; we visited the Bimini Biological Field Station, also known as the Shark Lab, in South Bimini. With his staff and students, we caught and tagged an adult tiger shark out in front of the lab, swam with the numerous reef sharks, and did an autopsy on a juvenile 6-foot tiger shark, the only one to have died of all the previous sharks we had tagged. This one had its tail bitten off by another shark while on the line. Interestingly, in its stomach were four different classes of animals: crustacea (mantis shrimp); fish (trunkfish); bird (a dead gull) and ray (yellow stingray), showing just how varied their diet really is.

So what is the history behind Tiger Beach? Jim has been diving with sharks all his life and, because he never speared any fish, he also has never had to deal with any awkward situations. He would organize fly-in trips for his customers to places such as Walker's Cay, where the famous chumsicle dives

LEFT

Jim Abernethy with Emma at Tiger Beach.

BELOW

This large female tiger shark wanted my Nikonos. Photo: Neil Hammerschlag.

ABOVE

A nimble loggerhead dodges the first rush by a tiger shark. Each shark has a unique color and stripe pattern. Some are gray, and the ones we encounter in the open ocean usually have a brown or tan hue with darker stripes. Acrylic on canvas.

FACING PAGE

Adding the final touches to the painting in my studio.

used to attract hundreds of reef sharks and blacktips. Very quickly, that number dropped to fewer than 100 as poachers in the area killed the sharks for their fins. Off Florida, Jim used to see big aggregations of scalloped hammerheads on the deep drop-offs and loads of sand tiger sharks during winter on the wrecks. They have all been caught by fishermen who killed all the sharks, believing the only good shark is a dead shark.

Jim first went to the Dry Bar on the west side of the Little Bahama Bank to shelter from a storm on his way back to Florida aboard his boat, *Shear Water,* in 2002. There is a little shallow area there that affords some protection from the east wind. His target species in those days were the great hammerhead sharks that came in for the grouper and snapper spawning aggregations, called SPAGs. With clients on board, while they waited out the weather, he put out a couple of milk crates with bait. Soon there was a big tiger shark checking them out, then another, until there were five circling the boat, all in just 8 feet of water—they looked enormous in shallow water.

Jim went home and did as much research on tiger sharks as he could. All the literature indicated that tiger sharks do not frequent shallow water. Had he discovered some new behavior? Jim named this place Tiger Beach, hoping to conceal the actual location from shark poachers by insinuating it was close to land. And the average size of the tiger sharks was big.

Over the next few years, Tiger Beach became one of the best places to interact with large species such as tigers, great hammerheads, lemon sharks and some bull sharks. Jim could show clients a dozen different species, but the real draw were

the tiger sharks. Jim quickly set up the protocols for continued safe interactions without a cage. These include how you dress—all in black, with your head covered—gloves and boots, and the bigger the camera housing, the better. If you did not have a camera, then you were given a 3-foot pole. The camera or the pole were effective in keeping a tiger shark from becoming too inquisitive.

Jim said: "Sharks don't have hands—they use their nose and mouth to check you out. Let them bite the camera. Put the stick in front of their nose so they bump that first. There is no need to hit the sharks.

"Your own behavior is the key," he continued. "Stay on the bottom; never linger at the surface. Stay with your buddy and pay attention to where a tiger shark is all the time. At this point, the reef sharks and lemon sharks are secondary. Point to where the tigers are so other divers know. If there are several tiger sharks, cover your buddy's blind spot."

Once the baited crates are situated on the bottom, the chum line is set up in the current. The divers stay on either side of

ABOVE

A drone shot of Shear Water *surrounded by mostly lemon sharks with some reef sharks and tiger sharks at Tiger Beach.*

RIGHT

The GHRI team with many of the students at the late Doc Gruber's Bimini Biological Field Station, aka "The Shark Lab," on South Bimini.

FACING PAGE

Andi Marcher wires a 300-pound blue marlin we caught on Shear Water *while crossing the Gulf Stream.*

the crates in a wide V so that the incoming tiger sharks swimming up the chum line on the runway have a clear path toward the source, which is guarded by Jim or a guide. The key is to prevent the tiger sharks from actually reaching the crates; if they get one in their mouth, they never let go and will destroy the crate. Jim will just rub their head or nose when they get too close to the crate, and they'll move away.

Typically, a new tiger shark will approach cautiously, and after an hour might swim up the runway, go up over the divers, and back around to the chum line. One of the most popular is named Emma, perhaps 15 feet long and probably weighing 1,200 pounds. She has grown a couple of feet since we first met in 2010. Emma knows the drill—she's a supermodel. When she first shows up, she shortcuts all the protocols that tiger sharks normally exhibit. She swims right up the runway, greets Jim (who might sneak her a whole barracuda without the other sharks noticing), does a swift overhead turn, and comes around in a tight circle back into the mix with great agility. There is no wide circle and five-minute pause to gather courage and return to the runway. She is in the zone all the time and can stay for hours.

I asked George Schellenger when he first heard about Tiger Beach. He said: "I was with Lawrence Groth from Great White Adventures. He told me about it when we were at Guadalupe with the white sharks in 2004. I never had a chance to go until 2007, when Lawrence Hastings was putting together a trip to Tiger Beach with a guy named Jim Abernethy. I instantly hit it off with Jim, had a brief encounter with Emma, and fell in love with Tiger Beach and the sharks there. I was completely blown away. Emma seemed like a cartoon character."

Hooks have always been a problem with sharks in the Bahamas. Fifteen years ago, every other shark at Tiger Beach had a hook in its mouth. Jim became proficient at removing them from eight different species, including tiger sharks. Over the years, he has removed four hooks from Emma.

During our trip in October 2010, Emma was present for most of the first and the third day with us. At Tiger Beach, she was very laid-back. Jim set the bait crates in 60 feet of water on the sandy bottom. All around were the usual amount of large lemon sharks, and out closer to the wall were many Caribbean reef sharks as well. I backed away just a bit to take in the big picture at a wider angle. There were so many bodies of different shapes, sizes and colors—all sharks—it was an amazing sight. I knew if the total protection of sharks was passed, the Bahamas would be working from a strong baseline compared with other Caribbean countries. Shark conservation was about

The mate **REMOVED THE HOOK,** *and the marlin swam off strongly—high fives all around. It was the* **PERFECT END TO THE EXPEDITION.**

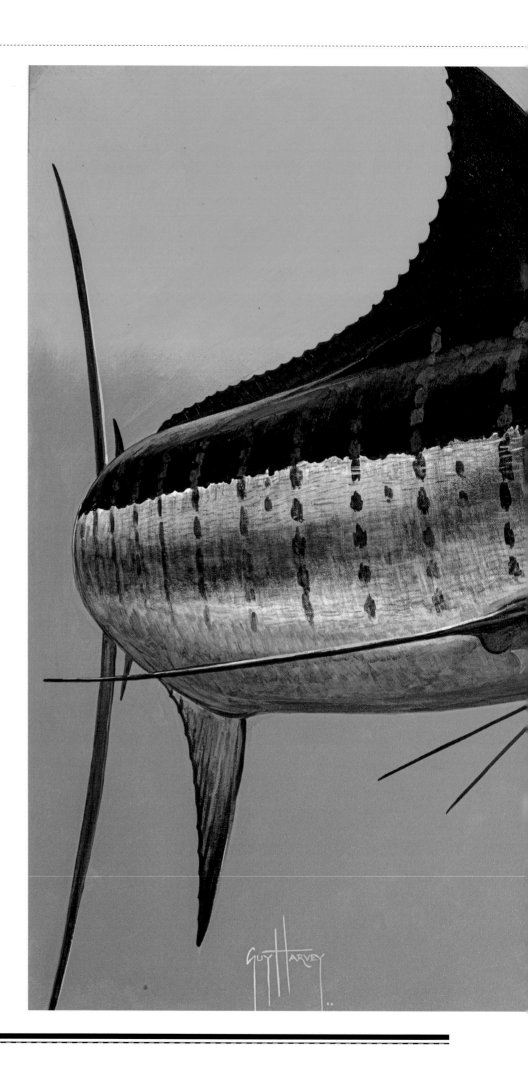

Apart from tiger sharks, the blue marlin is one of my favorite fish to paint. While traveling to and from dive sites anywhere in the tropics, we fish for blue marlin along the way. Acrylic on canvas.

The Formation of a Shark Sanctuary

IN 2017, DR. EDD BROOKS published a comprehensive paper on the value of shark ecotourism to the Bahamian gross domestic product. To summarize, at the time there were 44 dive operators specializing in shark diving, 29 of which were shore-based, and there were 11 liveaboard operations; four boats visited from the US. These operators brought in over 10,000 shark divers per year, generating $114 million per annum, or 1.3 percent of GDP. The species most divers interact with is the Caribbean reef shark, which generated 93 percent of the total income. Tiger sharks generate $2.7 million at Tiger Beach alone, although most of those funds stay with US-based operators. Rays generate $3 million, and great hammerheads generate about $1 million per annum.

Stuart Cove runs the biggest and most successful shark-diving operation out of Nassau. This interaction depends mostly on a healthy population of Caribbean reef sharks. In the early 1990s while his company was in operation, US-based longliners were making

a push to infiltrate the Bahamas. Michelle Cove wrote: "In the early '90s, we spotted a longline boat in the area and were horrified to find they had targeted our shark dive site overnight. We found a dead, finned shark at the site, and all of the regular population of sharks that visited the site daily were gone. We immediately reported this to the Bahamas Ministry of Fisheries and ultimately found out that this was not illegal; in fact, a well-known businessman and politician had applied for a commercial longline license. We realized that we were facing the possibility that this was going to become the norm in the Bahamas.

"Our task was to educate the public on the importance of sharks to the healthy balance of the marine environment and their value to the tourism industry. We achieved this by providing scientific studies, testimonials,

interviews and lobbying. The Bahamas Dive Association was instrumental in this as well. Sam Duncombe organized a public protest in front of Parliament—hundreds of people turned out, and eventually the prime minister addressed the crowd and assured us that longlining would be stopped. It took weeks to get any sharks back to the site. We have learned that sharks leave the area for weeks when there is a dead shark in the water."

According to Pericles Maillis, voluntary president of the Bahamas National Trust at the time, the Bahamian government had licensed Florida longline boats for scientific trials. He describes that the "experiment" was wildly successful: In a very short period of time, the longliners took more than 350,000 pounds of mixed grouper and reef fish species from the Berry Islands, just north of Nassau. Pericles said the groupers were temporarily wiped out.

Pericles continued: "What we came to call 'the longline war' is a longer story. BNT's scientific advisers and

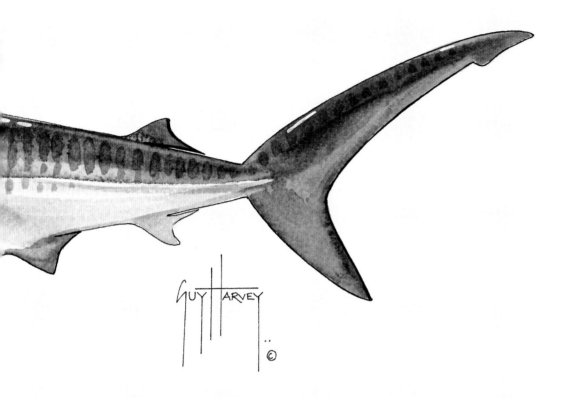

GUY HARVEY ©

council members, including Dr. Carlton Ray, Dr. Sonny Gruber, Dr. Alan Bolton and Dr. Karen Bjorndal, all backed the BNT in this campaign, which was the first time any such controversy with the government had ever happened. In the end, we reached into the minds and souls of our government and most of our people. When Parliament met to deal with the matter, the government confirmed the extent of public awareness and support for a ban on longline fishing. We stepped back into a sort of golden age of working with a conservation-inclined government. Unfortunately, if others don't tell of the BNT's role or of our tremendous efforts in the longline war, we get marginalized and forgotten. This was an important part of national and world conservation history and deserves due and proper credit. Forgotten or not, we still have the pride of the memory that we were in the right place and time to take up the longline fight and hold back the darkness—at least for a while."

Since the early 1990s, sustainable use of this marine resource has maintained biodiversity in the marine environment, bringing in tourism dollars and creating jobs for the long term. In 2011, GHOF/GHRI worked with the Pew Charitable Trust and the BNT to protect sharks in the Bahamas. Thanks largely to Pew, which supported the BNT, along with Stuart Cove, Gruber, Sam Duncombe and many other public figures, the commercial fishing of sharks in the Bahamas was banned on July 5, 2011.

Pericles sees a role for controlled noncommercial harvest of some species of sharks by locals and recreational release fishing, as the shark numbers have rebounded since 1993. The same argument has been made for goliath grouper in Florida, which have recovered well after 20 years of protection. There needs to be scientific evaluation of the shark population in the Bahamas before any such culling is contemplated. Unfortunately, the harvesting of sharks will open up a Pandora's box—there will be opportunities to supply the shark-fin trade, and down the slippery slope go sharks once again—and that slope is slippery with their own blood.

We must be careful not to succumb to shifting-baseline syndrome and enable the continued overexploitation of these species, particularly as other user groups are now a larger part of the equation. More socioeconomic benefits are being generated from the ecotourism activities with goliath grouper, sharks and reef fish than will ever be generated by harvesting these species. The respective pieces of legislation from 1993 and 2011 created a shark sanctuary in the Bahamas, and it will be incumbent on successive generations of Bahamians to keep it that way.

The survival of sharks in the Bahamas has come about through long-term research, management of marine sanctuaries, vision, enforcement and strong leadership. These are some of the few success stories in the history of our relationship with the sea and the creatures therein, and is enough to provide the hope that we can indeed do the right thing.

to begin in earnest in the Bahamas.

George produced the documentary *This is Your Ocean: Sharks*, narrated by Sylvia Earle. It was shown at many film festivals in the US, Canada and the Caribbean, and won the Special Achievement Award in Environmental Filmmaking from Freeman McGillivray Films.

The next step was to get an audience with members of the Bahamian government. This was facilitated by Eric Carey, managing director of the Bahamas National Trust since 2007, and the persistent work by Matt Rand of the Pew Environmental Trust in 2011. GHRI director Dr. Mahmood Shivji's work on tiger sharks in Bermuda and the Bahamas showed the vital connection between these distant islands in the annual cyclical migrations of tiger sharks between deep and shallow water. Earlier work by Doc Gruber, the Bimini Biological Field Station in Bimini, and subsequently by Dr. Neil Hammerschlag at the University of Miami was corroborated by Mahmood and Brad Wetherbee's work with Dr. Neil Burnie of the Bermuda Shark Project.

The end result was that the government of the Bahamas declared their archipelago a shark sanctuary on July 5, 2011. The scientific research showed how dependent tiger, great hammerhead, bull, reef and lemon sharks in the northwestern Atlantic are on the islands of the Bahamas, Turks and Caicos, and the Virgin Islands, making them essential habitat for half the year. Shark ecotourism was definitely a big factor in getting to that decision, and today the there are tens of thousands of divers who visit the Bahamas each year just to dive with sharks.

Earlier that summer, we had spent a week in Bermuda with Burnie tagging a dozen tiger sharks with SPOT trackers. We saw that many of them ended up in the Bahamas that winter. We quickly organized another short trip in December 2010 with Jim to tag tiger sharks at Tiger Beach. With Mahmood, George, Neil, Jay Perez and my son, Alex, we tagged four tigers, including the first male tiger Jim had seen there. As it turned out, some of these went all the way past Bermuda the next summer.

Going to Tiger Beach is an experience that never grows tiring. We returned in October 2012 with legendary wildlife sculptor and friend Kent Ullberg, Andi Marcher from Grand Cayman, GHOF board member and Hell's Bay Boatworks owner Chris Peterson, as well as Jessica, Madison Ryan—a young advocate for shark conservation—and George Schellenger. After a rough crossing to the Bahamas, we finally had some tiger sharks at a site called Hammer Time, when the east wind finally eased up and the current pushed out the dirty water. For Kent, Jessica and Maddy, this was their first encounter with tiger sharks.

The next day, the wind dropped

out and the action was nonstop all morning. One female tiger had the tip of her left pectoral fin turned up, as well as lots of recent mating scars. Another female had a SPOT tag on her dorsal. She was a tiger shark we had tagged with Jim two years earlier near Tiger Beach. It ended up being a wonderful day with five different tiger sharks visiting the crates. We moved that evening to another site called Crystal Beach and set up the crates to soak overnight.

On our final day, the great conditions got even better. We stayed in the same location and had six tiger sharks and about 60 other sharks around us—a mixture of lemons, Caribbean reef sharks and nurse sharks. We left Crystal Beach at 4 p.m. and cruised across the Gulf Stream toward Florida. I set out a spread of marlin lures as we were crossing some prime blue marlin territory on our way back to Palm Beach. After 20 minutes, a blue marlin came up fast on the stinger, dorsal fin high out of water, bill in the air over the lure—I could see this was a decent fish. I dropped back the lure as it ate again and hooked up. Chad, the mate, had never caught a blue marlin, so he was fitted with the harness and went to work. This was a big fish. It took a lot of line, not jumping at all. The fish went down, and in minutes we were down to a quarter of the reel, still losing line. The fish slowed and eventually stopped, with just 10 yards of line left on the big reel. We encouraged Chad as he began bringing up the fish. It's a job only the angler can do.

Eventually Andi got the leader. The marlin was perfectly hooked in the corner of the jaw. He held the marlin for photos in the fading light, and we estimated the fish at 300 pounds. He removed the hook, and the marlin swam off strongly—high fives all around. It was a perfect end to the expedition.

The last time we were at Tiger Beach was in 2016, with a

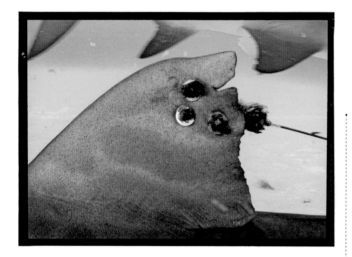

One tiger shark **HAD A LARGE LONGLINE HOOK** *in each corner of her jaw—we named her* **LUCKY** *and saw her three days in a row.*

group of high school students from Grand Cayman. As part of our Shark Talk educational series sponsored by the Kenneth B. Dart Foundation, we took five winners of a competition to Tiger Beach: Mateo, Cameron, Miles, Jack and Kai. The only prerequisite was they had to be certified divers.

The kids got a particularly detailed briefing from Jim and his crew. We began by diving with lemon sharks. Since my last trip, Jim had perfected the technique of quietly approaching lemon sharks resting on the sand. He would rub their head gently as they lay there, sometimes for 10 minutes. They clearly were not bothered by this; in fact, they seemed to enjoy the interaction. We all became proficient at doing this. I think the students enjoyed this more than any other part of the expedition.

Then the first tiger shark showed up, and we shifted gears with a different focus. The training kicked in. The students took positions by the runway and were able to see the tiger sharks come and go. Then two or sometimes three would come up the runway. One tiger shark had a large longline hook in each corner of her jaw—we named her Lucky and saw her three days in a row. For the kids, they were coming face to face with the reality of longlines and the meaning of bycatch. Jim tried to cut the hook with bolt cutters but was unable to complete the task before the shark spooked and left the area.

We moved to a couple of the deeper spots at Tiger Beach and had interactions with reef sharks, lots of lemons, nurse sharks, spotted eagle rays and stingrays. The action was continuous. On our last day, Emma arrived around midmorning with another big female. She stayed within 20 yards of us for the entire day, and was obviously hungry and therefore not as calm as she normally was. Jim had to fend her off the crates several times. Then another big female joined us. At one point, we had three tiger sharks next to each other on the runway like a group of fighter jets taking off. Nothing is more spectacular than spending time underwater with Emma.

On this 8-by-4-foot canvas, three tiger sharks gang up on a loggerhead turtle in the shallows. Our research work in Bermuda showed how tiger sharks are equally comfortable roaming the deep Atlantic Ocean as they are in the shallow reef environment. Acrylic on canvas.

Bermuda

A TIGER BY THE TAIL

IN EARLY AUGUST 2009, members of the Guy Harvey Ocean Foundation staff collaborated with the Bermuda Shark Tagging Project in tagging seven adult tiger sharks with pop-up satellite and single-position and temperature electronic tags on Challenger Bank, 15 miles southwest of Bermuda. Local Bermudians—veterinarian Dr. Neil Burnie and Choy Aming—were heading up this project on behalf of the Bermuda Shark Project, with assistance and collaboration from the GHRI/GHOF staff. We provided tags and participated in deployment along with analysis of these sharks' movements in the western North Atlantic. Guy Harvey Research Institute director Dr. Mahmood Shivji and Dr. Brad Wetherbee of the University of Rhode Island were on hand to calibrate the tags and assist with deployment; both have worked extensively on tiger sharks in the Bahamas and in the US Virgin Islands.

Neil's 34-foot Prowler, *Bones*, was the workboat; Capt. James Robinson assisted on his charter boat, *Wound Up*. The tiger sharks were caught on 130-pound-test line using

Tiger sharks are opportunistic scavengers and will feed on disabled and dead marine mammals, birds, fish and crustaceans. Acrylic on canvas.

BELOW

Capt. James Robinson wires a 10-foot tiger shark caught by Alex on rod and reel on Challenger Bank.

FACING PAGE, TOP LEFT

Neil Burnie always had his saxophone with him wherever he went: on the boat, in the airport, everywhere.

FACING PAGE, TOP RIGHT

A group of tag sponsors fights a big tiger shark on Wound Up, *with James at the helm.*

FACING PAGE, BOTTOM RIGHT

Yellowfin tuna, like this one caught by Alex, are a target species on Challenger Bank. Big blue marlin and wahoo also frequent the bank during the summer.

barbless 20/0 circle hooks; at the boat, they were tail-roped and restrained by a harness that kept them held snugly alongside the boat while Neil drilled small holes in the sharks' dorsal fins to attach the SPOT tag. This process takes about 10 minutes, during which time the shark's head is in the water and it is ventilating normally. The sharks are then released, and all swam off at a rapid clip. Rick Westphal and I filmed the releases in the water while Dee Gele filmed all the topside action for a documentary we were producing called *Tiger Shark Express*.

The results were so successful that we were able to track the sharks' daily movements away from Bermuda later in the season. When seawater temperatures dropped in October, they migrated south toward the Bahamas, the Turks and Caicos, and the Virgin Islands. The tracks showed that the sharks were not wandering aimlessly but rather headed in a straight line—they knew where they were going. For the rest of the winter months, they behaved like reef sharks, tracking along the edges of the deep island drop-offs. Their behavior in searching for food at or near the surface means that their dorsal fins were exposed, allowing them to communicate with the Argos satellite on a regular basis. Only a few oceangoing sharks exhibit this behavior, which allows us to use the SPOT tags to track them.

By April and May 2010, as the sea temperatures rose, all the sharks began their northward migration, some aiming straight for Bermuda. Again, they knew where to go. Not far away from the island, they started to wander away and out to the east of Bermuda, where some stayed in the vicinity for most of the summer.

On July 24, 2010, accompanied by my daughter, Jessica, and son, Alex, Neil and Choy took us out to Challenger Bank for six days of tagging. Brad and Mahmood were on hand to

Nova Scotia

Cape Cod

The Bahamas

Cuba

Turks and Caicos

Dominican Republic

Puerto Rico

Jamaica

Haiti

Tiger Tracks This track is for "Harry Lindo" (named after the tag sponsor in Bermuda), a 12-foot male tiger shark tagged on August 30, 2009. The tag transmitted for three years and reported for 1,168 days, during which time the shark swam a minimum of 27,421 miles. This provided GHRI researchers with the first data to show cyclical seasonal movements of this species. During summer, they roam the open ocean of the western north Atlantic, searching for prey such as loggerheads and dead marine mammals and birds. In winter, they spend time in the shallow reef systems of the Bahamas, Turks and Caicos, and the Virgin Islands, where they opportunistically feed on rays and fish. The tiger shark has adapted its seasonal preference to be in 10,000 feet of water or 10 feet of water. Few fish show this diversity of habitat use.

A tiger shark targets a logger-head turtle at the surface. Tiger sharks will track turtles as they approach the surface for air. As they lift their head out of the water to breathe, the tiger shark will shoot up from below and catch the turtle. Acrylic on canvas.

head up the science team. Robinson generously added his boat, *Wound Up*, to the mix again as a catch and support vessel. Starting out with one shark caught for each of the first three days, we got hot on the last three days, tagging three, four and two tigers.

Chumming was the key. We had an ample supply of fish heads, plus we caught bonito, ocean robin—a local name for an abundant mackerel scad—blackfin tuna, wahoo and barracuda on the bank to add to the mix. Half of a fresh barracuda got instant results. James would hook up and catch a tiger, transfer it to Neil's boat, and then return to the mooring to continue fishing while we operated on and released the shark. The GHRI provided 12 SPOTs, and Neil purchased four of the three-year SPOTs with assistance from Bermudian sponsors, some of whom rode along with James to experience the fight of a powerful tiger shark. Neil and Choy were doing a great job in Bermuda in getting local businesses involved and in producing a documentary to educate the public about their efforts and success with the project.

The Bermuda government was considering banning the landing of sharks, as are other countries in the Caribbean and western Atlantic. The results of our comprehensive study amazed the scientific community: Not only have the tags lasted so long, but the regular reporting by the sharks is shedding more information on their behavior and migration as well. They are not the strictly coastal sharks as was previously considered, but rather they make extensive journeys and lead an oceanic existence for much of the year. This knowledge has management implications, in that no country can consider these animals "their resource" because they have now been shown to make extensive migrations passing through the 200-mile exclusive economic zones of several countries in a given year.

The majestic tiger shark seems just as content in 8 feet of water chasing stingrays on the Bahamian sand flats as it is lurking near an oceanic bank 2,000 miles offshore hoping to detect a dead floating seabird, dead dolphin or loggerhead turtle. Several sharks provided tracks from two to four years in duration. These fish swam 30,000 to 40,000 miles during that time. We now have a much better idea of the life history of tiger sharks in the western North Atlantic and Caribbean Sea because of these studies.

The GHRI left several SPOTs in Bermuda with Neil and Choy in the hope that some female tiger sharks would show up later in the year. Brad said that the adults reach maturity after about 10 years, at about 9 feet long. The adult females do give birth to large numbers of fully formed juveniles, up to three dozen from one large female. Growth rates can vary depending on how well an individual shark feeds. Age and growth in bony fish have been determined by counting concentric rings in their scales, otoliths, fin rays or vertebrae. Because sharks and rays have only cartilaginous skeletons, it is more difficult to estimate their age.

Our research on tiger sharks demonstrated that they visit the Bahamas as an important overwintering region in their annual cycle of migration. This was a critical part of the argument that the Bahamas would be a vital shark sanctuary for tiger sharks and other species, such as reef sharks, bull sharks and lemon sharks, which visit the archipelago seasonally. We used this data in a presentation to the government of the Bahamas in January 2011 to help make the decision to ban commercial-fishing operations for sharks. The government protected sharks in July 2011, thereby helping to promote a burgeoning industry—shark ecotourism—in which tiger sharks play a critical role.

It was with great sadness that we learned of Neil's death on November 11, 2014. He drowned while assisting a friend recover a lobster pot in deep water. We all lost a great friend, a great veterinarian, a great conservationist, a great family man and a great human being.

ABOVE

Neil with Mikayla Harvey, Jessica Harvey and his son, Oscar.

FACING PAGE

A tiger shark with an entourage of cobia, bar jacks and rainbow runners. Watercolor and stippled ink.

Belize

THE GREAT SNAPPER SPAWNING

THE SECOND-LONGEST CORAL barrier reef in the world is off the coast of Belize; for decades, it's been a much visited dive destination and is also well-known for massive snapper aggregations, as well as the synchronized arrival of whale sharks at one of the spawning sites. My interest in experiencing spawning aggregations, or SPAGs, went into high gear in 2002, and I began seeking out various SPAGs in the Caribbean.

This particular destination is called Gladden Spit, located 24 miles offshore of Placencia, Belize. Because it is the only known site where whale sharks come in to feed on snapper spawn, it became a special protected zone in 2001. We had arranged to dive there with an outfit that my friend Bill Watts had dived with previously. We had invited friends from Spain, noted heart surgeon Dr. Alberto Iriarte and his wife, Maria; my photojournalist friend Bill Boyce; plus other friends from Cayman. It was also the first of many expeditions we did with brothers Steve and Jimmy Valletta from Phoenix, Arizona.

I had never been to Belize before, and on arrival, it reminded me of Jamaica in the 1960s. My wife, Gillian, daughter, Jessica, and son, Alex, all came on the expedition. Jessica had a couple of years of diving experience already under her belt. We drove several hours south, all squashed together in a rental van with our gear, past lots of orange groves and then to the Stann Creek district. Hurricane Iris had impacted Belize the previous October, and there was considerable damage along the coast and in Placencia. Soulshine Resort had just been reconstructed, and they were glad to have our business. Lodging consisted of rustic cabins on stilts and beautiful grounds, with great food and staff.

Bill Watts had booked the same dive operator they had used the previous year with good results. Unfortunately, we did not have the same experience, for which Bill was very apologetic. I understand the business is no longer in operation.

On our first day we had good weather, so we loaded up and ran out to Queen Caye, about 24 miles out, in an open 30-foot dive boat—12 divers on board, 24 tanks, two crew, definitely fully loaded. We were well south of the main barrier reef and

headed to the continental drop-off. Based at Queen Caye, there were other groups studying the snapper/whale shark aggregation. These included the Nature Conservancy, led by Will Heyman, and the Friends of Nature, a community-based organization that had a large presence, as did the Belize Department of Fisheries.

We did a wall dive, where we found good reef life—lots of fish, eagle rays and some large groupers. Far down the wall at 150 feet, I caught my first glimpse of the snapper aggregation: A long line of mutton snapper were swimming north at a moderate pace. They were too deep to reach, but it was a start nonetheless.

Because spawning activity happens late in the evening, we had the rest of the day to swim, snorkel and have lunch. We moved out to the zone around 4.30 p.m. There were already four other fully loaded dive boats there, all hoping for the same experience. We had a good drop, despite the boat not having a GPS or depth finder to locate the aggregations, and had a short swim toward the shadow that filled the water column from 150 feet up to 50 feet. It was a cubera snapper aggregation. Most of the cuberas one encounters while diving are very shy, hard to approach and live a solitary life on coral reefs. Like many other reef predators, they aggregate only during spawning. Here they barely moved aside as I went into the school. We were amazed. They were all different sizes, from 25 to 100 pounds. The bigger fish already had distended bellies as their eggs became more hydrated. Having large canine teeth, this species is also called dogtooth snapper, not to be confused with the beautiful dog snapper. Up close, they looked formidable indeed.

The fish were not moving as a group, just milling around

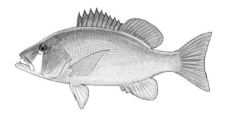

right on the drop-off. Below I spotted a large bull shark, then another. They were waiting for the action to begin, hoping to take advantage of a distracted fish.

There was no spawning activity that evening, and we saw no whale sharks. No worries—I was so excited to see the big cuberas in such a large group, and how nature had organized them to reproduce in an efficient manner, ensuring the long-term survivability of the species. This strategy certainly had worked for millennia. But all was not good; we had heard stories of how the SPAGs have been fished hard by poachers, not all of them from Belize.

We ascended and collected some of our team from Queen Caye, then headed back in. The trip back took 90 minutes; in the gathering gloom, we ran past reefs and cays and got back to the resort in the dark.

The following morning, we were back out at Gladden Spit. Although we were only a couple hundred yards from the other

In the open ocean from Mexico
south to Belize and Roatan,
large schools of sardines
attract the ocean's largest predators: finback whales, large
tunas, billfish, and silky and
whale sharks. Unlike other
oceanic predators, whale
sharks are keyed in to annual
spawning aggregations in the
region, such as the snapper
SPAGs of Gladden Spit, exhibiting diverse feeding strategies.
Acrylic on canvas.

BOTTOM

A portrait of a mutton snapper.
Watercolor.

RIGHT

On the shallow flats of Belize,
bonefish and permit dig in the
soft substrate searching for
buried clams and crustaceans.
The great barracuda can get
close using the "mud" clouds
generated by the feeding fish
as cover before the charge.
Mixed media.

dive boats, we did not find the snapper aggregation. With several hours to burn, we spent the time snorkeling. The reef was battered from Hurricane Iris, but there were signs of recovery. We left at 4 p.m. and took up a position to the west of other boats. We went in and swam and swam—no snapper, just a couple of bull sharks and a loggerhead turtle. We headed home dejected. It was dark by the time we ran out of gas near Lark Cay, about 4 miles short of Placencia. We were towed in by one of the other dive operators.

On April 28, we had a new dive guide, Alfred, who turned out to be a gem. It was rough by 2 p.m., but we joined some of the other dive boats, went in, and swam to the east along the drop and found the aggregation quickly. Alberto and I stayed with the aggregation while the rest of the group swam after a whale shark that had made a fleeting appearance.

The following day, we changed the format. In the morning, I hired Alfred in his own panga to take us offshore to look for whale sharks. The plan was to look for sharks offshore and then join the rest of the group for the afternoon dives at Gladden Spit. We headed out with Bill Watts, Alberto Iriarte and Alex.

Just outside the drop-off, we spotted terns flying over fast-moving tunas, and soon found what we were looking for. From 50 yards away, we could see a large brown amorphous shape barely moving, close to the surface: whale shark!

As we got ready to jump in, there were other smaller brown shapes around: silky sharks. No worries—we jumped in and swam toward the whale shark. It was about 25 feet long, a juvenile. All around were thick patches of sardines being

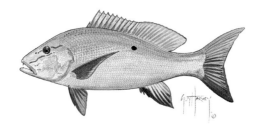

corralled by tuna. The whale shark was swimming very slowly, tail down, head up, with its mouth open at the surface, gulping bait as the fleeing fish packed up against the whale shark, trying to evade the rushing tuna. Isn't nature amazing?

Meanwhile, several silky sharks were also in the head-up position, mouth open, gulping bait. They were mimicking the whale shark's feeding behavior, and it was working. It was all happening: tuna, bait, sharks, good visibility and great light.

We swam and kept up with the shark for a while. It slowly moved off, so we got back in the panga and headed back in toward Gladden Spit. On the edge, we came across a couple of pangas catching large mutton snapper. We stopped next to them and watched them pull a big mutton into the boat, and then another. The fish box was full of mutton snapper. *This is madness,* I thought. I had seen the same activity at a mutton snapper SPAG off Bimini in the Bahamas, where no one seemed to be aware of the consequences of this unsustainable and illegal fishing. Catching adult fish in spawning condition while at an aggregation is a horrific waste of the brood stock.

We were joined by the rest of the group at Queen Caye and set off for the next dive. Soon Alfred found a school of dog snapper for us to film. It was a large group of this beautifully colored snapper, which have yellow fins and a distinctive pale triangle teardrop below their eyes. They were in a large, vertically orientated school like a tornado. I was glad to have content of another major snapper species at the aggregation. This showed that three species of snappers use the same spot at Gladden Spit.

We had a short surface interval, then we did our last dive. With Alfredo leading the dive, we were in the right spot. The main body of cuberas was closer to the surface and moving around excitely. We stayed at 50 feet near the group of milling snapper. As if a switch was flicked on, spawning began, and the snappers rushed to the surface in a big group; suddenly, they were shedding gametes in a big, billowing white cloud that quickly spread in the current, reducing visibility. I backed out and down to keep filming. Then whale sharks appeared out of nowhere, swimming through the haze, mouths open. A group of agitated spotted dolphins came through the whole scene, chattering excitedly.

At the surface, the outpouring of gametes calmed and actually flattened the surface of the ocean, as if oil had been

ABOVE

Dog snapper in a spawning aggregation.

FACING PAGE, TOP LEFT

A big cubera snapper on the move.

FACING PAGE, TOP RIGHT

Holding up two large mutton snapper caught from the SPAG by local fishermen. SPAGs should be fiercely protected by local authorities to protect the brood stock of spawning adults.

FACING PAGE, BOTTOM LEFT

Frigate birds roosting on mangroves that were ravaged by Hurricane Iris just months before.

poured on the water. I had seen this happen frequently in Piñas Bay, Panama, when 10,000 mullet snapper all spawn at once at the surface during daylight, turning bright red in their excitement before going down again. Presumably, dog snapper and mutton snapper spawn farther along the drop-off in a different location. We did not have time to look because it was getting dark and we were still 24 miles offshore.

In spite of the limitations of our dive operator, we were able to witness the spawning of the cubera snapper and the interaction of the whale sharks, which were all immature sub-adults, about 22 to 28 feet long. They must have been keyed in to the annual availability of fish eggs in this place at this time for thousands, if not hundreds of thousands, of years.

Egg production by the snappers must compensate for the early removal of their offspring—just part of the natural equation. What nature was not prepared for was the sudden removal of vast numbers of grouper, cubera snapper and mutton snapper brood stock by humans. All the commercially targeted species of grouper and snapper are long-lived, slow-growing species that lead a solitary existence, widely dispersed on coral reefs. Their reproductive capacity cannot compete with the unsustainable rate of removal during the past half-century. In the flash of a second in geological time, a successful species is put under great pressure through unsustainable fishing as the adults are caught and consumed while they are in the process of replacing themselves.

The following year, several organizations were successful in having some protections put in place under the auspices of Friends of Nature. The Gladden Spit and Silk Cayes Marine Reserve was established in 2003 to protect the fish-spawning aggregations as well as the whale sharks, which also have an ecotourism value. Nowadays the management of the Gladden Spit and Silk Cayes Marine Reserve is conducted by the Southern Environmental Association and the government of Belize.

One of the most important steps fishery-management agencies and governments can take is to identify the location of spawning aggregation sites and then throw a legal fence around that body of water. Once this is done, they can undertake more research, gather more data, and protect these sites for the entire year. Inclusion of SPAGs in marine parks covers a multitude of options for fisheries managers.

BOTTOM RIGHT

Alex checks out his digs: a cute wooden cabin on stilts at Soulshine.

GARDENS OF THE QUEEN

Welcome to the Gardens, and have a nice stay. This saltwater crocodile epitomizes the wild beauty and pristine nature of the marine park that is Jardines de la Reina.

THE ANCHOR CHAIN rattled off the bow as the anchor splashed into the clear turquoise water of the Caribbean. We were tucked in behind a low island at Cayo Boca de la Piedra de Piloto, close to the Canal de Caballones in the Jardines de la Reina—the Gardens of the Queen—just off the coast of Cuba. The wind was blowing hard out of the north as another cold front kept things cool on the water. We had finally arrived at our destination, having left Havana 12 hours prior aboard *Jardines Aggressor I*. We were looking forward to getting underwater tomorrow.

Earlier in the day, March 3, 2018, we joined Wayne Hasson, managing director of the worldwide Aggressor liveaboard dive fleet, on a bus with other clients driving six hours east from Havana to Jucaro. This is a small fishing village that is also the base for the Avalon, a sport-fishing and dive operation that

has operated here for a long time.

The Gardens of the Queen has been protected from commercial fishing for decades; some catch-and-release sport fishing takes place on the flats, targeting bonefish, tarpon, permit and snook. The dive business has grown rapidly under the Aggressor brand. The operation has several Cuban-built boats accommodating up to 24 guests that provide excellent weeklong experiences for avid divers.

Our first dive day, we were split into two groups of eight, received our safety briefing, and headed off to our first dive at a spot called Mogotes. We rolled in, and there were a couple of full-grown Caribbean reef sharks to greet us, sleek and fat. With our guide, Jorge, we slowly headed east and down a mini wall from 30 feet to 70 feet. I was doing a fish count on a slate and quickly noted large numbers of key medium reef predators: numerous black grouper of all sizes, and Nassau grouper as well. There were tarpon hanging in shallow caves and lots of schoolmaster snapper but few mutton snapper.

The coral was healthy and dense, as were soft corals and sponges. Several species of grazers were visible: parrotfish and blue tangs in big marauding schools. The drop at 70 feet leveled out to a sand plain that went south to the drop-off just out of view. No need to go there, though—all the life was right here.

We circled back, and the reef shark count went to seven different individuals, one of which was the biggest reef shark I had ever seen—7 to 8 feet, fat. They were all healthy, none with hooks or leaders in the corners of their mouths. We ended having a lot of playtime with some jumbo-size black grouper up

WE CIRCLED BACK, *and the reef shark count went to seven different individuals, one of which was* THE BIGGEST REEF SHARK I HAD EVER SEEN.

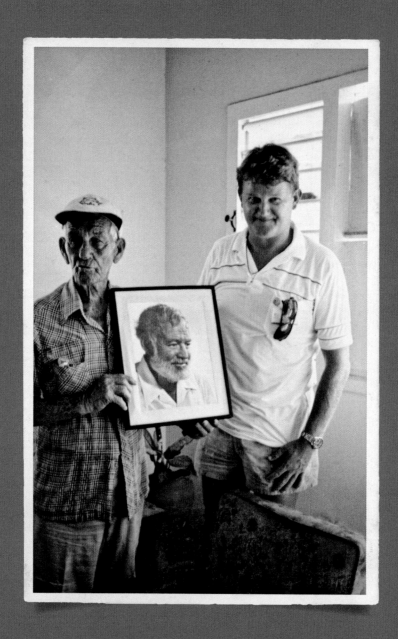

in the shallows at 30 feet. They were obviously very conditioned to divers and would hover close for wonderful shots. I sketched the face of a black grouper on my slate while George filmed. My tank was dry by the time I finished my safety stop and got to the boat—an empty tank meant it had been a fabulous dive. And we had not seen a single lionfish. The guides did not have spears, so the predators—black and Nassau groupers—must be controlling them.

After a warm shower, dry towels and coffee, Wayne asked if we wanted to film a saltwater crocodile in the wild. Sure! Off we went.

It was still blowing a cool north wind, but we were sheltered in the mangrove channels. Armed with some raw chicken parts, we went up a mangrove channel and stopped in a beautiful natural arena of low mangroves and banks. A huge barracuda immediately came up to check us out. The guides starting shouting: "Niño! Niño!" After a few minutes, an 8-foot crocodile appeared, cautiously swimming toward us, its tail weaving from side to side and the top of its head exposed. It stopped at the edge of the channel and stayed there, so some of us swam over to meet it. Jorge had a piece of raw chicken on a string, and used this bait to lure the croc into the deeper water, where it swam toward our panga. We fanned out, keeping a respectful distance. It swam straight to us. The contrast of the dappled gray and brown scales of the big reptile against the turquoise water was beautiful.

My daughter, Jessica, used her iPhone to take some underwater video close to the surface. The croc stayed for a while, and was rewarded with some raw chicken before it headed back into the flats. What a way to spend a surface interval!

Our next two dives, Cabezo de la Raya and Five Sea, followed a similar format, where we dropped in at 30 feet on top of the mini wall and went down the wall as far as needed. Since there were big schools of grunts, goatfish, blue tangs and schoolmaster snapper in the 30- to 40-foot depths, we chose to hang there for most of each dive. Black grouper and reef sharks were always around. There was good light, and we rarely get to see such large schools of reef fish like that anywhere in the Caribbean anymore, even in Little Cayman.

Jessica concentrated on some of the hogfish as well as the abundant big queen triggerfish. These are numerous here, but they're just as difficult to film as everywhere else because they are so shy. We rarely see this species in Jamaica or Cayman because they have been overexploited in the trap fishery. Already I was reminded about shifting-baseline syndrome—here the baseline was what it had once been for the Cayman Islands 30 years ago and for Jamaica 60 years ago. I was constantly reminded about this throughout the week.

Our first dive for March 5 was a ripper. The site was called Coral Negro and was on top of the main wall in 60 feet. There was a monstrous sponge like a giant vase standing 10 feet off the bottom, into which our guide placed a handful of sprats. Some hefty Caribbean reef sharks showed up immediately, and once they caught the scent of the fish, they circled the sponge rapidly, some even putting their heads down inside the big sponge. It shook like a tree but withstood the repeated knocks as it must have done hundreds of times before.

When the bait was finished, the sharks circled around us, posing for shots. We finished the dive with a safety stop, our view of the surface blocked out by the bodies of passing sharks. In the direct sunlight, their skin has sheens of pink, gold and bronze depending on the angle of the light. Their eyes were golden with tiny slit pupils, very mobile in small sockets. Their rounded noses, dotted with ampullae, and their countersunk nostrils in front of a barely open mouth gave them a purposeful look.

During the second and third dives, we experienced big southern stingrays and a species seldom seen in Jamaica, and never in the Cayman Islands, called the Caribbean whiptail ray. It has a square face with a tiny point, round disc and thick tail base. They are quite shy.

On the next dive at Cabezo de la Cubera, we swam north along the mini wall. I was not surprised to see a 40-pound king mackerel sculling along rapidly. Again, we do not see this species in Cayman waters, though they are all around us in Cuba, Jamaica and Mexico. This was a great dive for more black grouper, lots of Nassau grouper and a few tiger grouper; big schools of colorful porkfish mixed with grunts and

After **A WARM SHOWER, DRY TOWELS AND COFFEE,** *Wayne asked if we wanted to film a* **SALTWATER CROCODILE** *in the wild.* **SURE!** *Off we went.*

Jessica gets portraits of indigenous Cuban rock iguanas.

The 120-foot Jardines Aggressor I, *our home for a week.*

goatfish created a kaleidoscope of color. This was one of the best reef dives here.

The next day, we moved before sunrise about 7 miles to the northwest, to a spot called La Cana. Right at the top of the mini wall in 30 feet was a spectacular pillar coral surrounded by a dense school of Bermuda chub. Jessica and I went for a closer look, and the school opened up to let us in. There was one piece of the pillar coral that was bare of living tissue. It had been used as a place to rub by the chubs, probably for a long time. They were taking turns in rubbing their thick scaly bodies. We stayed for a while, fascinated by the process.

The second dive was the one we had been waiting for: the silky shark dive. The mooring, called Pipin, was a half-mile to the west. The silky sharks were gorgeous—rusty brown, almost copper-colored, with purple iridescence on the upper surfaces. Then a couple of big ones arrived, and it was time to dive. The sharks were conditioned to divers, obviously. They barely moved out of the way when we hit the water.

We all did a quick 360 to see what was around, just as big 10-footer came into my peripheral view a couple of feet away. Then another big one, and another, as they sucked up the sardines being thrown to them from the panga. Compared with other oceanic species, the bigger individuals have a quiet disposition, not bothered by the excitement, whereas the smaller 4-footers were zipping in and out of the action.

The last time I saw a 10-foot silky shark in the Caribbean was 50 years ago, when I was a young boy fishing with my dad, catching blackfin tuna in his 26-foot canoe off the south side of Jamaica. Big silky sharks would swim up to the side of the boat and pick off the tuna as we wound them in on our Penn 4/0 reels. Since then, longlining and the shark-fin trade have annihilated silky, oceanic whitetip, blacktip, reef, blue, and mako sharks in the Caribbean and western Atlantic.

I spent a lot of time absorbing the beauty of these elegant sharks: long, slim bodies, pointed snouts but flattened heads, small mouth slightly open, no teeth showing, golden eye, big shoulders, long pectoral fins and a proud dorsal fin. There are black tips on the underside of the pectoral fins. All 20 silky sharks we counted were females.

But it was their wonderful color that was really striking: bronze and purple on top turning to gold on the flanks. It was flat-calm and sunny, so wide bars of sunlight rippled down their lithe bodies as they swam. They were so elegant. Then our time was up when it felt like the party had just started. I wanted to do another dive there right away. Wayne said we would be back to that site tomorrow, so we ran in to the adjacent reef for a shallow dive.

Another blast from the past: In 8 feet of water, we encountered many wide growths of elkhorn coral, now an endangered species. For the second time in one day, I was seeing a species I had not encountered in such proliferation since the late 1970s in Jamaica. Each head of coral had its resident group of grunts

and large numbers of sergeant majors taking shelter among the branches, some as thick as my thigh.

The afternoon dive was gangbusters by any standard, but coming after seeing the silky sharks and healthy shallow reefs, it was amazing. We dived at Finca de Pepe, where a big school of horse-eye jacks dominated the blue. Our guide brought sardines to excite the black grouper, queen triggerfish and snapper, as reef sharks circled but kept a discreet distance. We were cold and tired after a monumental day, and elected to have a beer and watch the sun dip below a flat horizon.

March 7, my dad's birthday, was another excellent day of diving. Our first dive was at El Farallon. The silky sharks showed up as soon as they heard the boat arrive, but we descended through them to the bottom and swam through some tunnels and past some deep caves. Sure enough, this is where all the lionfish were hanging out. After a few minutes of looking at amazing corals, we were back in the silky sharks in 15 feet, enjoying the light.

The guides had a quick and easy way of putting a silky shark into tonic immobility. As a shark swims past, the tip of the tail is gripped firmly and twisted to one side. The shark stops swimming and may be held also by its dorsal fin, quite steadily, for up to 20 seconds. Letting go, the shark swims off to renew its circling. Soon we had each held a silky, then they left and came back around. This was a very cool experience.

For our surface interval, we did a drift snorkel on the incoming tide in a channel between the islands. Outside was shallow coral base rock studded with some healthy staghorn coral and

loads of fish. Once the current took us into the channel, it got deeper. A couple of giant nurse sharks bolted in front of us, and then a group of four evenly sized spotted eagle rays came closer, gliding over the bottom. Suddenly the whoosh was over and we found ourselves inside the lagoon, mangrove roots sheltering gray snapper, jacks and grunts in clear, slack water.

Back in the panga, we raced off to a nearby cay to check out the local iguanas. Jessica was beaming—she recognized this species of rock iguana but had not seen one in the wild. She worked in Cayman on the two local species: the blue iguana on Grand Cayman and the Sister Islands' rock iguana. We spent a while taking photos as they appeared out of the low, scrubby bushes.

For the afternoon excitement, we went back to El Farallon, this time with some bait. We hung a few feet below the surface as the silky sharks twisted and turned, sucking up the sprats. A couple of full-grown reef sharks joined the fun. We filled our cards with close-up footage, knowing these were the best conditions we would ever have for filming these rare sharks. A spotted eagle ray flew by 30 feet below, then a 50-pound king-fish made a rocketing pass at some creole wrasse. It was all happening right here.

After a hot shower, we stayed on the sun deck and watched the sun join the ocean in a cloudless sky and waveless ocean. It was so calm and the light reflected off the water so perfectly that it was difficult to place the horizon.

The comparative abundance and size of species in these reefs show how fishing has reduced populations of all reef species throughout the Caribbean. Here is the realistic baseline of abundance that we should be using to measure other islands' reef-fish biomass going forward. If the Cubans can keep it healthy by continued protection, the Gardens of the Queen reef system will not be impacted by pollution, agricultural overnutrification, coastal development, siltation and poaching. Wayne explained how only locals are employed by Avalon to run its fly-fishing and diving operations and are inclusive of the local workforce in the community. The great benefit is that poaching is kept to a minimum, self-regulation works effectively, and the tourism dollars keep the systems lubricated, even if a lot of that money goes to Havana.

A mother humpback whale keeps an eye on her frolicking calf while a hopeful escort lingers in the background. Acrylic on canvas.

HUMPBACK WHALES OF THE SILVER BANK

ONE OF THE FEW PLACES snorkelers can legally swim with humpback whales is on the Silver Bank, in the Caribbean Sea 90 miles north of the Dominican Republic. There is a wide area of shallow water where adult humpbacks spend February and March each year, having their calves and then finding another escort. After spending a couple of months there, they then swim north in late spring to the fertile fishing grounds off the northeastern United States and Canada, where they feed on schools of herring, sardines, sand eels and other small fishes.

All species of whales, including humpbacks, were hunted by the whaling fleets of the world for a thousand years, going well into the 20th century. Humpbacks were brought from an estimated level of about 200,000 worldwide down to just 5 percent of that number by the time whaling ceased in 1986. Today's estimates are from 9,000 to 12,000 humpbacks in the Atlantic, with the population slowly rising. "The transition from whale killing to whale watching has pricked the consciences of nations worldwide. The movement to save the whales may have been the greatest conservation story of the 20th century," according to whale researchers

Local artisanal fishermen have cleared out all the fish from the shallow reefs off the coast.

Taking a short break on deck with my daughter, Jessica, and son, Alex, between dives.

Aggressor Dive Fleet president and CEO, Wayne Hasson, and family friend Christina Gray.

Turks and Caicos Aggressor II *at anchor behind the reef on the Silver Bank.*

and authors Greg Kaufman and Dr. Paul Forestell.

We have seen humpback whales on many expeditions in the Pacific Ocean—from Panama, Costa Rica and Mexico to Hawaii and Alaska—but never had a chance to swim with them. We were invited on a whale-filming expedition by Aggressor Dive Fleet president and CEO, Wayne Hasson, in February 2004, with a group of his friends and family. In Puerto Plata, Dominican Republic, we boarded *Turks and Caicos Aggressor II,* captained by Piers van de Valt, then headed 85 miles north through the night to the Silver Bank. In the pre-dive briefing the next morning, Piers explained that we would typically see three different behavioral situations: a) a mother and calf together; b) sleepers or loggers slowly moving along and; c) a "rowdy bunch," several males chasing a female and competing with one another. The team was

split into two inflatable chase boats with guides. We went out moving slowly west, looking for the whales in between the bommies—very shallow coral-reef heads—in 60 feet of water. The mothers had given birth to their calves in the shallow reef areas between the bommies and stayed in that zone all the time, while the males typically were out on the bank jumping, fin slapping and generally putting on a show.

The best situation was to have a mother with a newborn calf. We would wait 50 yards away in the boat and time the breathing cycle of the calf, typically breathing every four minutes. Then the mother would surface to breathe every four or five cycles the calf made, about every 15 to 18 minutes. When the calf came to the surface, it would linger, play around and do some moves, which included breaching. Sometimes it would approach the quiet string of wide-eyed snorkelers before returning to its

*Humpbacks off the Big Island,
Hawaii. My first encounter with
humpback whales was fishing
there. This over/under painting
includes the dramatic scenery
in the background, unlike the
Silver Bank experience.*

mother. If mother was calm, then everything lasted for quite a while, hours sometimes. The mother surfaced like a submarine, her bulk impressive and highlighted by massive white pectoral fins like wings. The calves were gray in color, with big white pectoral fins and large expressive eyes. Sometimes they breached, wanting to play, but mother controlled the show. Or sometimes a male arrived on the scene uninvited and got between us and the mother and calf. Game over.

We had an action-packed few days. We intercepted the rowdy males a couple of times as they let off long, agitated blasts of bubbles from their blowholes. They swam rapidly along between the bommies, trying to get the mother's attention. Late one afternoon, we were generously called over to a mother and calf by another operator, on *Wind Dancer*. We took the opportunity to swim until late with these two. They

never left, just went up and down to breathe in a regular cycle, with no interference from any males. A pod of spotted dolphins blitzed us as we got back in the inflatable, then stayed for a while. What a finale! The dolphins showed up again the next morning, and we spent some quality time with them. Compared with bottlenose dolphins, Atlantic spotted dolphins are much more interactive and playful.

We returned to the Silver Bank in March 2005, with my daughter, Jessica, and son, Alex, in tow, plus legendary sculptor Kent Ullberg and friends Bill and Beverly Watts; Steve Valletta and his wife, Dana; and Jimmy Valletta. Underwater cameraman Rick Westphal was on board to document the expedition.

We were once again greeted by Piers Van de Valt aboard *Turks and Caicos Aggressor II*. We left at midnight and anchored up behind the reef early the next morning. Soon after breakfast and before the briefing, Piers noticed a mother and calf resting not 100 yards from the boat, so we quickly got our gear and headed out. Right off the bat, Rick, Kent, Jessica and Alex were in the water with their first humpbacks, chattering with excitement when they returned.

We spent most of the day east of the anchorage behind the reef, looking for opportunities to jump in. Most of the encounters were flyby swims: Piers would drop us in 50 yards ahead of a group of moving whales, and we would get a passing shot. He advised us that this late in the season there were more whales chasing mates and fewer mother/calf interactions. Plus the calves would all be bigger now. For the next couple of days, we had short swims with resting loggers, always with an escort in tow. To get the action shots, Piers was more willing for us to get in on the flyby situation, some of which were very dramatic.

PREVIOUS SPREAD

Dolphins often swim with their larger relatives; this was a common occurrence on the Silver Bank. Mixed media.

BELOW

A defensive escort whale rears above Kent and me as if to say, "Too close—back off."

FACING PAGE

A mother and calf shortly before they leave the Silver Bank. The calves consume about 100 gallons of milk per day and grow rapidly until it is time to leave the sanctuary of the bank.

Kent and I were able to start creating some art, having had some inspirational encounters. He had brought some modeling clay, and I had brought a large canvas to do some painting. It was wonderful being able to sit up on the sun deck and paint between dives, after lunch or in the evening, and watch the sun go down, while in the near distance whales were slapping fins and tails and presenting the occasional full-body breach. The breeze whipped the spray away in a billion golden droplets, and the loud report reached us a second later.

The wind was still blowing hard on the fourth day of the trip. Piers took us to the west in the morning and kept in close to the main reef to stay out of the chop. We had a couple of short encounters and then—bingo! We found a mother that was particularly calm, and we had a three-hour encounter. We were in and out of the water eight or 10 times, during which she moved very little and the calf kept coming right up to us, with mother staying 30 feet below. At one point the calf's face was just a few feet from us—we could see all the detail, the nodules, scrape marks and that inquisitive eye. Then it started swishing its tail sideways in a wide arc, getting closer, like trying to sweep us out of the way. We backed off, and then the calf returned to its mother.

We stayed with them from 11 a.m. until 3 p.m., at which time we called over our other chase boat to have a turn because we were cold, hungry and out of gas. What a day. That encounter

happened adjacent to a bommie in shallow water, so the light on everything was bright, bringing out all the colors of the reef: the pinks, purples, pastel greens, and yellows of the reef corals and sea fans, with the calf in the foreground and mother below, menacingly dark but with bright-turquoise pectoral fins reflecting the sunlight. That was what I wanted to paint.

The wind had dropped out for our last morning. We headed back east and went a bit wider of the main reef, and soon located a threesome: mother, calf and escort. The male remained in the background for most of the encounter. We got in and out at least 10 times over the next two hours; the mother moved only a little, with the calf surfacing every four minutes in front of us. The male was not pushing her but gradually became more involved. Then at one point, the male moved in deep below us and stayed. I could see his white pec fins out of the corner of my eye while filming the calf.

Alex was in the boat, while Kent, Jessica, Rick and I were all swimming and filming, and when I looked down, all I saw was the snout and jaw plate, loaded with sharp barnacles, of the male escort coming up at us—fast. The barnacles were bright white and getting bigger rapidly. *Abort!* was all I could think as I furiously backpedaled. The snout, head, and pectorals of the male reared up above us and crashed back down on the surface. We reckoned that was a clear warning by the escort that we were close enough. No harm done, but it does raise the question of what would happen if you were bumped by an adult whale or if one breaching actually landed on the chase boat.

We left with lots of good images and footage of humpback calves and their mothers—some rowdy moments, but most of all for a much better appreciation of the natural history of the species. Humpbacks visit the shallow reefs of the Silver Bank to have their calves in the calm, shallow, warm water away from any potential predators. Having put on thousands of pounds in just a few months, the calves then migrate with the adults several thousand miles north to their summer feeding grounds, running a gauntlet of fishing gear, ships and natural predators such as killer whales along the way. The calves are weaned by the time they return to the warm waters of the Caribbean, where the cycle begins again.

All I saw was **THE SNOUT AND JAW PLATE,** *loaded with sharp barnacles, of the* **MALE ESCORT COMING UP AT US—FAST.** *The barnacles were bright white and getting bigger rapidly.* **ABORT!** *It was all I could think as* **I FURIOUSLY BACKPEDALED.** *The snout, head, and pectorals of the male reared above us and* **CRASHED BACK DOWN ON THE SURFACE.**

Venezuela

A BILLFISH BONANZA

SOME PEOPLE ASK ME where the best places to fish are, and why. For 30 years, we have been repeatedly visiting several places because of the consistent fishing, and Venezuela is one of those places.

One of the most important studies on post-release mortality of billfish over the years was conducted by Dr. John Graves of the Virginia Institute of Marine Science at the College of William and Mary. With white marlin, blue marlin, sailfish and swordfish readily available, Venezuela was one place where John would have a lot of different billfish to tag.

Having fished there numerous times since 1987, we organized an expedition in late November 2002 aboard *Caliente*, a 60-foot Mikelson owned by Steve Potts of Scout Boats, who would also ride along with us. I had fished on this boat previously in an episode of *Sport Fishing Television*, hosted at the time by Dean Travis Clarke. The crew of Capt. Ryan Higgins and mate Bennett Griffin had been wonderful to work with. Our camera team consisted of Rick Westphal, James Petit and Andy Rowe.

Heading out it was windy at the famed La Guaira Bank. The first four white marlin that came in the spread were all window shoppers, not interested, but the bite turned on shortly afterward, and we hooked a couple of active whites on circle hooks. They were jumping like crazy, doing cartwheels in the air, and we were able to tag one with a PAT satellite tag.

Ryan got word from the other captains that a *ribazon*, or huge ball of baitfish, was forming offshore. We ran out 8 miles and found a school of bait with tuna all over it, so Rick and I went in with tanks. I went down to 30 feet, and there in the middle of the ball was the back and tail of a whale shark. I swam up next to the whale shark—the biggest I had seen, at least 50 feet long—which had its mouth open, sucking in sardines fleeing from the tuna. The shark stopped feeding and went deep, so we went back to the boat and resumed trolling, catching a couple of 50-pound yellowfins before hooking a really nice one of 140 pounds. We also found a big leatherback turtle to dive on for the first time. It was all happening in one area, which is why I love Venezuela.

The weather was calm the next day, and as we ran out we heard that another ribazon was forming just north of the bank. The tuna were thick below, those coming up to the surface in a constant conveyor belt of gleaming fish, pectorals out wide and the beautiful bronze band along their bodies glowing brightly. Their yellow sickle fins and finlets stood out against the dark blue water. The only billfish I saw was a blue marlin that came by 10 feet below us on the hunt.

Afterward, we moved to another massive bait school a half-mile away. So many tuna were feeding on sardines at the surface that they had turned the upper 15 feet of water white with foam. I stayed on the edges of it just as a Bryde's whale came up out of nowhere, mouth open like a garage door, and sliced through the densely packed bait, moving fast, maybe 20 knots. Then another whale went by on my right side, its throat pleats distended, slowing down as its tongue squeezed out the water, leaving only the bait to be swallowed. Sunlight dappled its great body. It turned, went down and turned around again for another pass, crashing through the surface before rolling on its right side as before.

A whale shark joined the action—it probably had been there all along but I just hadn't seen it. I now had a Bryde's whale and a whale shark in the same frame. It was an amazing experience, with more to come, as I retreated to the boat to hurriedly change my tank and the batteries for the camera. The cockpit was a frenzy of activity as we all reset for the next opportunity. Just then, another massive whale shark passed right under the boat. The school of bait took up its position, swirling like a tornado, above the head and front end of the 50-foot whale shark while the tuna attacked them from the side. I stayed with this shark for 20 minutes. I had no idea where the boat was, and so I surfaced low on air but exhilarated. Ryan was nearby, having been driving from the tower and following my bubbles. John was happy with the progress we'd made, so we arranged to return the following year to keep deploying PATs on white marlin, continuing the survivability study.

We organized another expedition on *Caliente* for early October 2003. We were shooting an episode on white marlin for the series *Portraits from the Deep*, then in its second season. I invited Kent Ullberg, America's—and perhaps the world's—most famous wildlife sculptor and a great friend, to go with us on the tagging expedition.

For the post-release mortality study, John was going to deploy more tags on white marlin, with some caught using J hooks and some caught on circle hooks. John emphasized that every white marlin caught had to be tagged, no matter their condition. Our first day, October 1, was a ripper right from the start. Out near La Guaira Bank on a calm morning,

Vast schools of small sardines bring predators from far and wide to the feast. A fast-moving Bryde's whale competes with the lumbering whale shark and swift tuna to scoop up bushels of baitfish with each pass. Acrylic on canvas.

the white marlin action was solid. Our first bite was a tripleheader on J hooks, and we converted two of them to releases. John tagged both fish. We then caught a couple of singles, tagging them before we switched to using circle hooks.

Midafternoon, a blue marlin came up on the long left ballyhoo bait. Wanting something bigger, it swiftly swam forward in the spread and creamed the left teaser. I pitched a horse ballyhoo, but the marlin went right to the center of the spread, then came left to eat the horse ballyhoo, missed it, turned on a dime, all lit up, and ate the bait on the short left rigger, head and shoulders out of the water—40 seconds of adrenaline-pumping action. On 20-pound-test tackle, Ryan raced after the marlin in reverse, and *Caliente* could really move. The marlin was jumping all over the place, then the fish went down. Harnessed up, I put pressure on the fish and brought it back up for lots more jumps, until Bennett got the leader and released the marlin. We finished the day with two more white marlin caught on circle hooks, and tagged them both. We caught eight white marlin out of 12 bites, went zero-for-2 on sailfish and caught a blue marlin.

The next day, we started out with a quadruple header of white marlin and caught a couple of them on circle hooks in calm conditions. John tagged them next to the boat in the water as Rick and I swam with them on release. Since there were so many fish around, I switched to jumping in on the white marlin as they came in the spread while the other anglers were hooking them. *Caliente* had a wide swim platform, which was a good place to wait for a bite, and which also made it easy to get back in the boat. It was so cool to be in the water with the teasers going past overhead and a couple of white marlin on them, fins up, stripes on their bodies so bright that they looked white against their dark bodies. White marlin have a broad bronze strip running along the flank just below the dark back, which is sometimes green and sometimes blue/black depending on the sunlight. They are very agile and could turn around in their own body length, thanks in part to oversize pectoral fins that look like oars.

Having caught six white marlin and deployed all the PAT tags, we turned our attention to swordfish. Ryan trolled west toward a spot where the shelf dropped steeply. We trolled past schools of tuna working bait, raised a couple of white marlin, and the radio was saying the bite was on. Decisions! We really wanted Kent to catch a swordfish though, so we went with the plan.

With a half-mullet rigged to a 12/0 J hook, a 16-ounce weight and a light attached to the leader, the main sacrificial weight was a mesh vegetable bag filled with stones from the beach. This was attached to the hook with a piece of 8-pound-test line, then lowered to the seafloor. When the bag hit bottom, we jerked the main line, breaking off the weight and leaving

THE MARLIN CAME LEFT, *missed the horse ballyhoo, turned on a dime, all lit up, and ate the bait on the* **SHORT LEFT RIGGER,** *head and shoulders out of the water.*

the bait hanging at the chosen depth. Soon we had a bite and Kent was in the chair, handling the rod like a pro. When the swordfish was close to the boat, I went in with a tank and filmed some of the action, staying well clear of the fish. It was purple-blue with silver flanks that reflected bright sunlight as it got closer to the boat. I got 20 feet below the swordfish because I thought they were going to gaff it right away, but it suddenly turned around and headed down at warp speed in a power dive, the tail beating rapidly like a skipjack tuna. Down it went and out of sight in the clear water, and I was glad to not be in the way of that rush.

Kent brought the swordfish back up to the boat, put John on the rod, and then he jumped into the water to have a look. The fish turned again and went down between us, zigzagging erratically. I really did not like being in the water with this animal—they are crazy.

At the end of the fight, the swordfish was gaffed and brought on board. Kent was thrilled to get his hands on his own swordfish, around 170 pounds. We spent the rest of the ride home looking at the anatomy of the fish, which is really quite different from the billfish family in so many ways. It was worth giving up a good white marlin bite to see this fish up close.

For our last day, we headed west to the swordfish drop and set two lines at 10:30 a.m. With little current—unlike fishing off the Yucatan or in the Gulf Stream off Florida—we did not drift much, and the baits stayed near the bottom. After an hour with no bites, Ryan moved and reset the lines. Then at 2:30 p.m., three boats around us hooked up with swordfish almost simultaneously. Ryan dropped me off close to *Bud Man* to film their sword being caught. Next, we went to a local boat with a bigger swordfish on the line. When they brought it in the boat, the fish went nuts: The mate lost his grip on the fish and jumped overboard, the captain flew up the ladder to the bridge, and the angler ran forward to the bow as the dying fish beat up the cockpit with its bill. You cannot afford to get in the

way of that sharp bill when its owner is swinging.

Back on board *Caliente*, we finally had a bite, and John was up. He did a great job on the fish, bringing it to color in about 45 minutes. We were going to release this one and follow it down for as long as possible. It lay quietly by the swim platform as we cut the leader, and the 200-pound fish slowly swam down right past Rick's camera. I grabbed the dorsal fin in one hand, camera in the other, as we went deep, fast. The fish was pumping now; its color had returned, and it was bright purple in my hands. It took only a few seconds, but it seemed like ages. I let go at around 100 feet as the swordfish kept swimming down strongly—a beautiful sight as it disappeared into the depths.

Hurricane Ivan hit Grand Cayman on September 11 and 12, 2004, and we were fortunate to still have a roof, though the storm surge was over 8 feet for much of the island. It was a long recovery time after the storm, so the last thing on my agenda was going fishing, even to Venezuela. Our next expedition was in November 2005.

Caliente had been sold; Ryan was now working with Viking and was on a 68-footer at the Portofino dock, so we chartered *Tropic Sun*, a beautiful 46-foot Merritt, from Venezuelan Luis

> *We started the day with an* **ACROBATIC WHITE MARLIN** *whose* **SILVER FLANKS AND WHITE BELLY** *contrasted starkly against the gray-black rain clouds in the background.*

Angel Rincon, who is also the owner of Mango Marina. John was back, this time with friend and dentist Dr. Ken Neill. My film crew of Ken Kavanaugh and cameraman Dee Gele was along to shoot the expedition as well.

We started out catching a sailfish, then a 200-pound blue marlin crashed the left teaser, and I hooked it with the pitch bait. The next fish up was a crazy blue marlin, again on the left teaser. I hooked it on a 50-pound-class outfit, and Capt. Wilfredo backed down hard on this 250-pound marlin as it went away doing lollipop jumps going down-sea. Wilfredo knew only two speeds: full stop and full speed, forward or reverse.

The next day, Wilfredo ran so hard in a rough sea that we broke an engine mount. We tagged two white marlin and missed three sailfish that day, but we finished early and came in on one engine. With *Tropic Sun* out of action, we were lucky to have Capt. Jimmy Grant on *Waterman* available for our next two days. Ken and I decided we had lots of footage catching marlin and so were going to tease and swim with billfish all day, which was fine with Jimmy.

In the cockpit, Ken was on the right and I was on the left. Two sails came into the spread but did not tease well. Next, another pair of sails came in—one teased very well right in front of my camera, but overall it was a slow day. At 4 p.m. a

300-pound blue marlin came up on the left teaser, so I went in and followed it over to the right teaser; it stayed around the stern for a while, charging the teasers being cast by the mates on spinning rods. The colors on the marlin were superb, with bright and vivid stripes along its flanks. Good stuff.

Still teasing and filming on the last day in better weather, we raised a white marlin that was initially shy but eventually came close. It was beaten up, with some scars on its body, and it had a broken bill. I imagine that marlin had some interesting stories to tell. Then we had a blue marlin stomp on the long right teaser and track it all the way in to the boat; Ken and I went in, the marlin swam at Ken, then crossed the wake coming straight at me, where I got the best shot of the trip: the fish bursting through the foam of the wake coming right at the camera. This made for our first grand slam on film. Soon after, a 350-pound blue came up on the right teaser. We jumped in, and rather than stop the boat, I asked Jimmy to keep going and bring the boat around 360 degrees while still teasing the

A sketch of a white marlin on a daisy-chain squid teaser. Ink drawing.

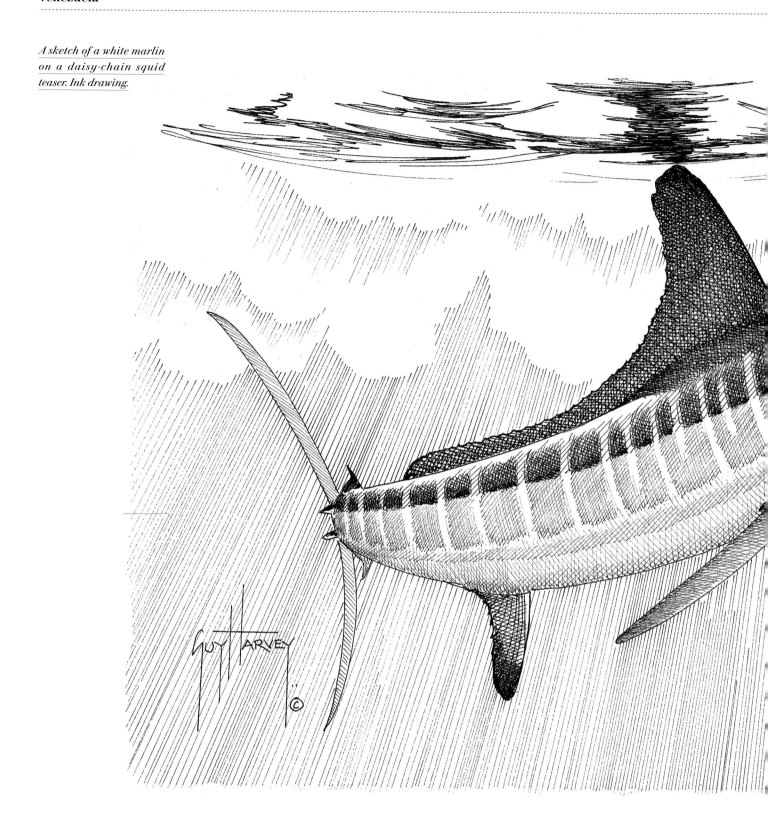

fish to bring the marlin right past us for the second shot. It worked like a charm, and the hot marlin came right past the camera on the second pass.

We all returned in 2006 for what was to be our last expedition to Venezuela. We were shooting an episode on all species of billfish for my final series of *Portraits from the Deep*. John was continuing the post-release mortality study, but now the focus was on blue marlin. We had chartered *Waterman* again; Dr. Ken Neill and Bill Watts were our anglers.

October 30 was windy and squally, with intermittent rain. We started out with an acrobatic white marlin whose silver flanks and white belly contrasted starkly against the gray-black rain clouds in the background and inspired several paintings. On our second day, we saw and caught several sailfish, and then a small blue marlin that unfortunately swallowed the J hook and was bleeding at the boat. John tagged it as part of the survivability study; we found out three days later that the marlin had died. That evening at Mango Marina, we

were chatting with Luis Angel, who had just returned from Australia fishing with Capt. Laurie Wright. Luis had caught a black marlin that Laurie said was the biggest marlin he had caught as skipper, well over 1,200 pounds.

Unfortunately, the politics in Venezuela have rapidly become more anti-US, so we stopped visiting this nation. I am sure the fishing is still good, although I hope the burgeoning artisanal fishery does not wipe out the white marlin and sailfish. As we know, catch-and-release sport fishing is a sustainable use of the billfish resource. With everyone using circle hooks as a result of the research work by Dr. John Graves and others, it is clear that they consistently maintain a very high survival rate at 98 percent; the value of a living billfish to the country of Venezuela remains much higher than if the fish were harvested.

Hopefully in the not too distant future, normalcy will return, and once again the marinas will be full of sport-fishing activity. Viva Venezuela!

Stingrays vie with turtles as the mascot of the Cayman Islands. Rays are never alone, and have bar jacks and yellowtail snapper in tow.

A NEW HOME

IN *PORTRAITS FROM THE DEEP*, I describe in its first chapter growing up in Jamaica, where my family has lived for 10 generations, since 1664. Yet even as I wrote that chapter in 2002, we had already moved our family to Grand Cayman in August 1999, and still considered ourselves fresh expatriates working to fully integrate ourselves into our new home.

We achieved Cayman status in 2003, which was a big step forward. Full integration, though, came as we invested ourselves in the local economy and habitat. The Guy Harvey Ocean Foundation and Guy Harvey Research Institute began actively conducting research in 2002, and the Guy Harvey Gallery and Shoppe opened on the waterfront in George Town in December 2006.

The GHRI and GHOF have undertaken a number of research and educational projects in the Cayman Islands, some of which are still current. The longest-running project is the study of the stingray population.

RAYS

Early upon our arrival, I identified a research opportunity on the stingrays that visited the sandbar, also known as Stingray City, each day in North Sound. Virtually nothing was known about these animals except that they were being fed by divers on a regular basis, starting in 1983 or '84. Large numbers of

transponder, called a PIT tag, during the first year of research.

The process involved catching all the rays by hand, putting them in a landing net, and then lifting them into a pool in the workboat. Here, after covering the spine, the ray was measured, weighed, sexed and tagged, and then a DNA sample was taken before it was marked as recorded with small wing clip.

Rays were recaptured on a monthly basis to measure growth and to determine pregnancy in females. All the rays did not visit the sandbar every day, but many did. Mark established nighttime behavior by sonically tracking individual rays for 24 hours, 48 hours and even 72 hours. Generally females stayed close by in the sand around the site, while the smaller males spent the night foraging as they do normally. It is likely they do not compete well for food with the much larger females at the site during the day, hence the need to feed at night. It was apparent early on that constant food supplementation had changed the rays' behavior from being nighttime predators to feeding during the day while resting at night.

In 2003, the GHOF worked with Diana Udel of Broadcast Quality in Coral Gables, Florida, to produce a documentary called *The Stingray Chronicles*, which told the story of the research work so far.

During the first two years of the work, the number of tagged rays reached 320 animals, including many wild rays as controls. Approximately 160 rays frequented the sandbar. Thereafter, other researchers came to study the rays using the baseline data we had collected over the first two years.

In 2004, Hurricane Ivan came through on September 11 and 12 as a Category 5 hurricane, and Grand Cayman was badly damaged. The island was closed for repairs for three months. No visitors came until December, so there was no one feeding the rays on a regular basis. From a research perspective, it was

people visited two sites on a daily basis, creating jobs for many locals in the watersports sector. The socioeconomic value of the attractions was obvious, but no one had any idea about the natural history of the species.

Under the terms of reference drawn up by the Cayman Islands Department of Environment, the GHRI had initiated a series of surveys that resulted in creating a database of the participating rays. Answers were needed to the following questions: How sustainable was the interaction? Are the rays now dependent on food supplementation? How many are males or females? When do they become mature adults? How many pups do they have? Is there a breeding season? What do they do at night? What are their predators? This research was the first detailed investigation into the influence of supplemental feeding on the movement patterns of a marine animal.

Under the supervision of Dr. Mahmood Shivji, director of the GHRI at Nova Southeastern University, Mark Corcoran began the survey in February 2002 as a master's student, with assistant Hillary Ganz. Mahmood said this would be the start of a long-term study. Like sharks, rays are long-lived animals, and to fully understand their life history, research must cover several years. With support from the GHOF and us personally, plus some volunteers, the entire population of rays at the sandbar was caught and tagged with a passive integrated a lost opportunity to determine if there was weight loss in the population or if they foraged as normal.

Surveys resumed in 2005. It was determined that the rays were in good health following Ivan, so they must have been foraging normally.

Meanwhile in 2007, the DOE limited the amount of food that each tour boat could feed the rays on each visit. This had the effect of reducing the number of rays visiting the site. Less food, fewer rays. Was that good for the rays? It certainly wasn't good for tourism. In the following surveys in 2008, it was apparent that the number of rays visiting the sandbar was reduced to just over 100 animals.

By 2011, it was obvious that the number of rays was falling to the point where tour operators were concerned about the population. In the January 2012 survey, we counted only 62. What had happened with the rays? Dr. Brad Wetherbee of the University of Rhode Island was helping us with the ray surveys and enlisted the assistance of three veterinarians from the Georgia Aquarium: Nicole Boucha, Tonya Clauss and Lisa Hoopes. They visited us for the July survey, in which we caught only 57 rays. We took blood from all rays and determined from analyses of stable isotopes and fatty acids that there was nothing wrong with the rays. They were fed mostly squid by operators, which showed up in the results. Squid is not in their normal diet, but it's cheap, which is why the tour operators use it.

Soon afterward, Tonya contacted me to say that the Dolphin Discovery tourist site had 10 rays in a pen next to the dolphin tanks. We informed the DOE, which then went to the facility with a scanner and found four male rays had our

PIT tags. Because we had demonstrated strong site fidelity in the rays, it is unlikely that the stories of Dolphin Discovery staff taking the rays from fishermen were true. Was sabotage one explanation for the reduced numbers of rays? The Dolphin Discovery management was instructed to hand over the four tagged rays to the DOE, but they refused to give up the other six rays because there was no law to prevent possession. These rays were so valuable to the country that legal protection was needed right away.

We had to wait for a change in government on May 22, 2013, before any meaningful action was taken. The incoming

By 2011, it was obvious that THE NUMBER OF RAYS WAS FALLING to the point where tour OPERATORS WERE CONCERNED about the population. In the January 2012 survey, we counted only 62. WHAT HAD HAPPENED WITH THE RAYS?

BELOW

The sandbar on a busy day in ideal conditions. This is one of the most popular tourism attractions in the Caribbean and needs to be protected for future generations to enjoy.

FACING PAGE, TOP

Scribble art of a ray, nice and simple.

FACING PAGE, BOTTOM

GHOF staff and volunteers lift a 130-pound female ray into the boat for measurements, an ultrasound and a blood sample.

Minister of the Environment, Hon. Wayne Panton, made the necessary changes to accelerate protection for all species of rays by May 2013. The survey count in July 2013 was still low at 61 rays. On July 12, all the rays from Dolphin Discovery were released back at the sandbar by the DOE. Well-known environmentalist and TV show host Jeff Corwin was on hand to film our work, getting the story out to a wider audience.

In 2014, we did surveys four times per year, with assistance again from three veterinarians from the Georgia Aquarium. The team included Dr. Alexa McDermott, who replaced Nicole Boucha in the ongoing project sponsored by the GHOF. Not only were the blood samples important for establishing the health of the rays, but they brought an ultrasound to test for pregnancy. Unfortunately, we were present on January 6 when a tour-boat operator revving his boat engines on a flat-calm day at the sandbar hit a mature female and chopped her up. In my mind, a $10 million matriarch was killed, with no consequences for the operator. The behavior of some tour operators who take the rays for granted had to change.

Regulations about boathandling and ray handling needed to be set and properly enforced. The DOE was not sufficiently well-funded to have a constant presence at the sandbar, which is needed, particularly on heavy cruise-ship days, Tuesday to Thursday. Thousands of people went to the site each day. The attraction was way beyond capacity from 2013 and the government looked the other way, beholden to cruise-ship companies. The tour operators were not benefiting as much as the cruise-ship companies were from this situation. The

visitors' experience was diluted, the rays left the site because of the heavy foot traffic, and those rays that stayed would be passed from group to group without a break. We received many complaints about the lack of controls at the sandbar.

This all came at a time when Jessica, who had worked at the DOE for nearly four years, joined the GHOF as project manager. One of her projects was to make a stingray-handling video with documentary producer George Schellenger that would help tour operators and the DOE with enforcement issues.

Thereafter, we continued to do the surveys twice per year, in January and July, with the help of resident veterinarian Dr. Ioana Popescu and other local vets and volunteers, many of whom were high schoolers. Jessica and Louisa Gibson built a comprehensive list of volunteers to assist with the surveys and with the shark-tagging projects. The numbers of rays rose steadily as the years went by. This was expected because about one-third of the mature females have pups at any time in the year. In addition, natural predation is low.

The current number as of this writing is approximately 115 rays at the sandbar, 15 at Deep Stingray City, 12 at Rum Point, and three at Coral Gardens, which are sites we have added to the survey. It is interesting how little the rays travel between these sites, even though they are geographically close together.

Bad weather early in 2020 kept us from conducting our January survey. While we were working the first day of the survey on March 22, we were escorted off the sandbar by the marine police due to the regulations regarding size of gatherings and social distancing during the pandemic that had been announced that morning. In the three months following, we were not permitted to feed the rays or take note of which rays came and went during the period of no tourism activity. Only DOE staff fed the rays occasionally. A tremendous research opportunity was lost after 17 years of working at the site and never having this situation occur.

Hopefully in the year ahead, we will learn more about how a monthslong stoppage on tourism affected the ray's attendance

A 10-foot tiger shark caught in North Sound, which Dr. Ioana Popescu measured and deployed a SPOT before release.

at the sandbar. Based on our experience with Hurricane Ivan, we anticipate the sandbar population should return. It will be interesting to see how quickly we get back to 80 or 100 rays.

This ongoing study is the longest-running survey of a marine interactive program in the world, centered on the most visited marine interactive site in the world. The GHOF produced a new documentary called *Stingray Chronicles II* in 2019 to highlight the research effort and also the progress made since 2003.

SHARKS

Mahmood tasked us with catching and tagging several species of sharks to add to our database, particularly tiger sharks, from Bermuda and the Bahamas. We discovered in Bermuda that smart position- and temperature-transmitting tags worked well on tiger sharks, so we began collaborating with Dr. Rupert Ormond and Dr. Mauvis Gore of Marine Conservation International, which had a grant from the Darwin Initiative to conduct research work on sharks in the Cayman Islands. Setting mini longlines in North Sound yielded several species, including tiger sharks, great hammerheads, blacktip sharks, Caribbean reef sharks and the occasional nurse shark. Rupert, Mauvis and their students placed sonic transducers in these sharks and used the array of sensors around the island to detect movements. Two tiger sharks were also tagged with SPOT tags.

In 2015, all sharks received protection under the new National Conservation Law, which was pushed through the Legislative Assembly by Minister Panton. Rays had already been protected in 2013 after the sabotage debacle. So now all sharks and rays were protected in the Cayman Islands, following Honduras and the Bahamas, which had achieved the same milestone. The BVI and Saba can now be added to this list. Sharks will not be safe in the wider Caribbean until all island states acknowledge the low numbers of sharks and the inherent value in protecting sharks and rays for the good of marine ecosystems and their own socioeconomic well-being.

With permits issued by the DOE, we continued our research on tiger sharks. Our efforts targeted tiger sharks using big hooks, heavy leaders and big baits fishing at night in 8 to 12 feet of water. We had several volunteers helping my team, led by Alexandra Prebble from 2014, including Ioana and Pete Foster-Smith. The best time of year to catch tiger sharks was from December through April. Heavy winds during that season limited our fishing.

In one week in early March 2016, we caught three large tiger sharks, the largest of which was 11 feet long. It was memorable because everything that could go wrong that night did go wrong. On March 1, we set the line at sunset in the usual place 500 yards south of the sandbar. On the first check an hour later, the bait was still on the first hook. On the second hook, a 6-foot blacktip awaited us. While we were handling that shark, the main line went tight, and in the gloom of our lights, a big shark reared up to our right, splashing, now caught on the first hook, next to the end buoy and anchor.

We decided to wait 15 minutes because the big shark was full of energy, just hoping it would get tired and calm down. Meanwhile we checked all the gear and discovered the drill battery was dead. Knowing we could not install a SPOT without an operational drill, we ran back into a canal to borrow one, and then headed back out to the line 2 miles away. On the way, a steering hose burst, rendering the steering wheel useless. Trouble! Now I was anxious to get back to the big tiger shark before she died on the line. In my 26-foot Dusky with a single Honda 225, Pete sat on the transom and held the engine straight with both arms, and I slowly guided the boat in the direction of the waypoint on the GPS in the darkness.

The shark was now tangled in the main line, which luckily held up. Pete and I got the tail rope on the tiger, and Ioana went to work. She drilled the holes for the SPOT tag in the shark's fin, took the DNA sample, and measured her at 3.4 meters fork length. We cut the hook with bolt cutters, and she swam off quickly. Tiger sharks are tough! We called David Carmichael for a tow in at midnight. What an experience. We named the shark Ioana, and she reported well for a couple of years afterward.

As you can see from the tracks generated, these tiger sharks gave us some long tracks, but we did not see the cyclical migrations experienced in the Western Atlantic around Bermuda and the Bahamas from the 50 tiger sharks tagged there from 2009 to 2014. The Cayman sharks stayed in the Caribbean mostly, and only one, Petey, ventured into the northern Bahamas, and one swam into the southern Gulf of Mexico. For the amount of effort we put in, our sample size was small.

Following the work done in the Bahamas on oceanic

whitetip sharks with Jim Abernethy, the dream team of Mahmood, Derek Burkholder and Brad came to Grand Cayman to help us with tagging OWTs. Knowing they were few and far between in a big blue ocean, we approached local experts for assistance in catching these sharks. Franklyn Thompson, president of the Cayman Islands Angling Club, and various tournament organizers—particularly Chris and Daniel Kirkconnell, who organized the Kirk Slam—joined the cause. The plan was to reward anglers $1,000 for an OWT they might catch and hold for us while we ran out with a chase boat to transfer the shark and then tag it.

With 50 participating boats in the tournaments working all sides of the island, we had four chase boats, each manned by volunteers and a GHOF staffer, to deploy tags. Andi Marcher (*Here Fishy Fishy*) and Bart Hedges (*Volatility*) were two key

volunteers, along with charter-boat owner Derrin Ebanks (*Hit 'n' Run*). My 26-foot Dusky, *Makaira,* rounded out the chase boats. The system worked well. We had several members of the local press who came with us to report on the collaboration. Before sharks were protected in 2015, many anglers would have killed an OWT or silky shark if it threatened to take their dolphin or tuna.

We ran out of tags the first year and deployed SPOTs on 10 mature OWTs. Each angler who donated a shark received $1,000 and a shark print at the awards ceremony to publicly acknowledge their support and participation. Two boats caught two OWTs, and one owner, Tom Guyton, kindly donated the reward money back to the GHOF. As time went on, our shark-tagging projects attracted the attention of several corporations, which donated to the research,

When a big blue marlin shows up chasing other fish beneath a log, the action is fast and furious—predator/prey inter- actions at their most exciting. Acrylic on canvas.

education, and conservation undertaken by the DOE and GHOF. These include James Mansfield of the Cayman Islands Brewery, which makes a local lager beer appropriately called White Tip. Cayman Islands Brewery donates 5 cents from each White Tip sold to shark conservation, so drink a beer and save a shark.

Other major sponsors of our work in the Cayman Islands include the Kenneth B. Dart Foundation (Chris Duggan), Sunset House, Tortuga Rum, Kirk Freeport (through the TAG Heuer Guy Harvey watch edition), HSBC, the Market Street Group and several individuals who make annual contributions. We successfully operated this system of tagging OWTs for several years during the dolphin tournament and the Cayman Islands Angling Club International Tournament. In all, 22 OWTs were tagged.

BLUE MARLIN

My favorite fish is the blue marlin. From a very early age, I have been fascinated by them and have caught many in different locations around the world. When we moved to Grand Cayman in 1999, I was lucky to get my 1994 26-foot Dusky center-console towed over from Jamaica to Grand Cayman. Over the years, we caught 51 blue marlin in that boat before it was stolen in 2016. I also had a 28-foot Scout, a beautiful boat that I bartered for in 2007 by trading advertising space on my television show at the time, *Portraits from the Deep*. We caught 10 blue marlin on that boat before it too went missing.

I eventually replaced the Scout with a 33-foot Dusky, also called *Makaira*, on which we caught 16 blue marlin in the first year, which was 2017/2018. I now keep the boat at the Cayman Islands Yacht Club.

*During the pandemic, the sand-
bar was closed to the public,
so the Dept. of Environment
and the GHOF were tasked with
feeding the rays daily. With no
other boats there, we learned
that the sandbar was not only
home to rays, but also several
blacktip, nurse and reef sharks,
as well as large fish.*

BELOW TOP LEFT

Unhooking and releasing a typical Cayman Islands blue marlin of 150 pounds.

BELOW BOTTOM LEFT

Alex hooks up to a blue marlin just a quarter-mile off Rum Point.

BELOW RIGHT

Jessica removes the hook from a 250-pound blue marlin she caught off Little Cayman.

MY FAVORITE FISH IS THE BLUE MARLIN. *From a very early age, I have been* **FASCINATED BY THEM** *and have caught many in different locations around the world.*

The GHOF tagged about two dozen blue marlin with pop-up archival transmitting tags in the Cayman Islands over a few years, mostly by my own fishing activity and some during the tournaments held each year.

Our best day of blue marlin fishing occurred on October 21, 2016. My son, Alex, and his friend, Trent Christie, went with me on the 26 Dusky for an afternoon of fishing. Between the northwest point and the seamount at 12.30 p.m., we had a blue marlin take the right short lure, a big pink-and-white chugger. Trent was up with Alex, coaching him on his first marlin. It was flat-calm, and I raced around to chase the 200-pound fish, which was jumping far away. Eventually we caught up with it, and as we got the leader, the hook came out—so, no photos. We continued trolling toward the seamount and were on the first pass right on top of it, when a marlin ate the right short again. Trent grabbed the rod. It peeled away, and a couple of seconds later, another bigger fish ate the left short, an old Pakula hard-head lure. Alex was on this fish. Doubled up!

Trent's fish started jumping behind the boat while Alex's went around the right, keeping away from the other marlin. Driving, I worked on Trent's marlin first because it seemed about 175 pounds and was staying up at the surface a lot. Meanwhile, Alex moved around to the bow. I backed up on Trent's fish, and he was now an experienced angler fighting his second blue marlin in one hour. After 25 minutes, I got the leader, grabbed my camera, and fired off some shots with Trent and his fish. The fish rolled, I pulled out the hook, and it swam off strongly in a perfect release. We turned our attention to catching Alex's fish. Alex fought the marlin for another 20 minutes and brought it up on the port side. It was a long fish, easily 275 to 300 pounds. We tagged it with a PAT and took photos before releasing it. In three hours, we had caught and released three blue marlin, converting a double—a great afternoon of blue marlin fishing!

Our best year for blue marlin was 2008, fishing mostly on the 26 Dusky. Fishing for blue marlin in the Caymans is not like fishing the seamounts in Costa Rica, where in one day you can catch all the marlin you would catch in a season in most other locales. Here we get one bite per day, if that, so you'd better keep them on! Typically, if we catch a marlin in January, we make a push to try to catch one in every month of the year. That means lots of fishing, and in 2008, we nearly achieved it, with marlin caught every month of that year, January through November. We ended up going 17-for-24, with three doubleheaders, converting one, and a tripleheader, catching one. Pretty good for a 26-foot outboard boat.

LIONFISH

The year 2008 was also the year that divers began seeing a lot of lionfish on a regular basis. We had seen this invasive species already in the Bahamas, where it was causing untold damage to reef-fish populations. It would do the same in Cayman.

Lionfish are native to the Western Pacific and Indian Ocean. As a beautiful reef predator, it was a favorite species of the aquarium trade. People purchased lionfish and put them in their tanks, not realizing that they grow fast and eat everything else in the tank. People subsequently disposed of them in canals that lead into the sea. This happened frequently

replacing overfished snappers and groupers as the preferred "green" fish to consume. Restaurants proudly served lionfish; it quickly became a favorite.

At the same time, the GHOF supported research on lionfish natural history, behavior, growth rates and reproductive rates conducted by the Central Caribbean Marine Institute, based in Little Cayman. Up to 100 different reef species, many as juveniles, were found in the stomachs of lionfish, which grew to twice the size they attain in their native waters. They have become a formidable force and invaded every aspect of the marine environment, from the shallow mangrove habitat and seagrass beds to the reef and deep coral walls, more than 1,000 feet down.

Humans remain the only predator for now. The organized culls in the Caribbean, Bahamas and Florida are the one controlling mechanism of the creeping dominance of this species, which has been causing immeasurable damage to the Caribbean fish populations. Lionfish are here to stay as we continue to overexploit medium reef predators such as groupers, large snappers and reef-dwelling sharks, which have the capacity to control lionfish. There is evidence now in Little Cayman that Nassau grouper and nurse sharks are preying on lionfish. After three months of no diving allowed because of the pandemic and less diving generally in the second half of 2020, will the lionfish population in the Cayman Islands come back strongly?

MARINE PARKS

Since moving here in 1999, we have witnessed successive administrations in the Cayman Islands continue to neglect the environment. Overexploitation of fishery resources continues. Governments have been complicit in the destruction of coastal habitats through overdevelopment, which increases the pollution of the sea and groundwater due to an inadequate centralized sewage-disposal system. Where is the vision and the long-term planning, the leadership? Apart from Wayne Panton, successive Ministers of the Environment have done a terrible job.

However, we are fortunate to have a DOE staff who are dedicated to their work. With an inadequate budget, they carry out their jobs with pride and professionalism. The consistency of research, education and enforcement carried by the DOE over the past 30 years has enabled the marine environment to

enough to enable the species to reach a population threshold. With a rapid rate of reproduction, they suddenly exploded in an ideal marine environment with no predators and so much food available. No Atlantic or Caribbean fish recognized the lionfish as a predator; the medium reef predators did not recognize the lionfish as potential prey.

In the Cayman Islands, where snorkeling and diving is a major activity, the threat was quickly recognized, and the DOE instituted a culling system. After completing a lionfish training and spearing course, the registered diver was issued a short Hawaiian sling spear with three points just for lionfish. Catches were reported to a database, and lionfish culling became well-organized. The fish were good to eat, even

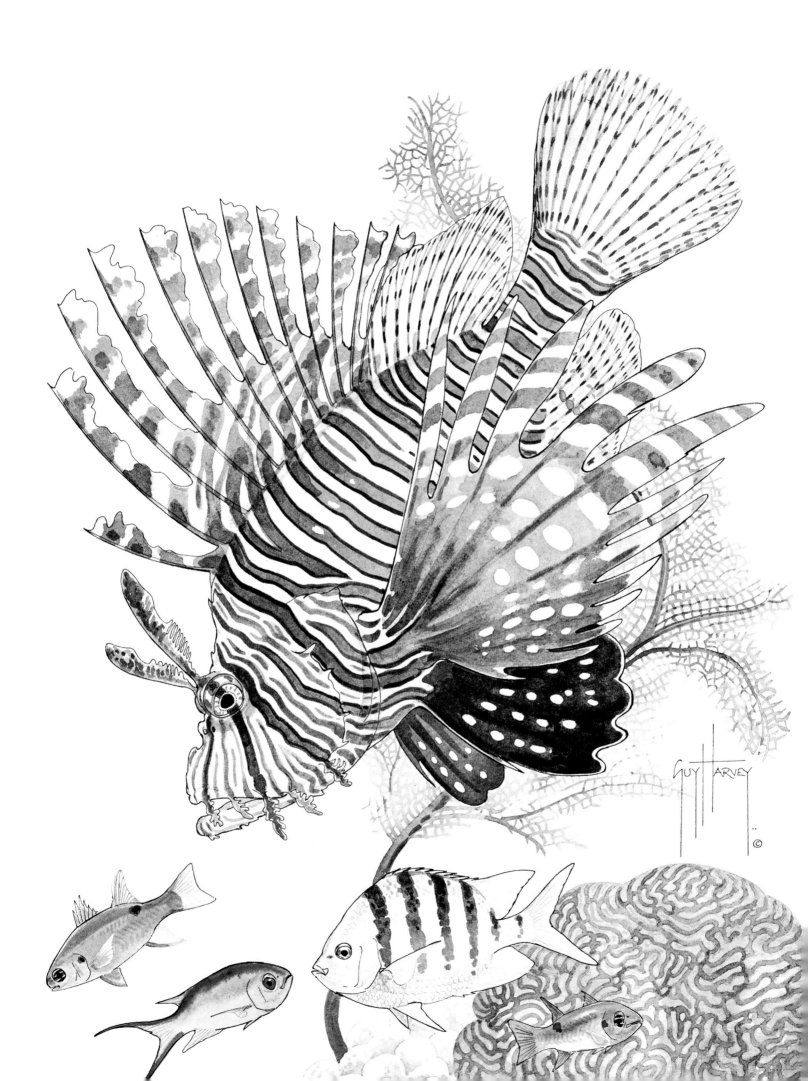

Guy Harvey

Marine parks are now an essential component of well-managed coral-reef ecosystems. Regulated fishing can exist with protection, but exploitation without protection will not work in the long run.

accommodate the high level of nonextractive use in the snorkel and dive industry, which is a focal point of the tourism product. Having 360 mooring buoys around all three islands for boats to tie up to instead of anchoring has been a game-changer. Compared with many of our neighboring countries in the Caribbean and Central America, we have an enlightened approach to the management of our limited marine resources. The Cayman Islands are tiny specks in the vast ocean, so responsible management for this small area is critical.

However, regulations regarding hook-and-line fishing, bait-fishing, spearfishing and trap-fishing have been inadequate in conserving the commercially important species. We must acknowledge that snappers, groupers, parrotfish, jacks and grunts are more valuable to us alive than cooked. However, our fish, lobster and conch resources continue to diminish, so more controls need to be put in place. Rather than protect individual species, it is much more cost-effective to expand the complete protection of marine habitats of

high value, and regulate extraction in neighboring areas where fishing is permitted. As more demands are placed by a growing population, it is necessary to plan for the future accordingly. Otherwise we will consume the icons of our marine heritage, and there will be nothing left.

Quoting from the Executive Summary of the Enhanced Marine Parks Proposal of 2011: "Research conducted by the Department of Environment and Darwin Project Partner, Bangor University, shows that the implementation of the existing Marine Parks thirty-plus years ago and their continued support have been effective in protecting the marine environment and coasts of Cayman, but that they now require enhancement to halt or even reverse evident declines in our marine resources. Our coral reefs are in poor health, the physical structure of the reef is degraded, fishing pressure is higher than previously believed, and our fish stocks are declining to critically low levels. Further, climate change, national population growth, development trajectories and economic growth will continue to apply pressures on our marine environment.

"Given that they have a variety of biological, fishing, economic and management benefits, the DOE believes that an enhanced system of Marine Parks which is underpinned by increasing the area of 'no-take' reserves to between 40 to 50 percent of shelf area (combined with species-specific fisheries management as needed; for example, Nassau grouper) is the optimal management tool to ensure the Cayman Islands marine resources are better able to resist or recover from existing and emerging threats. The proposals call for increasing the amount of 'no-take' area on each island.

"The justification for Marine Park Expansion was properly planned and researched, based on science, and has been considered by the DOE since 2011. There were many exhaustive rounds of public consultation and public input from 2012 to 2014. Then with the entry into force of the National Conservation Law, the Marine Parks system now fell under the new Protected Areas legislative regime, so another round of public consolation and revision was conducted in 2015. The plans were submitted to the cabinet in 2016 and again in 2018."

Feedback indicated that the majority of the public recognized the need for the enhancement of existing marine parks (currently at 10 to 15 percent of area). However, politicians do not grasp the concept of shifting-baseline syndrome, and typically listen to a few vociferous constituents and not the public at large. Unfortunately—predictably?—the Marine Park Expansion plans never made it to the cabinet's agenda.

Until, that is, Prince Charles visited the Cayman Islands from March 20 to 21, 2019. The government decided then to agree to the Marine Park Enhancement proposals because these would provide Charles with a positive environmental development to announce. As heir to the British throne, a world figure and an outspoken environmentalist, his opinion matters. His keynote speech reiterated the value of living reefs to human well-being, to small-island economies and to maintaining biodiversity. The concept is one on which we all can agree, but it still seems so difficult for politicians to grasp. What would our reefs look like now had the expansion plans been expedited back in 2011?

Male Nassau grouper in spawning color phase, crowding a female just moments before they all shoot up in the water column spewing gametes. Acrylic on canvas.

Little Cayman

UNDER THE GROUPER MOON

LITTLE CAYMAN IS ONE of the best places to visit in the Caribbean: small, quiet, civilized and perfect for anyone who wants to be close to nature. Topside are the world-famous red-footed booby and frigate bird nesting colonies, lots of indigenous rock iguanas, and beautiful beaches. For the fly-fisherman, the bonefish lurking in South Hole Sound or around Owen Island present a real challenge. Underwater, the 8-mile-long island has vibrant coral reefs with limited fishing pressure. With just under 200 people living on the island, it is like going back in time.

The crown jewel for divers is Bloody Bay Wall on the north side, which drops from 15 feet straight down to more than 1,000 feet. Swimming among the beautiful reefs are Nassau grouper—lots of them. Groupers and snappers spawn annually in the same place at the same time of year, called a spawning aggregation site, or SPAG. Unfortunately, fishermen, not only in the Cayman Islands but all over the Caribbean, have discovered these SPAGs and plundered them systematically. One site on the western end of Little Cayman remained untouched

until January 2001, when it was fished heavily, and again the following year. Approximately 2,000 spawning adult groupers were caught and taken to Grand Cayman for sale. The island's population was outraged, and the government banned fishing at these SPAGs. A research project was launched, and enforcement efforts began in earnest.

The Grouper Moon Project was initiated and conducted jointly by the legendary husband-and-wife research team of Dr. Brice and Dr. Christy Semmens from REEF and the Cayman Island government's Department of Environment. The director of that department, Gina Ebanks-Petrie, and her team of Tim Austin, Phil Bush, Bradley Johnson and Dr. Croy McCoy, were the key players in organizing research and logistics over many years. In addition, a group of the most dedicated fishery scientists and marine-sanctuary managers such as Dr. Steve Gittings of NOAA, Dr. Scott Heppell (Oregon State University), and many students and volunteers came each year to Little Cayman for the annual grouper spawn. Through the generosity of local hotel owners and dive operators, the project has been co-sponsored by numerous local residents and businesses. Peter Hillenbrand, owner of Southern Cross Club, was one of the project's biggest supporters. Little Cayman Reef Resort supplied free nitrox for countless dives each year for the research team, and local dive operators were invited to

experience the evening spawning events. The site is closed to public access.

We were finally granted access to film the Nassau grouper spawning aggregation in Little Cayman in 2011. For George Schellenger and our Guy Harvey Ocean Foundation team, the aim here was to tell the story of the recovery of the species under the unique conditions of research, cooperation and oversight. It was called *The Mystery of the Grouper Moon*. The moon is significant because the groupers gather during the full-moon phases in January and February and spawn generally three days afterward.

The biology of the larger grouper species works against them when they are overfished. They are long-lived, slow-growing species. Nassau grouper grow to 50 pounds and live for 20-plus years, living a solitary life as a medium reef predator until it is time to spawn. With this dispersed range and behavior, it is, theoretically, hard to overfish such a species.

In an island situation, reef fish will migrate to a place where their eggs and larvae have a high chance of dispersion, and consequent settlement of juveniles, while avoiding

ABOVE LEFT

Sir Richard Branson and daughter Holly about to do their first dive on the Nassau grouper SPAG in Little Cayman.

ABOVE RIGHT

Peter Hillenbrand's Southern Cross Club is the perfect getaway in Little Cayman for people who love to dive and fish.

FACING PAGE

Bonefish are a challenge to paint: a silver fish on a white background. Clear blue water over the seagrass flats helps to provide the contrast needed. Mixed media.

Here I am filming the main body of Nassau grouper spawning stock in "banding" mode. They spawned for the next three evenings.

On a flat-calm, clear day, they saw the thousands of heavily laden adults banding in a dense group off the bottom. The visual impact of all these large fish in different stages of coloration is one of the most amazing things to witness in nature. Then in the evening, we dived on the year's first spawning event as the grouper all turned black and white and began spawning, shooting up to the surface in rocketing pillars of fish and clouds of spawn. Sir Richard was justifiably impressed, if not overwhelmed. He kindly did a couple of interviews on camera with Schellenger and myself for our follow-up documentary, *Grouper Moon, the Next Phase*.

predators. In a continental situation, adults might migrate 100 miles along the shelf to a suitable spot, such as seen for several snapper species at Silk Cayes Marine Reserve at Gladden Spit in Belize. We visited this location during the snapper spawning to see cubera, mutton and dog snappers all do their thing. The larger females are more fecund, producing more, higher-quality eggs with a better rate of survival. Killing large females of any species, not just grouper and snapper, for a couple of fillets is the worst possible management policy.

Of the 10 years we have been visiting the Little Cayman SPAG, two years in particular stand out. In 2012, there were a lot of one-year-old Nassau grouper in the shallow back reef areas of Little Cayman. We helped the REEF team catch, tag and film these juveniles for that first documentary, *The Mystery of the Grouper Moon*. We knew in five years that these little guys would be showing up as first-time spawners at the SPAG, and sure enough, they did. Coincidentally, I had invited Sir Richard Branson and his daughter Holly to dive with the research team on the SPAG in 2017. Sir Richard wanted to see how it was all being done so he could share the scientific knowledge and encourage the British Virgin Islands government to adopt similar measures and get a grouper-restoration project started.

It was a memorable trip. Sir Richard and Holly flew in to Cayman Brac, came over to Little Cayman, and joined my daughter, Jessica, and myself for the afternoon dive.

The spike in numbers that year was astounding. Some 3,000 new spawning adults were added to the population in that one recruitment from 2011. It was as large as the combined recruitment from the 10 previous years. Semmens said that the same spike in recruitment was experienced all across the Caribbean. It was clear that recruitment does not happen on an even basis; there are lots of slow years punctuated by some good years.

TOP

Guide extraordinaire Chris
Gough with a bonefish he
caught on fly on the beach in
front of Southern Cross Club.

BOTTOM

Outside of the spawning season,
adult Nassau grouper live a
solitary life on their home reef.
The closed season is December
to April in the Cayman Islands.

Why is this population of Nassau grouper important to the wider Caribbean? The Little Cayman population of Nassau grouper is the largest in the known geographic range of the species. The research efforts of the Department of Environment and REEF are now being used as a template for other Caribbean countries as a model for what can be undertaken in restoring grouper populations. It begins with the research effort, finding out what is remaining, and how best to manage, conserve and utilize that resource in a sustainable manner.

Additionally, if this population continues to expand, there is a significant possibility that it will repopulate Cayman Brac and Grand Cayman with more individuals. Now in its 20th year, the Grouper Moon Project has continued to record the recovery of the species. Some of the tracks developed on spawning nights show where eggs and larvae may have ended up. Some tracks have shown that larvae could settle out in Grand Cayman, Cuba and Jamaica. If other

Caribbean governments can benefit from the Cayman experience, then many of the predatory reef species will have a chance to bounce back and restore reef ecosystems. According to the work done by McCoy, 27 other species of fish use the SPAG at Little Cayman at different times of year. SPAGs around the Caribbean should be identified, researched and included in any designation of marine parks in order to be better protected.

In the Cayman Islands, the current regulations protecting Nassau grouper states that there is a closed season, so no take of any Nassau grouper is permitted between December 1 and April 30. Outside of that, there is a slot size of 16 to 24 inches long that may be taken, up to five fish per person or per boat per day, whichever is less. For a species listed as critically endangered by the IUCN, harvesting this number of fish is too much too soon. The SPAGs themselves were included in the new plans for the MPAs, but because of political objection, they were removed and so are no longer protected except during the closed season. This is a shortsighted policy after all this research work has been done. A more sustainable policy would include all known SPAGs in marine reserves where fishing is never permitted. We look forward to the triumph of science and data in better management practices going forward. It is just common sense.

02

For many reasons, it's an island at the crossroads. It's located where the Gulf of Mexico meets the Caribbean Sea. It's set amid a migratory highway for our oceans' apex predators. And thanks to conservation efforts, its future is looking bright.

Isla Mujeres

MEXICO'S MAKO MADNESS

THE FIRST TIME I heard about mako sharks showing up on a regular basis off the Caribbean coast of Mexico was during a chat with legendary captain, Vernon "OB" O'Bryan. I used to charter OB every year in late April or May on *Sea D* to catch sailfish and white marlin off Isla Mujeres. Every so often there would be a story or photo of a big mako shark taking out a hooked sailfish. OB said that Capt. Anthony Mendillo, who runs Keen M Blue Water Adventures, had encounters with makos on a regular basis. As it turns out, Anthony has long known about the numbers of makos that lurk in the swift, north-flowing current off Mexico's Caribbean coast. They attack his dredges when he is fishing for sails and white marlin, occasionally grab a hooked sailfish, and also love to chew on the jumbo-size bonito that frequent these waters.

Anthony has been fishing his 41-foot Fitz, *Keen M*—a single-engine sport-fisher and the best dayboat I have ever fished on—off Isla Mujeres for more than a decade, concentrating on different species at different times of the year. The run of mako sharks in March and April has been added to the sailfish season in the early part of the year, white marlin in May and June, whale sharks from June to September, and swordfish when it is calm enough to catch them.

I discussed the research opportunity with Dr. Mahmood Shivji, director of the Guy Harvey Research Institute, and Dr. Brad Wetherbee. There was a big hole in the knowledge about the life history of the shortfin mako shark in the Caribbean, Gulf of Mexico and northwestern Atlantic. We already knew that the mako was a long-lived shark but with a slow reproductive rate. Because of the mako's great speed, it is an apex predator of all other large oceanic species, such as swordfish, billfish, tuna and amberjack. The shortfin mako shark is a cosmopolitan species found in all tropical and temperate oceans around the world. They generally lead an oceanic existence and can be found along the continental shelves and oceanic islands where there is an abundance of fish. They are one of four species in the family Isuridae, the mackerel sharks. They are generally rare in the Caribbean, and so my prior experience with mako sharks was nil.

LEFT

A series of jump shots I took of an acrobatic 250-pound male. Not all the makos we hooked jumped, but this one was spectacular.

BELOW

We deployed a PAT tag on this 300-pound female mako shark that fell for the flopping dolphin bait, one of our most effective.

Anthony and I started fishing together in January 2007 when we did a sailfish expedition with wildlife photographer Amos Nachoum. The subject of makos came up, but the GHRI did not field a mako tagging expedition until March 2012. Mahmood thought the best option would be to fish out of the Yucatan, deploy pop-up satellite tags on some makos, and see what happened.

With restaurateur friend Andi Marcher and film producer George Schellenger in tow, we had three days of dedicated mako shark fishing with Anthony, beginning on March 28, 2012. He said the best bite was usually over the full moon in March and April. Unfortunately, there is a lot of commercial shark fishing in Mexico; Anthony arranged for us to see the cold-storage room in the local fishing cooperative before we headed out. One of Anthony's crew, Capt. Rogelio Delgado, was a converted commercial fisherman and still had all the contacts.

The floor of the 20-by-30-foot cold room was covered with different species of sharks. They were all whole and had their fins. There were several very big great hammerheads up to 18 feet long, a few bull sharks, reef sharks, tiger sharks, a nurse shark, and a white shark of about 1,500 pounds, even though white sharks are protected in Mexico. George and I called it the Chamber of Horrors—very sad indeed. The sharks fetch around $2 per kilogram (roughly 2.2 pounds) and are sent to Mexico City whole in refrigerated containers.

LEFT

Makos are top predators of all the other oceanic predators. Their attacks on our rigged dolphin baits and dolphin decoys inspired this painting. Acrylic on canvas.

ABOVE

A sketch of a mako taking out a sailfish. Ink.

The next day, we headed out to go fishing. Our mates, Gallo and Rogelio, put out a spread of dead baits until we found the bonito, and then we put out three live ones. We did not wait long for a bite—Andi was on the first shark, which jumped high in the sky, cartwheeling in the air before the hook pulled. We stayed with the bait and frigate birds, and soon had another mako on, around 100 pounds. We tagged this one with a PAT and released it, filming the shark's departure underwater. They seemed to be pretty tough animals. The last bite of the day was on a dead bonito, but the hook pulled after just a minute. We were 1-for-3 the first day, and it was an encouraging start.

The conditions on the second day looked good. We started with slow-trolling dead baits this time. A splashing 10-pound dorado was Anthony's favorite bait, although a swimming bonito was also effective. Anthony deboned the bonito, rigged them with two hooks and a chin weight, and trolled them slowly to keep the bait swimming below the surface. He said the makos would not touch the bonito if they were splashing but would pounce on a skipping dorado. He had obviously fished for makos here quite a bit.

It was a beautiful day, but we did not see a mako, so George ate a tequila scorpion at the corner bar that night to change our luck. The weather on our last day was wonderful. We found the bonito and started out with two live baits and a flopping

dorado on the right short rigger. It wasn't long before a small mako creamed the dorado in a burst of spray. After a quick fight, it was tagged and released. At noon, we had the same half-eaten dorado bait out, and a much bigger mako swirled on it, came back and pounced on it. This had me convinced that dorado is definitely the best bait because the shark passed up two live bonito for it. The mako thrashed at the surface but was really quite tame compared with what I thought might happen, and Gallo wired the impressive shark. This was a real one: pointed face, black fathomless eyes, big teeth and beautiful purple-blue back like a swordfish. Between the blue back and the pale flanks was a hint of bronze, a metallic sheen that changed color in the light. Beautiful.

I could not get the tag in, and neither could Rogilio when he tried, so I used sharp knife to quickly cut the skin at the base of the dorsal fin. I could then put the sharp point of the applicator deep into the muscle. It was a decent fish of more than 300 pounds. Rogilio cut the cable leader, and the big mako swam off rapidly.

We were back in Mexico for March 2013, with Dr. Brad Wetherbee, shark biologist, GHRI consultant and professor at the University of Rhode Island. Around that time, Mahmood learned that the smart position and temperature tags that GHRI had sent to New Zealand in a collaborative study for deployment on makos there were working extremely well. One shark in particular named Carol covered 9,000 miles from northern New Zealand to Fiji and back in a few months, making headline news. So the decision was made to switch from PATs to SPOTs for the Mexican makos.

At the same time, our GHRI scientists were deploying

ABOVE

Makos will attack sailfish, white marlin and swordfish, usually by cutting off their tails first, then returning to consume the now-immobilized prey. Acrylic on canvas.

Nova Scotia

Cape Cod

The Bahamas

Mexico

Turks and Caicos

Mexico

Dominican Republic

Jamaica

Haiti

Puerto Rico

Long-Distance Runner This 200-pound male mako named "Tough Guy" was tagged off Isla Mujeres in April and, unlike most of the other southern Gulf of Mexico and western Caribbean makos, went east and eventually left the Caribbean, and headed north through the Bahamas, past the mid-Atlantic region, on its way to Nova Scotia and then to the Flemish Cap. Then Tough Guy turned back, headed south, and spent considerable time in the bountiful mid-Atlantic before the tag finally stopped transmitting.

BELOW LEFT

George Schellenger checks out the new cage. This would allow us to get closer than ever before to makos.

BOTTOM RIGHT

Keen M, *in the zone, drifts and chums with the cage deployed and divers in the water.*

SPOTs on makos caught in Ocean City, Maryland, and off Montauk, New York. From our previous studies on tiger sharks in Bermuda and the Bahamas, we now know that these species of sharks spend a great deal of time at the surface, allowing the SPOT to transmit its exact location to a satellite. This device gives a much more accurate fix on the shark's position—within 5 meters—than a PAT tag.

We caught only three makos during the 2013 expedition. We battled horrendous seas for four days but still managed to deploy three SPOT tags. The makos were brought into the cockpit so we could work; it was too rough to keep them in the water and do it the easy way. We placed them on a rubber mat, covered their eyes with a damp towel, and irrigated their gills with a powerful saltwater deck hose while Brad implanted the tag, measured and determined the sex of the shark, took a fin clipping for DNA, and then we released it back out the transom door. Not as easy as it sounds though.

I booked Anthony for 10 days at the end of March 2014. Little did I know that Anthony had embraced the project in a large way, and had built an aluminum derrick and lifting platform on the stern of *Keen M* before we arrived. No more sharks in the boat—good move. Having the movable platform on rollers across the transom would allow us to load the mako on the platform and then raise the shark out of the water. The scientists could attach the SPOT easily and without having 200 pounds of charged-up shark actually in the boat.

Dorado, aka dolphinfish or mahimahi, were scarce in the western Caribbean this time of year, so the solution was to make a decoy dorado. I arrived in time to help paint the decoys, add some spots and eyes, and make it realistic, with the idea

being to bait-and-switch: raise the mako on the decoy, then pitch a bonito chunk on a circle hook. The following day found us trolling two hookless dorado decoys on the right short and right long rigger. On the left side, Anthony was pulling swimming dead bonito baits armed with a large single J hook on each one. We were working on the edge of the current line in 200 to 300 feet of water and—*kaboom!*—a 400-pound mako shark skies on the short decoy, going completely airborne with the decoy firmly in its jaws not 30 feet from the transom. It arched and flipped in midair to land heavily and then mounted another attack on the decoy in a burst of foam. Wow—air mako! Not happy with the taste of pine, it jetted across the wake like a blue marlin and grabbed the swimming bonito. We were hooked up, and line poured off the Shimano reel as the mako raced away on the surface, throwing curtains of water. George and I filmed all the releases in the water and watched as the chunky mako took off into the deep blue—very gratifying. On our first day we had four bites but caught just one shark.

Graced with beautiful weather, we trolled decoys and bonito with astonishing results. While a few makos would sneak up and just bite the rigged bonito, the majority—particularly the bigger fish—would launch on the dolphin decoy from underneath or by coming across from the inside out and crashing the decoy just as crazily as a 500-pound blue marlin. There

BELOW

*The formidable business end of
a big mako shark.*

*The formidable business end of
a big mako shark.*

BELOW

Colorful pangas line the beach next to Ballyhoo's Bar.

BOTTOM

Capt. Rogelio Delgado rigs a bonito bait for mako fishing.

was never any warning. Famed gamefish photographer Scott Kerrigan was aboard for several days and waited patiently for the bite sitting on the flybridge, but none of us were fast enough to get that first jump.

Latin television fishing-show host Diego Toiran joined me for a day and caught a fine 200-pound mako for an episode of his show, *Fishing the Keys*. His shark is named Diego and has carried its tag for two years. Typically we would catch 1-in-3 makos that we raised; many simply pulled the hook or were even hooked several times and still managed to get away. Sometimes I thought they were just holding on to the bait, not wanting to let go. We did hook a couple of makos using the pitch bait, so bait-and-switch fishing off the decoys did work to a certain extent. We caught and tagged 11 makos during this expedition from 32 bites and 36 raised—not great catch numbers but some incredible action, and we built a good library of content for the next documentary on mako sharks.

By 2016, Anthony had changed everything. He went back to the tried-and-tested technique of chumming and chunking, the most important component being lots of chum. The local bonito population was the source of a lot of bait, which was ground up and frozen in 5-gallon plastic jugs. Hung over the side in the water, the chum slowly thaws and sets up a wonderful line of tiny fish bits and scent.

Another piece of intrigue was added to the experience: a cage. With this, we could film free-swimming makos underwater; if they stayed around, we could then hook them, offload the cage, catch the shark, tag it on the platform, release it, then retrieve the floating cage and begin the process again.

SeaWorld had come on board as a collaborator with GHOF and sponsored five SPOT tags each year. They also had their own two TV series, *Wildlife Docs* and *Sea Rescue*. Dr. Dominique Keller from Busch Gardens in Tampa, Florida, was on the expedition, along with the film crew directed by Jeff Androsky. The only issue was the weather, which was never flat-calm, so there was a lot of motion in the cage.

On April 13, we had sharks of all sizes come in the chum line. One 350-pound female was very amped up and biting at everything—the chum jug, baits, even the buoys floating the cage. We

were in the cage filming everything for 20 exhilarating minutes, then the call was made to catch her, so we needed to get out of the cage and back on the boat. After a quick catch-and-tag process, she was back in the water smartly.

The next day we were on a drift, and around 1 p.m., a big mako shark came up on the chum barrel—and it was already tagged. It was the same big female from the previous day and only about a quarter-mile from we were saw her the day before. The SPOT tag on her dorsal fin was clearly visible. She hung around for a few minutes and then departed, not wanting to play any further games with us.

The important part of this whole project is to learn more about the abundance and migrations of this species in the western Atlantic and Gulf of Mexico. According to latest catch statistics, approximately 500,000 mako sharks are killed each year in the North Atlantic. Of all the sharks commercially harvested, they have the best-quality meat, plus their fins and teeth also fetch a high price. One of our tagged makos called JoAnn was caught by a commercial fisherman from Isla Mujeres in March 2015, after being at large just short of a year and providing the GHRI with some valuable data. Two makos tagged off Ocean City in 2015 were caught and killed by commercial fishermen in Nova Scotia at the end of the summer.

At the time we did not know this was the beginning of another aspect of the mako research project. By 2018, we had tagged 106 shortfin mako sharks in Mexico and in the mid-Atlantic region of the US. The Mexican makos rarely left the Gulf of Mexico or western Caribbean, with a few exceptions. However, the American-tagged makos traveled much greater distances, and in doing so faced more-intense fishing efforts, particularly off the northeastern US and Canada. Many SPOT tags ended up on land in Mexico, Cuba, the US, Canada and Spain. The sharks therefore had been caught. The research over eight years showed that the makos traveled through the 200-mile EEZ waters of 17 different jurisdictions, and 30 percent of the makos we tagged were caught and killed. The highest rate of capture was in the northeastern US and in Canada off Nova Scotia. This mortality rate shows how intense the fishing for this species has become.

In 2018, NOAA took note of this research work, which set off all kinds of alarm bells. They mandated a change in management of the species; fishing for shortfin mako sharks was now unsustainable and had to be limited. This was achieved in part by NMFS increasing the minimum size from 55 inches to 83 inches and requiring the release of any mako sharks that were still alive on the haul-back of commercial gear. To complement this measure, shortfin mako sharks were afforded listing by the Convention on International Trade in Endangered Species.

Isla Mujeres

SAILFISH AND FRIGATE BIRDS IN MEXICO

WE HAVE BEEN fishing in Mexico for many years—my family and many of my friends caught their first sailfish and white marlin fishing with the late Capt. Vernon "OB" O'Bryan and his wife, Charlene, from as early as 1990 in Cozumel. Then OB and Charlene moved their fishing operation over to Isla Mujeres with their beautiful 55-foot Merritt, *Sea D*. We had some interesting experiences over the years. Once, we were catching lots of sailfish, so my daughter, Jessica, and I jumped in with a few that were teased up to the boat. It was such fun that we did that with many sailfish during the day, only to discover later on there was a lot of sea lice in the water. That evening, both of us were struggling with the irritation—big welts everywhere but mostly on our torsos where our shirts had been, not on our arms and legs. It was so bad that OB sent us to see a local doctor the next morning. He was going to give me an antihistamine shot in my bum with an old, large metal syringe with a 4-inch needle—it looked like something a vet would use on a horse. Jessica screamed with fear and burst into tears, but it did work.

On another occasion, we were out catching sails, and I was taking underwater video with my Sony. It was my son Alex's turn to jump in with me. A white marlin showed up on the left daisy-chain teaser, and as we jumped in, Charlene slid back a ballyhoo. She hooked the fish, and the marlin started jumping. This fish could have gone anywhere, but it came right at us instead, greyhounding along in and out of the surface. I held my breath in fear as it jumped right over Alex and me. We decided it would not have been cool to have been perforated by a jumping white marlin.

The expedition from May 3-6, 2004, with Dr. John Graves did not get off to a good start—all of Rick Westphal's camera gear was confiscated by Mexican customs authorities in Cancun. Not only was it a Sunday afternoon, the following day was a public holiday, so Tuesday was the earliest we could get the show going, and we were due to fly out the day after. The focus of this expedition was to collect the remoras off sailfish for a genetic study being conducted by John's student, Jan McDowell. Jan would collect the remoras off the fish, and

BELOW

*Frigates close to the water in a
tornado formation signify
a sardine baitball trapped at
the surface with sailfish below.
This is what you look for off
Isla Mujeres.*

FACING PAGE

*Sailfish caught with circle
hooks on 20-pound-test line put
on some great aerial displays.*

John would get a fin clip from the host sailfish and then put it back in the water.

The first day was great—even though a front came through and it was cloudy and rainy, we went 13-for-27 on sailfish. Charlene was great at dropping a sinking ballyhoo back after the first bite and getting another, doubling up. The following day, Rick went with an agent to recover his gear in Cancun. He called later and said it wasn't happening, so we headed out at the crack of 2 p.m. for a quick fish. Shortly afterward, OB found a big group of frigates and sailfish working on bait, so I went in snorkeling and was just mesmerized by the sight. Very inspiring. In the morning, I changed the painting I was working on to show the baitball and sailfish before we went fishing.

The next day, we found another baitball with six sailfish on it. Then it got better: OB spotted a commotion ahead of the boat, and we slid up to see what was going on. There were two manta rays chasing a larger one. I went in and they turned toward me, swimming fast close to the surface. With the camera running, I thought I was going collide with a 2,000-pound, 20-foot-wide female. I literally sucked in my breath and tried to walk on water as they zoomed past just inches below me before diving out of sight.

June 1, 2006, was the first time I met Capt. Anthony Mendillo. He had kindly let me swim on a hooked white marlin his client was fighting that morning. We went into town that evening to meet Anthony and his wife, Kin, at Ballyhoo's Bar. OB said that since they would not be returning to Isla Mujeres, he recommended we charter and work with Anthony going forward—it turned out to be sound advice, with many years of friendship, research and adventure to follow.

On January 19, 2007, it was still dark when we left the dock at Ballyhoo's in Isla Mujeres. The wind was already up and blowing spray over the bow of the 41-foot Paul Mann *Keen M* as Anthony pointed the boat into the northeast wind. *Going to be another ripper,* I thought to myself. We had to go out about 8 to 10 miles as the light came up. World-renowned underwater photographer Amos Nachoum was my guest this expedition—for all the sea creatures he had photographed, dived with and escaped from (including polar bears), he had never dived with a billfish. Rick, our professional cameraman for *Portraits from the Deep,* was with us as well.

Arriving at a spot with frigate birds working over sardines, we strapped on our gear as we raced to get closer. Anthony watched for a minute to gauge the speed and direction of the baitball, then said, "Go, go, go, now!" He dropped us ahead of the moving school of fish—a couple dozen sailfish hounding the sardines, close to the surface. The lateral light was hitting the flanks of the sails as waves broke overhead, all edged in the gold of the early light. It was incredible. The bait was using our dark stationary bodies and the cloud of bubbles above us for protection.

The sailfish seemed hesitant to break into the bubbles, but then a 60-pound wahoo arrived and made a lightning pass through the sardines, triggering the sailfish to swoop in. The wahoo struck again and then left. The sardines crowded our bodies—one squeezed itself between my mask and regulator;

The lateral light was hitting the **FLANKS OF THE SAILFISH** *as the waves* **BROKE OVERHEAD,** *all edged in the* **GOLD OF THE EARLY LIGHT.** *It was incredible.*

I could feel it wriggling. The sailfish had broken off a smaller group of sardines and began to work on these close by.

The sails engaging with the sardines were using a premeditated swing with their bills against the crowded baitfish. Underwater we could hear the bill slap against the bait and see the puff of scales as they registered a hit time and time again. They grabbed the bait between pointed jaws, crushed and then swallowed it, whirling around to get back into the action. Their dorsal fins were fully extended and pelvic fins lowered, making the sailfish seem much bigger than they really were. Their flanks were bronzed, cut by regular spotted stripes that glowed iridescent blue, their eyes were very mobile in their sockets, searching out prey and locking onto the fast-moving targets. Amos, whose website is all about big-animal experiences, was ecstatic. He was so enthusiastic about the encounters and the long interaction with the fish that he wanted to bring people down to see what we had experienced.

The next day, the weather was the same—another cold, windy day. We were out there before the frigate birds and got in on the first baitball at 7:15 a.m., where we spent a full hour with the sailfish. The water that day was milky, but the action was continuous. When the air ran out of the pony tanks, we would float at the surface, where the bait always came closer,

seeking refuge. Their little eyes seemed wide with fear, almost pleading for safety. No quarter given here—enemies were below and in the sky above. The bite shut off at noon. We raised only a couple of sailfish while trolling, so we headed in at 3 p.m.

We began the third and last day as the others had begun. We were a bit farther offshore when we found the first tornado of frigate birds at 7:15 a.m. The visibility was fantastic—we swam with the sailfish for 40 minutes. It was very rough, but the breaking waves in the background above the fish provided drama, and each wave was trimmed in yellow and gold.

Several years later, the next expedition targeting sailfish out of Isla Mujeres was during a joint tagging and filming expedition in a cooperative effort with Dr. Molly Lutcavage of the University of Massachusetts at Amherst in January 2015. I was longing to return to the water to swim with the feeding sailfish.

"Hold it...steady...OK...go, go, go now!" We were back at sea on the 48-foot Cabo *Chachalaca*, with Anthony at the helm. We dropped into the big blue swells of the western Caribbean, swimming hard and looking up at the surface to check my position with the signature flock of frigate birds overhead. Suddenly, there they were: flashes of silver against the blue, large silhouettes moving rapidly, changing direction, and in

PREVIOUS SPREAD

Sailfish feed on a wide variety of small baitfish, including ballyhoo, mackerel scad, needlefish and jacks. Acrylic on canvas.

ABOVE

Capt. Anthony Mendillo's eldest daughter, Lilly, swims with a freshly tagged and released sailfish.

FACING PAGE

Jay Perez with a big sailfish, which contributed to a grand slam for us that day. Mates Gallo and Pasqual released the fish.

Dr. Molly Lutcavage activates PAT tags on Chachalaca *before they are deployed on sailfish.*

the middle of all these bodies, a large, glinting shadow: baitfish on the move. Sailfish and sardines—the ultimate open-ocean diving experience, and I was right in the middle of them again, shooting the amazing interaction of predator and prey.

The large school of about a thousand sardines raced toward me. I sank to 15 feet as the school of bait kept moving like agitated mercury, round and round, back and forth as the lean sailfish carved their way through the school. The bait school locked in on me as a potential refuge from the charges of the unrelenting sailfish. Cameraman and producer George Schellenger and others were snorkeling above me, enjoying the interaction. For Molly, this was her first close encounter with sailfish.

We kept station with the baitball and watched as the sailfish methodically picked off the sardines on the fringe of the school. A sailfish would sprint in, brake, all fins erect and stripes glowing, and take a well-aimed sideways swipe with its bill. More often than not a sardine was knocked out of the bait school in a puff of scales, and the sailfish would spin around and inhale the disabled bait. Sometimes the bill would strike more than one sardine, and a following sailfish would scoop up the hapless bait. On one occasion a sardine was impaled on a sailfish's bill, the host shaking its head to knock it off and then promptly swallowing the baitfish. The school was quickly consumed, and then the sailfish all went into cruise mode, dorsal fins tucked down. Now dressed in pastel colors, they looked like javelins, propelled by their large forked tails as they headed off into the blue.

Back on the boat for a much needed rest and change of air tanks, we were elated and discussed the feeding behavior, the coloration changes, and the effectiveness of this feeding

Behavioral Notes on Sailfish

HERE ARE A FEW notes on my observations of sailfish feeding behavior:

TEASERS

From an angling perspective, sailfish behave quite differently when presented with a bait or a moving teaser towed behind the boat compared with the behavior seen in a natural baitball feeding situation. And while baitballs are quite rare occurrences, I have spent 25 years diving with teased sailfish and marlin as they are raised into the spread of baits behind a boat. In every instance, the fish has overtaken the bait or teaser and grabbed it between its pointed jaws— it has not used its bill to strike the bait. I believe this is because the target is moving in a straight line at a constant speed, and so the predator does need to use its bill to stun the prey.

BAITBALLS

Sailfish and other predators, such as bonito, tuna, bottlenose dolphins, etc., acquire the baitball—sardines in this case—in the daylight hours, and then carve out a smaller group from an even bigger school, making it much easier to control. The sailfish use their incredible speed to get under the bait and drive them upward. Usually more than one sailfish is doing this, some-times several. Others linger in the background but will be galvanized into action if the bait escapes in their direction. The sailfish then drive the sardines, now in a tight bunch, toward the surface, where they are trapped, and the sailfish can work on them at their leisure. In the air above are the ever-present frigate birds, swooping

FOR MEXICO, *sailfish are a* SUSTAINABLE SOURCE OF INCOME *for local businesses; anglers travel great distances, stay in local hotels, eat in local restaurants, use taxis, shop and* GENERALLY SPEND LOTS OF MONEY.

method. We rejoined the group of 50 or more sailfish and bait for more footage before going into fishing mode.

Isla Mujeres is famous for the large numbers of sailfish, attracting anglers from around the world from January to May each year. This is a catch-and-release fishery: Circle hooks and dead bait are mandatory, and anglers can expect 30 to 50 bites per day, with many multiple hookups. Live bait is not permitted. For 15 years, Anthony and his family have operated a successful charter business out of Isla Mujeres, catching and releasing tens of thousands of billfish during that time. He said it would be great to learn more about the migrations of the sailfish that visit the productive waters of the Yucatan. For Mexico, sailfish are a sustainable source of income for local businesses; anglers travel great distances, stay in hotels, eat in local restaurants, use taxis, shop and generally spend lots of money. The socioeconomic value of the living sailfish is very high throughout its range in the western North Atlantic. Current Mexican laws allow for one sailfish to be taken per day, but catch-and-release is the main appeal, and local fishermen target food species such as tuna, bonito, mackerel and bottomfish rather than sailfish.

Over the years, a great many conventional spaghetti tags have been placed in sailfish caught here by recreational anglers. The system depends on the tag card being completed and returned to the tagging agency, as well as the sailfish being recaptured and the tag cut out and returned. The result is a straight-line displacement that shows where it was tagged and where it was recaptured, but it cannot provide information about where the fish spent that time or how it used the habitat.

On previous expeditions to the Yucatan with Anthony, I have accompanied Dr. John Graves of the Virginia Institute of Marine Science in conducting post-release survivability studies on white marlin, which frequent the Yucatan in April and May. We deployed PATs on a number of white marlin using both J hooks and circle hooks to test post-release mortality. The PATs were programmed to pop off in 10 days. John's

in to easily pick a sardine from the surface in midflight.

The baitball is constantly moving and zigzagging, making it difficult for the sailfish to pick out an individual fish. Feeding begins with one sailfish swimming up, thrusting its bill into the ball with a deliberate sideways swipe and injuring one or more sardines, knocking them out of position so they are easily overtaken and consumed. There is no wild slashing—the swipes are deliberate and well-aimed. Underwater you can actually hear the swift movement of the fish's bill in the water and the sound of the bill striking the sardine. Scales are dislodged from the sardine, signifying a hit.

The color of the feeding sailfish will be vivid blues, bronze flanks with stripes lit up in powder blue, and various parts of the body glowing blue or silver, particularly the tail. The dorsal fin, pelvic fins and anal fin are all fully extended for rapid changes in direction, and to startle the prey. With all its fins extended, a charging sailfish looks three times larger than it really is. Several sailfish together, with fins raised in this fashion, will present a visual barrier or wall to the baitball. In comparison, sailfish not engaged in the chase are drab black, bronze or pastel blue, almost the color of the water.

THE BILL

Sailfish with broken bills will also try to strike the sardines; apparently, they do not realize their bill has been broken. However, these individuals do not appear thin and must feed successfully in other situations—the bill is therefore not absolutely necessary for feeding. About 1-in-20 sailfish have a shortened or broken bill, but all are healthy individuals. The bill acts as a breakwater in high-speed swimming, and is also used in defense against predators, such as large mako sharks, large blue marlin, orcas and false killer whales.

Two sailfish working on a school of ballyhoo. The explosion of bait gives the painting a lot of movement and drama. Acrylic on canvas.

results from 60 white marlin tagged showed a 98 percent survival rate for white marlin caught on circle hooks and only a 66 percent survival rate for those caught on J hooks. It is reasonable to assume similar survivability for sailfish using the same tackle. However this was not a survivability study, and only the healthiest sailfish were tagged in this expedition.

Using 20-pound-test, we trolled dead ballyhoo bait rigged with 7/0 circle hooks and chin weights. Anthony pulled two dredges, which imitate bait schools as teasers; we fished an area 6 to 12 miles north of Isla Mujeres looking for telltale vortexes of frigate birds to show us where the concentrations of sailfish were located. When the sailfish were hooked, fought and brought to the boat, our mate, Ruben Garrido, grabbed the bill of the sailfish and flipped it into the boat onto a plastic-covered foam mat. The fish's eyes were covered with a wet cloth and the saltwater deck hose placed in its mouth to irrigate the gills. Molly and her assistant, Eric Jacquard, measured the sailfish, a mini PAT was placed carefully in the right shoulder, and the fish was jetted back into the water in less than 50 seconds. We had much more control over tag placement when the sailfish was in the boat as opposed to trying to tag the fish in the water. They move around a lot and are hard to control on a light leader, so correct placement of these expensive tags was a priority.

One of us was in position in the water to shoot the release and accompany the sailfish for as long as we could keep up. They recovered very quickly and would swim away strongly out of sight. Anthony's 13-year-old daughter, Lilly, not only caught a bunch of sailfish, but she also accompanied me in the water as the sails swam off. Other team members, Valerie and JD Gaynor, caught sails, helped with the tagging, dived, and helped acquire footage.

It would be as long as six months before the tag released from the fish and sent its information to the waiting Argos satellite. Each tag costs about $4,000, so we are taking a gamble; anything can happen between release and the tag detaching and floating to the surface. No news is good news, because to hear from a tag early would mean that the tag came off the fish for a number of reasons: The fish did not survive, it was eaten by a predator, or the tag just pulled out. Large mako sharks frequent the area as well and have the speed to take on a sailfish.

From this study, we obtained several long tracks with sailfish, which were spending time in the Gulf of Mexico and in the western Caribbean. One fish went to term, with its tag staying on for 12 months; it traveled to Brazil and returned to Mexico, covering 16,000 miles in the year.

*Two swordfish chase squid near
the surface at night using the
light of the full moon to hunt.
Mixed media.*

THE FISH OF A LIFETIME

IN 2012, I WAS on the third consecutive shoot in Isla Mujeres, Mexico, for a documentary about the marine life off the Yucatan Peninsula. In January, we had started the project by fishing and diving on sailfish aggregations with Capt. Anthony Mendillo of Keen M Sport Fishing, who owns and operates four charter boats based there. With the help of Dr. Molly Lutcavage, we tagged 12 sailfish with pop-up archival satellite tags to better understand their migratory paths after they leave the Yucatan. We had also tagged two dozen white marlin and about four dozen mako sharks working with Anthony and his team over the previous eight years. Very little

BELOW LEFT

Jessica works on the big sword-fish while Andi Marcher turns the chair and mate Gallo waits patiently for the leader.

BELOW RIGHT

Jessica fought the swordfish on 80-pound-test line for over three hours. The fish dived to the bottom twice during the battle.

BOTTOM

The swordfish was 14 feet long, and while not an IGFA world record, it remains the largest ever landed by a female angler on rod and reel in the Atlantic Ocean.

FACING PAGE

The huge fish jumped completely clear of the water just once, an amazing sight that left all on board speechless. Watercolor.

FACING PAGE

The crew with Jessica and her fish of a lifetime at the public fishing beach. Not a scrap went to waste, and the swordfish fed scores of people on the island.

BELOW

Capt. Anthony Mendillo's children—Lilly, Sonny and Andrea—with Jessica.

is known about the migrations of these large pelagic species in the western Caribbean and Gulf of Mexico. Film producer George Schellenger accompanied me on all expeditions.

Summer in the Yucatan brings the whale sharks; thousands of eager snorkelers flock to the region to swim with these docile monsters. On any day in July and August, the whale sharks that gather at the surface can be as few as a dozen, but if conditions are right, as many as 300 are spread over several square miles of ocean. Our group—which included myself, along with two staff members, my friend Andi Marcher from Cayman, George and my daughter, Jessica—had the cameras rolling all day for three consecutive days of this trip. Jessica, who had just graduated from Edinburgh University, Scotland, with an honors degree in zoology, was thrilled to spend so much time in the water photographing whale sharks.

We planned to go fishing for swordfish for the last day of this expedition. Anthony took us out on the 48-foot Cabo *Chachalaca*, owned by Lawrence Berry from Texas. Our two mates for the day were Ruben and Gallo, and the weather was flat-calm, ideal for drifting for swordfish. Anthony had a few good spots offshore where he deep-drops Florida-style in 1,400 to 1,800 feet of water. Similar to Florida's east coast, the Gulf Stream roars north past Isla Mujeres, squeezing between the west end of Cuba and the eastern tip of the Yucatan. We were not fishing IGFA rules here, using 80-pound-test braided nylon line with a 100-foot top shot of 200-pound-test monofilament—the goal was simply for us to try to catch a swordfish on rod and reel.

The fishing technique is unique to the area because of the strong current. Anthony kept the boat moving ahead into the current at 3 knots while Gallo let out the line. Some 1,500 feet below, the bait is actually moving north at 1 knot in a 4-knot current, just off the bottom. If a fish is hooked, then the primary weight breaks away because it is attached with very light line. An electric drill is used to wind up the bait and weight when checking the line for tangles, which really speeds up the whole process.

Jessica was up when we got the bite just a few minutes after 10 a.m. on the first drift, when the rod tip began

bouncing and the line began flying off the reel. Ruben and Gallo helped set her up in the chair with harness and gloves, bracing for what could be a long duel. Anthony spun the boat around and began to give chase with a big grin on his face— he knew from 15 years of fishing for swordfish that this was a good-size one. Jessica worked hard on the fish, and after an hour, it came to the surface and did one massive jump, leaving all on board speechless. Ruben said, "It's 500 plus!" and Anthony simply nodded in agreement. We backed down hard and got close to the big swordfish swimming just beneath the surface, vivid in purple and blue. The hook was in a good spot in the left corner of the jaw—no one wants to fight a big swordfish that is foul-hooked.

As we got closer, the swordfish became galvanized and spurted away with great sweeps of its tail as line dumped off the reel. Jessica shrieked in exasperation, all her hard work melting off the spool in a few seconds as the great fish

Calamari dreaming: Swordfish grow to over 1,000 pounds by feeding on the abundant schools of squid in the deep scattering layer, or on cutlassfish near the bottom in complete darkness. Acrylic on canvas.

sounded. As Anthony turned the boat this way and that, Jessica kept heavy pressure on the fish, and we cruised past the two-hour mark when again the leader came up on the rod and the great fish was swimming just below. Gallo had the leader to hand, but again the swordfish turned on the afterburners and paddled off into the deep as if the fight were just beginning. Sweating, tired and sore, Jessica redoubled her efforts; Anthony instructed her to add more drag while keeping pressure on the reel with her gloved left hand. Over the next 50 minutes, this added pressure worked, and Jessica pumped the swordfish to the surface.

The crew quickly went to work, and soon the swordfish was ours. It took six men to slide the 14-foot-long fish into the boat. The bill was past the cabin door into the salon, and its tail was touching the transom door. Anthony popped the cork on a bottle of champagne, and the celebrations started—he said it looked at least 100 pounds bigger than anything he had ever caught off Isla Mujeres or in Florida, so we decided to run in and weigh the fish.

The giant was too big to unload onto the dock, so it was pulled into the water through the boat's transom door and swum across to the public beach by many willing hands, as an expectant crowd helped to pull the fish up on the wooden gantry for photos. After an hour, the fish was taken down, measurements were made, and then Anthony and crew cleaned the fish. The chunks of meat were all weighed as well as the rest of the backbone, head and fins, totaling 625 pounds. With the loss of blood, bodily fluids and scraps, the swordfish was clearly in the 650-pound range. The meat was shared among crew, family and friends—not a scrap was wasted. Anthony kept the bill for himself and had a tail mount made for Jessica.

Back home, I contacted the IGFA inquiring about other large swordfish catches by lady anglers. The last catch of a swordfish over 600 pounds was a 772-pound fish by Mrs. Lou Marron in Chile in 1954. That was before I was born! While it could not be considered as any sort of official IGFA record, it remains the largest swordfish ever caught on rod and reel by a lady angler in the Atlantic Ocean.

Isla Mujeres, Mexico

MIGRATIONS: WHALE SHARKS AND MANTA RAYS

WE HAVE BEEN FISHING off the Yucatan Peninsula in the Mexican Caribbean for probably 25 years. In April, May and June, while trolling for sailfish and white marlin, we would usually encounter whale sharks, sometimes several at the surface, feeding. Little did we know in the early 1990s that this phenomenon would blossom into the great ecotourism attraction that it has become today. In the past 15 years, encounters with whale sharks have been promoted from Isla Holbox and, more recently, from Isla Mujeres- and Cancun-based tour operators. These gentle giants are the charismatic mascots of the entire Yucatan region.

A few years ago, we attended a conference on whale sharks held at the Georgia Aquarium. Working with Dr. Alastair Dove, vice president of research and conservation, the Guy Harvey Ocean Foundation was a co-sponsor of the event during which we showed a recent documentary about the Yucatan experience. We met many other researchers involved in studying the biology, life history and particularly the migrations of whale sharks, and learned a lot. Scientists have identified other

SeaWorld's Dr. Mike Price and Guy Harvey Ocean Foundation staffer Louisa Sax with a cooperative whale shark at the surface.

locations around the planet, including the eastern tropical Pacific, Gulf of Mexico, Red Sea, Arabian Gulf, the Philippines, Western Australia, the Seychelles and Indonesia, where whale sharks aggregate in large numbers to feed. As a result, many more countries are now protecting this species.

Although the whale shark is the largest of all fish, the species has remained inaccessible to researchers except in a few locations. In Taiwan, where whale sharks have been harvested for a long time, there was a valuable source of biological data of whale sharks because humans consume them there. One question scientists had: Are whale sharks batch birthers, spitting out groups of juveniles as they become big enough to swim? Whale sharks, like so many elasmobranchs, are long-lived, as long as 120 years, as recently discovered by Guy Harvey Research Institute research teams working in Mozambique, Africa. If they produce such large numbers of offspring, where do they give birth? What species prey upon juvenile whale sharks?

The Georgia Aquarium purchased several whale sharks from Taiwan. They were being held in pens there and slated for consumption, and they would have perished but for this intervention. They were flown to Atlanta on a UPS Boeing 747 in a tank and cared for on the way by Georgia Aquarium veterinarians. Whale sharks seem to adapt well to captivity and feed well, living for a long time in tanks that are specially designed to help break up a circular swimming pattern. Several other aquaria now have live whale sharks. For millions of people who cannot afford to snorkel or dive with these creatures in the wild, this offers a unique opportunity to experience their huge size, wonderful coloration and the placid nature of the planet's largest fish.

Each July, we would book a few days with Capt. Anthony Mendillo and his crew at Keen M Bluewater Adventures. In the early years, the experience was not regulated, and as the number of visitors grew, more guidelines and restrictions were sensibly put in place to protect sharks from boats and to protect people from other people. Common sense is uncommon, especially out in the middle of the ocean, where one needs to have lots of it.

Without any specific agenda, we would just enjoy the experience and get what film footage we could. Generally, if the weather was calm, a lot of whale sharks would be feeding, with their dorsal fins and tail sticking above the surface and the open mouth pushing a small bow wave. This was the ideal situation. If the ocean was choppy, then generally there would be fewer

sharks feeding at the surface, and several dozen pangas would be jockeying for position to get their clients into the water.

Usually the tour boats leave the feeding zone by 11 a.m. Some stay later, but all have to depart each day by 2 p.m. to allow the whale sharks to feed uninterrupted for the rest of the afternoon. Aerial views on calm days with lots of sharks often show 200 to 300 sharks, all feeding at the surface. Then add to this scenario just as many big manta rays, and you have an extraordinary experience in the open ocean.

There were more whale sharks reported from this area than for any other area in the ocean. Why are all these massive plankton feeders aggregating in the same area during the same three months? Most animals that are highly migratory do so for food or reproduction. Because most of the whale sharks we saw were juveniles, reproduction might not be the answer. Taking a close look at the top 6 inches of water at the surface, we could see loads of plankton in a pinkish layer mixed in with fish eggs. Apparently little tunny—commonly called bonito— were mainly responsible for the fish eggs. This made sense because the largest numbers of bonito I have seen in the Caribbean are found in the waters off the Yucatan Peninsula.

There was also an overabundance of sargassum for the previous few years in the western Atlantic and Caribbean. How does a giant plankton-eating filter feeder swimming right at the surface avoid ingesting this bright yellow-orange floating algae? What about floating plastic debris, or microplastics? More questions to answer. We swam beside many whale sharks for as long as we had the energy, filming their feeding behavior. Because the greatest density of plankton and eggs was in a layer just below the surface, the lip of the sharks' upper jaw broke the surface, their lower jaw down and their mouth open, lined with fine teeth. They looked like an oval jet engine swimming along. The sunlight dappled the intricate markings on their skin, the white spots merging with ambient light. Everything

LEFT

Snorkeling with whale sharks in the deep ocean is one of the greatest interactions one can have with any marine creature. Each shark has its own flotilla of small fish following along. Acrylic on canvas.

ABOVE

Host Matt Gutman interviews SeaWorld's Mike Price aboard Lilly M *for an episode of* Sea Rescue.

Cape Cod

The Bahamas

Cuba

Turks and
Caicos

Mexico

Dominican
Republic

Jamaica

Haiti

Nova Scotia

The Trail of Milo
This whale shark named "Milo" was first tagged by Rafael de la Parra on July 30, 2018, off Isla Mujeres. After being tagged, Milo spent considerable time feeding in the plankton-rich waters off the Yucatan before taking a long journey via the Straits of Florida, through the Bahamas and out into the wider Atlantic, going east of Bermuda. We do not know why these migrations happen. Milo then returned to the Caribbean through the Windward Passage and headed straight back to the zone off Isla Mujeres. He spent the next year in the southern Gulf of Mexico and western Caribbean, then went back to the feeding area we call essential habitat, where he spent most of the summer. We encountered Milo several times in August 2019 while filming there. After the first tag lasted 473 days and 8,768 miles, Rafael replaced the tag on Milo in August 2020. This was just before Milo left and went back into the western North Atlantic, traveling far north to a point several hundred miles east of Cape Cod out in the Gulf Stream.

These tracks and data for Milo and other sharks tracked by the GHRI can be seen at ghritracking.org.

Bermuda

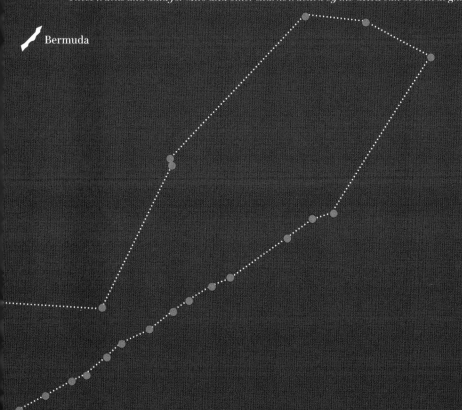

Puerto Rico

BELOW LEFT

Louisa goes head to head with a whale shark off Mexico.

BELOW RIGHT

Rafael de la Parra deploys a SPOT tag on a whale shark with help from his son.

FACING PAGE

Big manta rays, some up to 20 feet across, would swoop by in trains of up to 10 individuals. Acrylic on canvas.

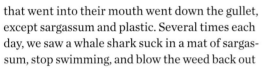

that went into their mouth went down the gullet, except sargassum and plastic. Several times each day, we saw a whale shark suck in a mat of sargassum, stop swimming, and blow the weed back out of its mouth—reverse thrust. I would imagine the same process gets rid of bits of plastic and floating debris as well. The sharks typically avoided the large mats of weed. Once we saw a shark get under a weed mat and then push its head out of the water shaking it, sargassum flying everywhere.

We went to film the sharks for six days in August 2017, the first two days of which the film team from SeaWorld shot an episode of *Sea Rescue* with host Matt Gutman and producer Aidan Pickering, and it was one of the most amazing weeks I have ever had out on the water. Not only was the weather excellent, but the plankton and fish eggs were thick. Every time we got back in the boat, we scraped a few ounces of fish eggs out of our hair and off our dive suits. There were lots of sharks and many more giant manta rays. The rays were jumping, doing somersaults and flips, landing on the water with a loud report like a cannon going off. Each morning, we looked for the whale shark aggregation by finding the jumping mantas—we could see the splashes from 2 miles away.

Sometimes there were five mantas to every whale shark. They came swooping by in trains of eight and 10 individuals, each looking like a jet engine powered by a pair of flapping wings. You could dive down in front of the lead manta and stay there at 20 feet as the rest of the train passed overhead like a flight of jet fighters: graceful, silent, peaceful. Sometimes they would do barrel rolls right in front of us; other times, the

mantas would stay inverted and continue feeding, going along for 100 yards, white belly shining up in the bright sunlight. We would be focused on a group, looking down at them from the tower of *Lilly M*, and suddenly—*whack!* An explosion of water just behind us as a flying manta landed its 3,000-pound body on the surface.

Dr. Al Dove, vice president of research and conservation at the Georgia Aquarium, and Dr. Bob Hueter of Mote Marine Laboratory and their collaborators have conducted research on whale sharks since 2004. Tracks of their migrations have been established using PATs and SPOTs that were attached by a long tether rather than actually implanted in the body of the shark. By using a tether, the shark does not actually have to reach the surface for the tag to transmit its location. But with the ever-increasing amounts of sargassum on the sea surface that could foul the tether and the tag, a better way of more accurately tracking whale sharks had to be utilized.

In 2018, we formalized our relationship with Mexican marine scientist Rafael de la Parra, the executive director of Ch'ooj Ajauil AC, the Whale Shark Research Project. Rafael had also been helping us on our billfish and mako shark tracking studies, and he has also worked with the Georgia Aquarium team on whale sharks. Having had great success with the amount of data we collected from mako and tiger sharks tagged with SPOT tags, Rafael wanted to tag the whale sharks

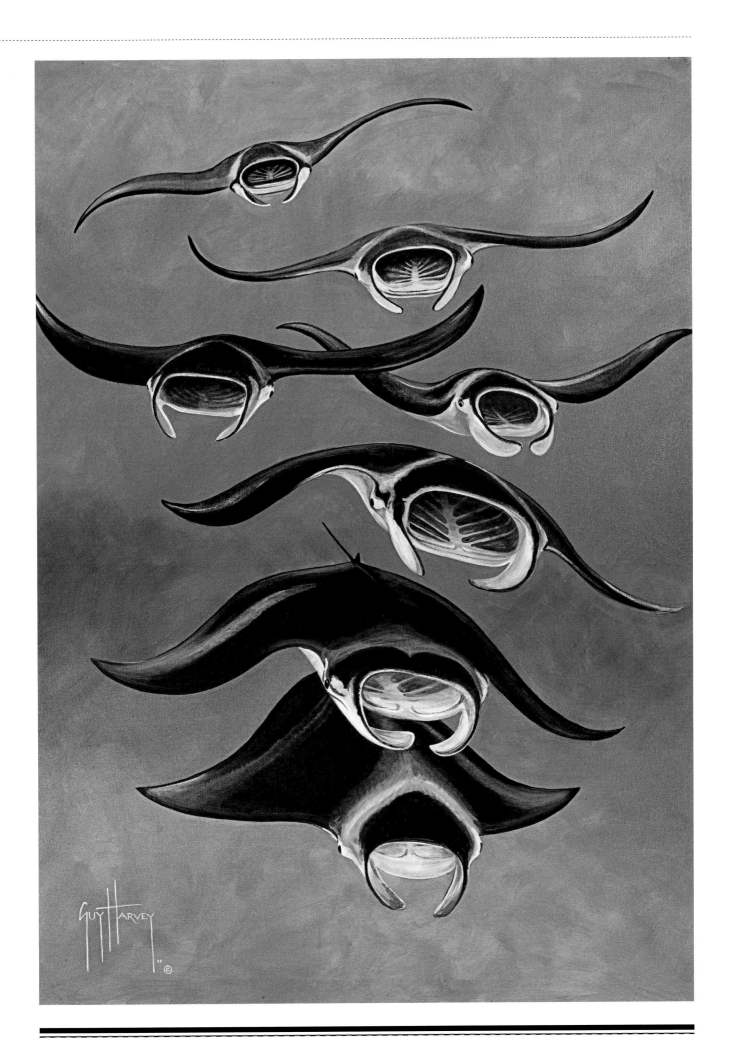

BELOW LEFT

The whale shark named Milo, with a SPOT tag deployed on its dorsal fin from the previous year.

BELOW RIGHT

Rafael and his family and crew with Jessica, tagging whale sharks.

BOTTOM RIGHT

Rafael's tagging boat, Grampus, *working with a cooperative shark.*

with the same devices. GHOF came on board as the main sponsor, and the data would be shared with all subsequent scientific publications. But just how do you attach a SPOT tag to the dorsal fin of a whale shark? A small whale shark is 20 to 25 feet long and weighs thousands of pounds—there is simply no way to catch one to attach the tag, as we had done with the tigers and makos.

Working with Anthony Mendillo, Rafael devised a method where a scuba diver would dive on a suitable shark and use a pneumatic drill fed by air from the dive tank to drill small holes through the top of the fish's dorsal fin to attach the tag. In 2017 Rafael, working with his family, deployed two SPOT tags, sending us some video of how this was accomplished. So in 2018, GHOF sponsored more tags and asked that we tag along to film his work the following season.

In July 2019, we were out in the zone next to Rafael in his work boat, *Grampus.* With help from his sons, Luis, Eugenio and Emilio, as well as his wife, Beatriz, on occasions, Rafael would choose a shark he considered a suitable candidate. He held on to the dorsal fin while swimming along to see how the shark responded. If the shark was tranquil, he started the process, drilling the holes for the tag in the top of the shark's dorsal fin. Just getting in one bolt securing the tag was the initial goal, particularly if the shark spooked and took off. For safety, Rafael put a small float on the tag in case it fell off.

Completing the bolting process sometimes took two or three attempts. No worries, Rafael said, if the shark moved off, it soon returned to feeding nearby. Occasionally he did not complete securing all four bolts in the late afternoon, so the team would return the next day, locate the same shark,

complete the process, and remove the little safety float. Very cool, but try doing that with a tiger shark or mako shark.

Rafael tagged two sharks in 2018; one male was called Milo. On July 7, 2019, while we were all in the water filming Rafael and Carl at work, Milo swam right next to our group. It is just amazing to think he had traveled 8,000 miles in the Caribbean and western Atlantic before coming back to take advantage of the abundant food supply right here. He knew where he had to be and when, just like all 1,317 other whale sharks so far individually identified that visit this region.

Milo has a distinctive chop out of the trailing edge of his dorsal fin. We even cleaned the algae off his tag. The data showed he stayed in the area feeding for nearly two months. As Rafael continues to tag whale sharks, we will learn a lot more about their habitat use and the range of this species.

After we departed in 2018, Rafael tagged a female named

BELOW RIGHT

Jessica, with our captain,
Rogelio Delgado, and a wooden
carving he made.

BOTTOM RIGHT

Rafael is a passionate marine
researcher and conservationist.

Rio Lady, which had been tagged twice before in the previous 10 years by the Georgia Aquarium team using PAT tags. Rio Lady continued to provide fine-scale detail on her migrations for the past two years. Whale sharks are very large, long-lived fish with no predators other than humans. Several sharks have chops in the dorsal and tail fins, probably caused by a ship's propeller or other collision. We have no idea where this species mates or gives birth to its young, which arrive as fully formed, perfect 3-foot-long miniatures of their parents.

Rafael considers there are three distinct groups of whale sharks that visit the feeding grounds of the Yucatan. More research might confirm his theory, but certainly this is the largest aggregation of whale sharks known on the planet. Meanwhile shark ecotourism in the Yucatan is growing, and is also considered a sustainable use of a protected marine species that provides income for licensed tour operators and their dependents. For three months of the year, tour operators put aside their fishing gear, where they harvest just about everything that swims, to take tourists out to swim with the whale sharks. During this time, they are killing nothing and providing a bucket-list experience to tens of thousands of people per season. During these three months, they make more money than they do the rest of the year fishing.

As humans, we are predictable in the way we exploit natural resources. We hope that the Mexican authorities continue to monitor and regulate the tourism opportunities that shark ecotourism provides. In the few years this interaction has been operating, overcrowding has become an issue. According to Hueter, the Mexican authorities must enforce accessibility and the level of interactions with the whale sharks. By comparison, the government in the Cayman Islands has lost control of public access to Stingray City in Grand Cayman. This world-famous 40-year-old attraction has gone way beyond daily capacity, particularly when more than two cruise ships are in the harbor. The patron's experience is diluted, and rays are subject to overhandling by tour guides and patrons. The GHRI has conducted the biannual stingray surveys since 2002, and has seen the attraction reach capacity—and then go beyond capacity now—for four days per week.

Mexico is in a great position to be a leader in conserving sharks, as has been done in the Bahamas. To achieve success in conservation of highly migratory sharks in the Caribbean, there has to be a regional approach. If we tag a tiger shark, oceanic whitetip or silky shark in the Cayman Islands, and then it swims west 300 miles to Mexico and is killed, this is a complete waste of time and money. Another positive development is the proposed designation of shark sanctuaries in the Yucatan. These sanctuaries could also generate sustainable income through shark ecotourism, as seen in other jurisdictions, providing alternative employment in the ecotourism sector that has been refined in the Bahamas since 2011.

Shark ecotourism is about saving sharks and helping educate people about the importance of top predators in marine food webs.

WHITE MARLIN: THE RACE AND THE CHASE

MEXICO'S YUCATAN PENINSULA has a wide variety of pelagic fish pass by at different times of year. We learned that mako sharks were there in March and April each year, and then white marlin showed up in May and June. The white marlin story is one of declining numbers year after year for decades. The areas of local abundance in Venezuela, the Dominican Republic, the Bahamas and the mid-Atlantic region of the United States were all becoming severely depleted. Marlin and sailfish were caught as bycatch in the lucrative tuna and swordfish pelagic longline fisheries. In addition, artisanal fisheries for billfish in Venezuela and small island states in the Caribbean and Central America also take their toll on the billfish populations.

The white marlin is a small species of billfish found only in the Atlantic Ocean, the Caribbean and the Gulf of Mexico. It closely resembles the roundscale spearfish, which is a species rarely encountered in the Caribbean and is more commonly found in the cooler waters of the Eastern Atlantic.

There had been tracking studies previously conducted by Dr. John Graves on white marlin from Venezuela when that fishery was accessible. A lot of tracking work has also been done in the Greater Antilles, some in the Bahamas and in the mid-Atlantic region, but very little in the western Caribbean and Gulf of Mexico. The tags we put out in 2003 were on the white marlin for only 10 days because this was a post-release mortality study: Every marlin we caught was tagged no matter what the condition of the fish. We learned they were tough. Even the few that were tail-wrapped and we had to revive survived the trauma of the capture and release, and then traveled 250 miles in 10 days. But where did they go from the southern Gulf of Mexico?

On Cinco de Mayo—May 5, 2014— we headed out of Isla Mujeres, Mexico, aboard *Keen M* with Capt. Anthony Mendillo and mates Gallo and Enrique "Tito" Can Osorio. As anglers, we had Guy Harvey Ocean Foundation staff member Alexandra Prebble and Jodi McCord from Texas. George Schellenger was filming for the new documentary about white marlin. We raised a couple of sailfish early, and Alexandra reeled in her

*More Atlantic grand slams
come out of the Yucatan fishery
these days than from Venezuela.
How often do you see a grand
slam in the spread, with all
three billfish species at once?
Mixed media.*

first one, a big fish for here at around 60 pounds. At 1:30 p.m.
we had a doubleheader of white marlin, real aerial acrobats
and great actors on the ocean's stage. We decided to take Jodi's
marlin first, so we boated the fish and placed it on a wet mat
with a saltwater hose flowing over its gills and its eyes covered
with a wet cloth. We removed the hook, measured the fish, and
Anthony implanted the tag in the shoulder. Still working on
landing the second white, I got some photos as they put the
first marlin back in the water. George was already in the water
to film its departure into the blue. They are so beautiful in
the water: a long, lean body with vivid stripes, big blue eyes
and rounded fins that seem oversize. The crew got the second
marlin in the boat, where Anthony put in the tag. George and I
were in the water and followed the fish as it swam off carrying
the electronic package. Doubleheader tagged and released—
good going, team!

The next white marlin was a full-grown one. It came up
on the left short bait, then dropped back to the left long and
inhaled it. When it started jumping, I thought it was a small
blue marlin—jumping, jumping and more jumping—great
long graceful leaps going around to the left and ahead of the
boat. This white marlin was close to 100 pounds, fat and long.
George and I were in the water for the release after our third
tag had been placed. This was our poster-child white marlin,
and it swam off strongly. Thinking back on all the large whites
in Venezuela, the mid-Atlantic and in the Bahamas, and
the hundreds of white marlin I have encountered, this was the
biggest of them all.

We were not finished yet. We caught another white marlin
at 4 p.m., which Jodi fought and we were able to tag. Another
hungry fish hit the teaser 30 minutes later and then dropped
back in the spread. Anthony hooked it on the stinger, passed
down the rod, and Alexandra caught it; we tagged and released
it, going 5-for-5 on Cinco de Mayo. What a day! We brought

only five PAT tags and got them all out in one day. The pressure was off.

My restaurateur friend from Grand Cayman, Andi Marcher, was at the dock waiting for us. He rolled his eyes when he heard about the day; he was still looking for his first white marlin. We enjoyed celebratory mojitos and some fresh dolphin at Ballyhoo's Bar that evening as the sun went down, the sky on fire.

On May 6, we arrived at the zone at the crack of 10:30 a.m. We hooked a sail right away, lots of jumps, then missed the next two sailfish as the action slowed. The next day, we switched boats and went out on the 48-foot Cabo *Chachalaca*, owned by Lawrence Berry. Andi started out by catching two sailfish, with lots of jumps. There were some wahoo around and we caught one, but it was slow fishing for white marlin. Finally in the afternoon, Anthony spotted several frigate birds low on the water. As we got closer, a white marlin ate the lure we had out for a blue marlin. Andi's first white was a scrappy fighter, with lots of jumps, and we were able to successfully release it. After circling the area, we had a bite on the short left and then the long left, and hooked another white marlin, which Andi caught after lots of jumps. I have never seen a white marlin caught that did not jump. George and Alexandra spent a while in the water filming the white marlin, the last one for the expedition.

We needed a larger sample size, so we followed up with another white marlin tagging expedition on May 5, 2015. George and I, accompanied by staffer Jay Perez, returned to fish aboard *Keen M* with Anthony and two mates, Gallo and Pasqual. The difference from the previous year was the amount of sargassum weed—it was pretty dense. We were pulling in the dredges to clear them of the grass every few minutes, and by the end of the week, we all had gotten some serious exercise.

It was a slow day, so Anthony made some calls to the captains fishing down south off Playa del Carmen and Puerto Aventura. We made the decision to move south and headed out the next morning, packing a bag of extra clothes as we cruised past Cancun and Puerto Morales toward the Mayan Riviera. We kept in close up on the shelf so we were not running against the northerly flow of the Gulf Stream.

We passed Cozumel to the east and started fishing at 1 p.m. about 5 miles north of Puerto Aventura. The weed was bad here too, but at least there were more fish. We fluffed a white that came up on the left teaser—I dropped back a ballyhoo that was immediately fouled with weed. Exasperating! Then a massive wahoo crashed the left teaser before cutting off the left flat line. It crossed the wake to the right teaser, then jumped back across the wake and hit the left teaser again, looking like a fish mounted on the wall—a monster—but no hookup. At 4:25 p.m., a white marlin came up on the stinger bait, dorsal up and flapping in the breeze. Anthony hooked it on the bridge rod and passed it down to Jay. The fight was on, with lots of jumps and cartwheels like crazy, as if this marlin were allergic to water.

We were using 80-pound-test leaders to get more bites, so Gallo held the leader carefully, gently bringing the marlin to the boat before grabbing the bill and, with Pasqual's help, laying it in the cockpit on the mat. Anthony put in the tag, George went into the water to film the release, and everything went like clockwork.

The next morning, we left the dock at 7 a.m., armed

AFTER CIRCLING THE AREA, *we had a bite on the short left and then the long left,* AND HOOKED ANOTHER WHITE MARLIN, *which Andi caught after lots of jumps.*

ABOVE RIGHT

White marlin always put on a dramatic show, including dozens of jumps. Get your camera ready as soon as there is a hookup.

FACING PAGE

Capt. Anthony Mendillo measures and tags a white marlin in the boat with help from Gallo and Pasqual. Tag placement is much more accurate with the marlin in the cockpit.

BOTTOM

White marlin portrait: a sleek fighter with oversize fins for excellent maneuverability. Watercolor.

with hot coffee and breakfast. Capt. Anthony put out the riggers, and we started fishing just 100 yards offshore from the entrance to Puerto Aventuras, where we had spent the night. There were no early bites, so we moved north, fishing close to the wall that drops off steeply just offshore. Then a sail took the stinger, and Jay was on it. It jumped repeatedly, with the beach and shoreline close behind—just surreal. It was Jay's first sailfish, a good-size fish at 70 pounds. At 10 minutes after 10 a.m., we hooked a white that jumped like crazy; we tagged this one with a satellite tag, and George swam with it for a while.

Around midafternoon, a blue marlin crashed the right lure, as they are supposed to, but there was no hookup. We waited those anxious seconds for the marlin to come back, as we knew it would, but it came up on the right flat, a small ballyhoo instead of the big lure. Gallo hooked it, and the blue raced away, tearing down-sea, but unfortunately the double line broke at the wind-on leader. That's marlin fishing.

At that point it was decision time whether we were going to go back up to Isla Mujeres or stay an extra day in Puerto Aventuras. I knew Anthony wanted to stay and have another chance at a blue marlin, so we were all in for the extra day.

At 2 p.m., we hooked our third white marlin—by now it was a windy afternoon, and the surface of the ocean looked like crumpled aluminum foil. We completed the catch, tagging, releasing and then filming the marlin's departure underwater.

At 3:20 p.m., another blue marlin crashed the right lure—*kaboom*! It happened so quickly that one had to be looking at the lure to see the bite. This one was hooked properly and tore off 200 yards of line before turning and jumping toward the boat. The marlin went out to the right and then turned to the left, still jumping. Anthony turned the boat to chase because the fish had taken out a lot of line. Afterward, George said that the marlin jumped continuously for one minute and 20 seconds. It was spectacular. Jay put the heat on the marlin and brought it up tired. Gallo had the leader, and I put in the PAT tag in the right shoulder. The hook was in a good spot in the upper jaw and was removed. We revived the marlin, estimated at 175 pounds, and let it go. Now Jay had his grand slam—sailfish, white marlin and blue marlin—all in one day. It was the first Atlantic grand slam I had seen since our days in Venezuela. We finished the day with one last white marlin, making it four whites, a sail and a blue. Tremendous action.

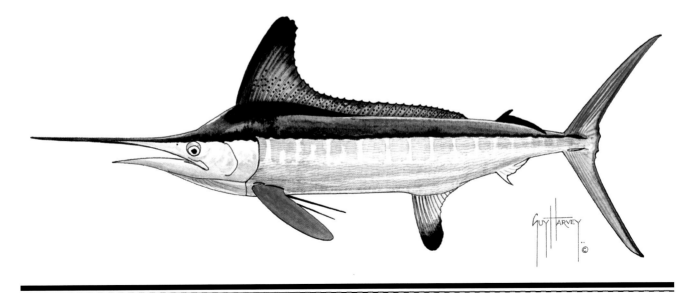

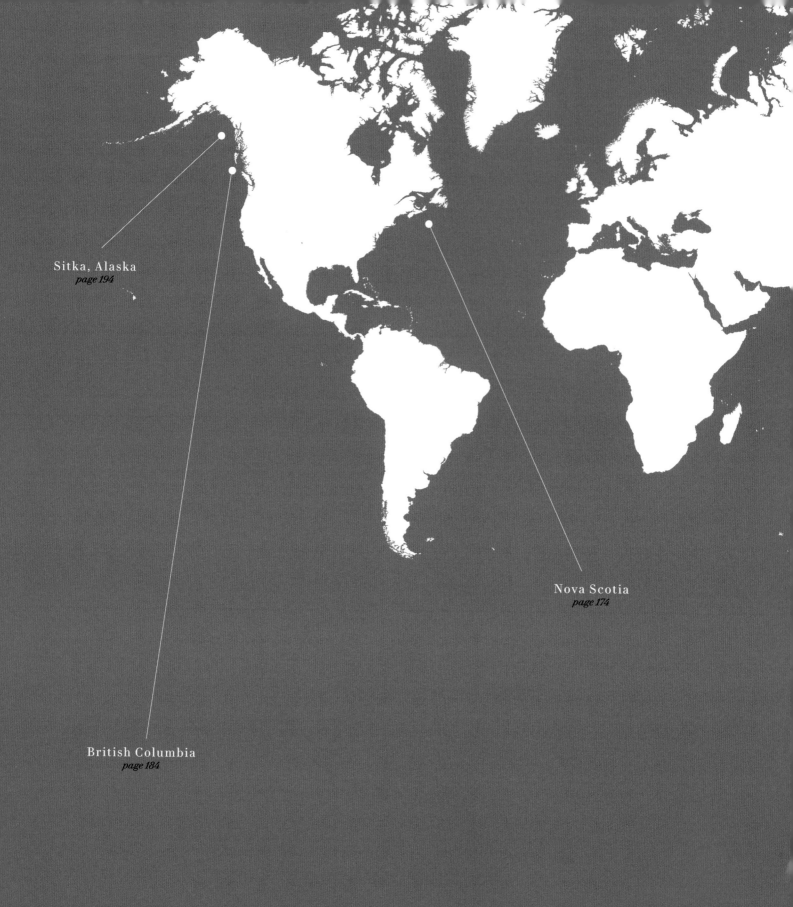

Sitka, Alaska
page 194

Nova Scotia
page 174

British Columbia
page 184

03

Big land, big water. It's home to healthy, well-managed fisheries where long, reel-screaming runs come one after the next. A region where salmon gleam in the Alaskan light like polished silver. A place that has inspired some of the best art I have ever created.

Nova Scotia

A SEA OF GIANTS

THE COLD, CLEAR GREEN water got my heart pumping as I turned to face the oncoming fish. It rose out of the green abyss, silent and purposeful, eyes wide, mouth slightly agape; the dorsal fin suddenly raised, pelvic fins lowered, and the gills flared as it inhaled a slowly sinking herring. It turned sharply, and the afternoon sun momentarily caught its bronze flanks, giving the surrounding water a golden glow. The fins and tail cut the surface, and the bubble stream followed the fish down into the green depths. Then another one rose up, then another. One came by really close in a rush to suck up the drifting herring, popping gills the size of trash can lids. Then a blur of bright yellow finlets as the huge fish passes. The average size of these giant bluefin tuna is 800 pounds. Yes, giant is the correct terminology.

These fish are up to 12 feet long with a 7-foot girth. Several fish that swept by me were in the 1,000-pound range. I panned my video camera as they glided past, unhurried, gobbling up the chum that kept them close to the boat. What a thrill to spend 40 minutes in the water with these magnificent creatures and their brilliant colors and movement! These were the visuals I needed for my next painting, although I would need to prepare a much bigger canvas.

In late summer and fall, these remnants of a once-larger population of bluefin tuna take advantage of large schools of herring that spawn in the Gulf of St. Lawrence and around Nova Scotia, Canada. They put on weight prior to undertaking lengthy migrations south to the Gulf of Mexico or across the Atlantic to the Mediterranean Sea.

We were on board *Fin Seeker*, a 50-foot lobster boat from Wedgeport, owned by Eric Jacquard and crewed by sons Joel and Camil. They have a permit from the Department of Fisheries and Oceans to take 5,500 pounds of dressed bluefin each season. Eric was very selective about which tuna were taken (they harvested only five in six days of fishing), and the rest were tagged and released for science. The fish that were harvested were meticulously cleaned and iced down before being shipped by air to waiting markets in Japan.

There were two research efforts underway in Nova Scotia, one being conducted by Dr. Barbara Block of the Tuna Research and Conservation Center, based at Stanford University's Hopkins Marine Station. The Guy Harvey Ocean Foundation co-sponsored this research organization with a grant to assist efforts at Port Hood in the northern district of Cape Breton.

The other research effort was being conducted by Dr. Molly Lutcavage of the Large Pelagics Research Center based at the Natural Resources Conservation Department, University of Massachusetts at Amherst. Molly's team was based in Port Mouton in the southwest. The GHOF has also sponsored some of her work in Canada. Both teams have spent the past decade in the field tagging and tracking the migrations of bluefin tuna along the eastern seaboard of North America, into the Gulf of Mexico and across the Atlantic to Europe.

Their results have indicated main feeding areas, spawning areas, and trans-Atlantic migrations for the species that conservationist Charles F. Holder described as "living meteors that strike like a whirlwind and play like a storm." The two researchers have also assisted in the sometimes-controversial management of this species by the International Commission for the Conservation of Atlantic Tunas, the organization that manages quotas in an attempt to regulate commercial fishing.

Harpooning these "horse mackerel" was the typical way of catching bluefin tuna in Nova Scotia until Zane Grey made the pilgrimage in 1924 and caught a 758-pound fish with rod and reel. Eleven years later, Michael Lerner (founder of the International Game Fish Association) and legendary captain Tommy Gifford

caught a giant tuna at Soldier's Rip near Wedgeport. This kick-started a rush of wealthy anglers attempting to catch a giant. Lerner perfected the technique of catching tuna from a skiff, rather than a larger motorboat, and being towed around by the fish until it was caught, coining the phrase, "Wedgeport sleigh ride." Very exciting but not for the faint of heart. Thankfully, tackle technology has advanced quite a bit since then.

Tuna catches in Nova Scotia declined in the 1950s; it's been claimed that the causeway built out to Cape Sable Island affected the herring's migration, so the tuna moved. Bluefin were still in the Gulf of St. Lawrence, and when boats went offshore to harpoon swordfish, they often encountered lots of them.

In the early 1980s, demand for fresh tuna in Japan grew exponentially, and so fishing for bluefin was greatly increased. Industrial-scale longlining and purse seining in the Mediterranean and western Atlantic were added to the trap and harpoon fishery. Consequently, the populations of bluefin

ABOVE

In the 1930s, Michael Lerner caught 21 giants in just eight days of fishing, for a total of 3,677 pounds, out of Wedgeport.

FACING PAGE, TOP LEFT

Eric Jacquard's main quarry is the lobster—the bigger, the better. We fished for giant bluefin on his lobster boat, Atlantic Angler.

FACING PAGE, BOTTOM LEFT

Camil Jacquard unhooks an 800-pound giant, which has just been tagged with PAT tag by Capt. Anthony Mendillo.

FACING PAGE, RIGHT

Mark Davis with a 600-pound giant harvested under the Jacquard's annual quota. Camil, Anthony and team members from the Large Pelagics Research Center assisted with the catch.

declined to the present-day levels where some authorities consider the species close to commercial extinction.

However, Molly says there's evidence of large numbers of fish—both giants and juveniles—in the northwest Atlantic. Assuming compliance with ICCAT management objectives, she is confident in saying that bluefin tuna are not on the edge of extinction. From her independent data gathered over many years, she said that if the quota system is properly regulated (as it certainly appears to be in Canada), then this fishery has the potential to be sustainable in spite of the huge worldwide demand for bluefin tuna as sushi.

Along with my documentary producer and cameraman, George Schellenger, we spent three days in 2012 with Capt. Anthony Mendillo and legendary angler Mark Davis on *Fin Seeker*. From December to May each year, *Fin Seeker* targets the lucrative lobster fishery. From June to August, it shifts

to the swordfish harpoon fishery. For our trip during bluefin tuna season, we watched willing anglers use ultra-heavy tackle while sitting in a modern fighting chair. They caught, tagged and released some two dozen giants in two nights. Pop-up archival tags were deployed on many fish following capture. The hook was removed using a dehooking device, and the tuna swam free. The PATs record the migration of the tuna, as well as depth and temperature data along their routes.

In bluefin tuna, a special physiological adaptation called a countercurrent heat exchanger allows metabolic heat to be kept in the body and not lost through the gills. This maintains the body temperature well above ambient water temperatures, allowing faster swimming speeds in areas rich in prey species. Being a "warm-blooded" fish, these giant tuna, often called superfish, can penetrate the cold northern latitudes and dive to great depths in search of fish and squid.

In October 2013, Andi Marcher, George and I fished for three days with Jennifer Gray, Molly and her assistant, Michele. Jennifer was working to put together a sizzle reel to host her own travel and fishing show, so Anthony, George and I helped out by including Jennifer in our expeditions.

In the cold, productive waters of the North Atlantic, humpback whales and minke whales locate schools of herring or mackerel, with big tuna following in close proximity, taking advantage of the bait schools trying to avoid the onrushing whales, whose mouths are as big as garage doors.

After spending time in the water with many giant bluefin teased up under the hull with loads of herring, I was inspired to paint this 10-by-4-foot scene of tuna as they compete for a trolled bait. Bluefin tuna are the ultimate prize for big-game anglers around the world. Acrylic on canvas.

ANTHONY said that a tuna or two had been CUT OFF BY WHITE SHARKS while being bled in the recent past. REALLY? DIDN'T WE JUST GO SWIMMING with the tuna?

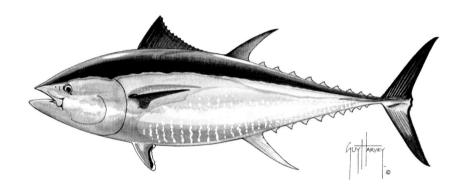

The scientific research and fishing action only added to her impressive credentials, which included being a weather anchor for CNN.

So why are the bluefin tuna in that area for that specific time? Eric explained how the herring moved into the gravel beds in early October to lay their eggs on the bottom, where the males fertilize them. At night, the herring boats set four gill nets on the bottom, each measuring 60-by-18 feet. After soaking for 30 minutes, they are hauled. In doing so, some herring fall from the nets, and the tuna mop them up. This is why tuna boats fish close to herring boats when possible.

After losing a day to weather, we set off the next morning to find the tuna. We had a bite at the Midway Ledges off Liverpool at 10:30 a.m. Jennifer fought the tuna for 30 minutes before the hook pulled at the boat. After no further bites, we moved northeast to Indian Island. Nothing. We went back to Midway Ledges again and had a double bite just as the sun went down. Andi had one on for 10 minutes and lost it. Jennifer fought the other tuna for 80 minutes; at 700 pounds, Eric said it was too big to land. Anthony tried to tag it, but the leader broke.

At dusk's last light, Andi hooked a 600-pounder, which Eric boated because it was the best size for his customers. He prefers the smaller to midsize tuna—350 to 600 pounds—because they are more easily sold as a whole fish. The big fish, over 600 pounds, are usually released. The whole process of butchering the tuna is fascinating to experience. The fish is bled for a half-hour in the water. Anthony said that a tuna or two has been cut off by white sharks while being bled in the recent past. *Really? Didn't we just go swimming with the tuna?* The head and entrails are taken out, ice water is funneled into the main dorsal artery, then the body is immersed in an ice-slurry bath.

We returned in October 2014 so Alex could catch a giant tuna. Unfortunately, the weather deteriorated over the first three days, and we finally fished on our last day. There was still a big swell from the front but no wind. We set up in 21 fathoms on the herring grounds and waited. Minke whales were blowing close by. Tuna were busting on schools of sauries. It was looking good. We moved a little deeper and marked some tuna on the depth finder. Anthony got a bite as he was letting out the bait. Alex was in the chair and fought the tuna for 30 minutes. While trying to tag the tuna at the boat, the leader broke.

We hooked up five minutes later. Alex was on again, fighting the tuna in the chair. After 10 minutes, the line broke. Anthony was beside himself—two equipment breaks on successive fish! We had another bite, and Alex was in the chair yet again, finally catching this one in 35 minutes. Anthony got the tag in, and we called it 650 pounds. Finally!

We will be back to follow in the footsteps of Grey, Lerner and other great anglers who pioneered this fishery. We will continue to support the research of this most remarkable of all fish, the superfish. Catch-and-release fishing for giant bluefin tuna has proved sustainable and a viable alternate source of revenue for commercial tuna operators.

British Columbia

THE SALMON RALLY

WHILE I HAD FISHED in Alaska for various species of salmon as far back as 1997, we traveled to British Columbia in June 2003 to produce an episode of *Portraits from the Deep*. The production team was headed up by Angelo Bernaducci, who had directed and produced the series *Walker's Cay Chronicles* with fly-fishing legend Flip Pallot. Our host, Raleigh Werking, was on the hunt for salmon world records on light tackle, and had discovered a guide who had access to big chum and pink salmon on a regular basis.

Four planes later—Grand Cayman to Miami to Dallas to Vancouver to Terrace—we met Raleigh and the production crew, Rick Westphal, Jim Petit and Andy Rowe. Our fishing guide, Gill McKean of West Coast Fishing Adventures, drove us to the Desiderata Inn, his small fishing lodge. I had shipped a blank canvas ahead because I planned on painting while I was there, as I had for all *Portraits from the Deep* episodes.

Our first day was on the Skeena River, the so-called River of Mists, known for its jumbo-size chinook (king) salmon. It was a total bust. "Hey, this is fishing," Gill said, the river high

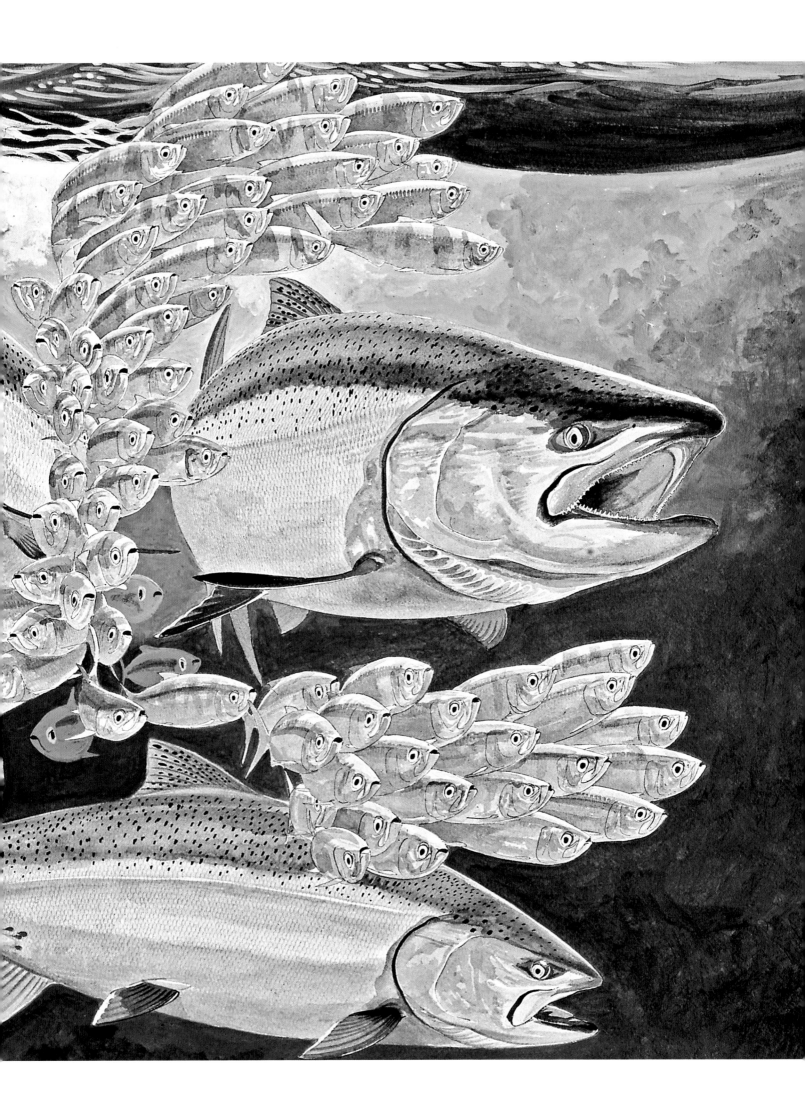

Fishing for salmon in the rivers in British Columbia was a completely different experience from fishing for them in the sea in Alaska, slow-trolling a spinning herring for bait. In BC, we either bottom-bounced or back-trolled downriver for the fresh run, or "chrome" fish heading upriver. We released the fish to continue on their way to the natal stream. As salmon spend time in fresh water and move upstream, they all change color. Pink salmon have green backs and pink flanks. Sockeye turn bright red. Coho turn pink and red. Chum develop colorful bars of red and pink on a bronze background. The large male king, shown here, turns a coppery bronze, retaining its vivid spots as the kype develops into very curved jaws. From an artistic perspective, the colors of all river-run salmon species are spectacular compared with their countershading with green backs and silver flanks in the ocean. King salmon are very active on the line, making strong runs and jumps, which opens up the opportunity to paint the surrounding habitat: cold, green water, leaves changing color, and mountains in the distance.

and fast from the recent rains. But the views were incredible, the river shining in the intermittent sunlight.

The next day, Gill and his younger brother, "Splash" Gordon, took two drift boats on a 30-minute drive to launch on a smaller river called the Kitimat. The Hyne drift boats are an unusual design specifically made for this sort of river fishing: fiberglass with a high bow, about 15 feet long, and with three seats, one for the guide in the middle and two for anglers.

It was a wonderful way to go slowly downriver. Splash had the film crew on board his boat; Raleigh and I went with Gill. We stopped where a tributary called the Ouida joined the Kitimat. There was a long, rough beach just down from the fork. We left the boats and hopped into the clean, green water and started casting while wading. We were "bottom-bouncing": using a 3-inch lure with a spinning head and dark skirt, a small weight 3 feet up the leader on a three-way swivel so the lure works close to the bottom. We cast into the river, the lure sinking and bouncing its way across the current. Large chinook rolled in front of us. So far we'd hooked a few logs but no fish.

Raleigh hooked up, and the salmon jumped like crazy. It was over 40 pounds, a beautiful chrome fish that put up a tremendous battle. The other drift boat closed in to get the action

on camera. Soon after we continued back-trolling downriver, and I had a bite on the right rod from another fine sea-run chinook. Gill skillfully maneuvered the boat around obstacles as I kept in touch with the fish. We ended up across the river and netted a salmon estimated at 35 pounds, which we then released. That evening, I started the episode's painting: a chinook salmon in the Kitimat River.

Day Three was cloudy and spotted with rain. Once again, Gill went back to the Kitimat. And once again, we beached just below where it forks with the Ouida and started wading from the shore, casting and bottom-bouncing. At 2 p.m., I had a solid bite. The fish swam across the river straight at me. I could not reel fast enough, so I backed up in the shallows and walked onto the bank, dodging tree stumps along the way. The fish then headed downriver, and I ran about 200 yards around stumps and logs to gain back some line. My heart was racing! Gill stayed with me, grinning, until I finally steered the fish into the quiet water, where Gill did the honors with the net. Tremendous!

The next expedition was a year later. Raleigh had said to come back in July to experience the chum and pink salmon. Our family was part of a big group that included Terri and Mike Andrews, the owners of Tropic Star Lodge in Panama,

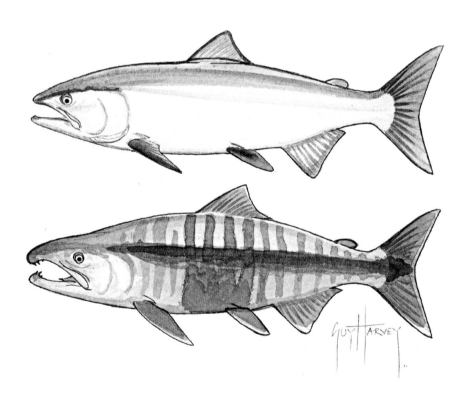

ABOVE

The colors of chum salmon change remarkably from being in ocean (top) and then heading upriver (bottom).

FACING PAGE, TOP LEFT

Jessica nets a big chum salmon in the Kitimat River for Alex.

FACING PAGE, TOP RIGHT

Gill McKean guided me on my first steelhead trout.

MIDDLE LEFT

Jessica loved the beauty of the British Columbia wilderness.

MIDDLE RIGHT

"Splash" Gordon holds the big chrome king salmon caught by Jessica.

BOTTOM LEFT

Alex and I pose with a pair of pink salmon caught where the Ouida meets the Kitimat.

BOTTOM RIGHT

Gill holds up a junior angler record chum salmon caught by Jessica.

Canada & Alaska / British Columbia **189**

Several brown bears came out of the bushes and began **CHASING SALMON IN THE RIVER.** *They kicked up spray, chasing fish left and right. It was the Pacific Northwest version of* **A BLACK MARLIN CHASING BONITO.**

and their son, Zane. I asked Ricky Westphal, who worked on *Portraits from the Deep*, to join us to gather B-roll for future episodes. As a family we were going for some IGFA junior angler world records on chum and pink salmon, which were wide open at the time.

It was a bright, sunny day, so everyone was in waders and short sleeves. At a beach known as Raleigh's Run, Gill taught Alex and Jessica the technique of bottom-bouncing. We all hooked chum salmon, a powerful, deep-bodied fish that thrashed at the surface and made long, reel-screaming runs. We would amble after them in our waders, shuffling over the rough pebbles, avoiding fallen trees. With every fish caught, I marveled at their colors: olive green backs, pink and bronze flanks barred with vivid bands of dark maroon and pink. Their coloration was a complete contrast to the green backs and silver flanks of the ocean-run fish.

Jessica caught a potential record chum of 19 pounds. Alex's next fish bested it at 19.5 pounds. Then Zane beat that with a 20-pounder.

We followed the same drill the next day: back to Raleigh's Run, where Raleigh hooked a chum on his first cast and caught 19 on the day himself. Meanwhile, Jessica, Alex and Zane were casting away, each fish besting their records from the previous day. A 20-pounder caught by Jessica was one of the largest females any of the guides had ever seen. Later that afternoon, Mike fought a large chum on 15-pound line, eventually landing it by jumping in a boat and following the fish before getting it in the net. It was a massive 29.8 pounds. It went through our common process: weigh, measure, photograph, release. We paddled downriver and stopped to scope

out another good location where the Ouida joined the Kitimat. The seam created by the meeting of two bodies of water was loaded with fish. The pinks were thick in the shallows, and big chum drifted on the edge of the deeper water.

That evening I did sketches from a male and a female chum salmon. Having the actual specimens there was great for reference.

The following day, we drove several hours through the mountains to Stewart, Alaska. Unfortunately it was very cloudy and started to rain as we got close, so there was no view of the spectacular vista where the mountains met the sea. We crossed the border at a little town called Hyder. I snapped photos of Jessica and Alex with one foot in Canada and one in the United States. Now it was time for a beer at the famous Glacier Pub before enjoying an Alaskan king crab dinner at the Prince George. Then it was off to see the bears.

At a place called Fish Creek, there's an elevated boardwalk above the shallow river. We watched chum salmon heading upstream until the rangers said to clear the river because the bears would be arriving soon and advised us to keep on the boardwalk.

Several brown bears came out of the bushes and began chasing salmon in the river. They kicked up spray, chasing fish left and right. The salmon would panic, going in every direction at once, white water flying everywhere. It was the Pacific Northwest version of a black marlin chasing bonito.

When Jessica was in high school in Victoria, British Columbia, I came to visit her at the end of May 2005. The morning after I arrived, Gill, Jessica and I drove a couple of hours to the Ishkinish River in the neighboring watershed

of the Nass River Valley. We walked the last part from the dirt road to a beautiful river. Gill set me up with a small lure that resembled a small bunch of salmon eggs with a float to keep it near the surface. We had only one bite from a fine 8-pound female steelhead. At last, I had my reference to undertake an authentic steelhead painting.

Three months later, Alex and I returned to Terrace, British Columbia, with Raleigh and my friend Dennis Hunter, from Grand Cayman. The Andrews family, from Panama, were on the trip as well. We fished the same spots from the previous year, but the configuration of the river had changed quite a bit. There were more fishermen this time as well. Apparently the news had got out about the Kitimat's chum and pink salmon runs.

On Day Two of our five-day expedition, we were at Harvey Run by 9 a.m. No one else was there, and the bite was on. The river was full of fish. We hooked several large chinooks, which kept the anglers running back and forth along the beach. Alex had a 40-pounder on that gave him a great workout. It eventually ran around my leg and broke off. Everyone got a slam before noon.

There was heavy rain overnight, but it cleared by the time we were back on the water. The morning chum salmon bite was good as we cast constantly under the watchful eye of our guide, Josef. Zane got the fish of the day by catching a 24-pound chum, a beautiful golden fish and the new potential junior angler record. That's how good the fishing was: the junior angler chum salmon record had been improved upon five times in two days. Alex rounded off the day with a 25-pound chinook, which completed his grand slam.

With more overnight rain, our last morning was not looking good. We considered going to the Skeena River, but Gill and Josef said the Kitimat might be the better option because it had been so consistent. Luckily the rain cleared up shortly after leaving the dock, and we ran swiftly down the swollen river to the spot where the little Ouida joined the Kitimat. The clear green tributary merging with the fast gray water of the Kitimat was holding *a lot* of fish.

The pinks were bunched up in the clear shallows, and the chum were in the deeper gray water of the Kitimat. It was obvious that they preferred the clear water. Josef went off to help Dennis catch a chum on fly. I stayed with Alex and Zane, who fished for six hours straight, hooking a salmon with almost every cast. Zane was the first to catch a pending junior angler world record pink salmon: a fine humped male of 10 pounds that was measured, weighed, photographed and released. The two boys were on fish for the whole day. It was some of the best salmon action I've ever seen. The chums were hard to land. If you did not fight them with a heavy drag, they were impossible to stop. Twice my reel got spooled; I just broke them off before they got too far away.

The day was full of bent rods, jumping fish, photos in bright sunlight, and excited chatter from two 12-year-old boys who just love fishing.

We ran swiftly down the swollen river to the spot where **THE LITTLE OUIDA JOINED THE KITIMAT.** *The clear green tributary merging with the fast gray water of the Kitimat* **WAS HOLDING** *A LOT* **OF FISH.**

A pair of chum salmon swimming upriver to their native stream along with pink and king salmon. Mixed media and watercolor.

Sitka, Alaska

KINGS, BEARS AND BARN DOORS

OUR FIRST INVITATION to visit Sitka, Alaska, came from Ricky Smith and Jay Gustin, who had a salmon fishing charter operation on Baranof Island. We first met Jay at the Miami International Boat Show in 1997. He wanted me to paint a fish from their region, so that June we went aboard Jay's 60-foot Delta, *Adventurous*. What followed were many repeat trips to Alaska and the Pacific Northwest, and some of the best art I've ever created.

Upon arrival, we went straight to Ricky's beautiful home on a private island called Thunder Bay. Coming from the Caribbean, Gillian, Jessica, Alex and I were enjoying the change in scenery: snowcapped mountains, eagles, trees, otters. Ricky showed us a chart of the area. The plan was for Jay and mate Travis Peterson to take us south to various fjords to fish for the four main salmon species—king (chinook), silver (coho), chum (dog) and pink—plus a variety of other species.

The next morning, we headed out on *Adventurous*, kicking off several epic days of salmon fishing using single-action reels with herring as bait on downriggers. We were surrounded by rocky headlands, with seals, otters, sea lions and eagles, and humpback whales breaching nearby. At ages 7 and 5, Jessica and Alex were having a blast.

We learned how to rig the baits from Travis and deploy the downriggers at different depths. Occasionally Jay would look back to say, "Fish at 30 feet," "50 feet," as he marked individual salmon on the depth finder. Invariably we would hook a king and the fight was on, then we'd bring in the rest of the gear so it didn't tangle the fish we were fighting.

I was taking lots of photos and making notes of the coloration of the salmon: the metallic silver flanks etched with pink, gold and turquoise, depending on the light, with black spots like confetti on the upper part of the body and tail.

In late afternoon, we anchored up in an unnamed fjord in Whale Bay and set out a few deep shrimp traps armed with a salmon head. Each morning we hauled the traps on a winch and spent an hour sorting the catch, which was a spectacular amount of bright red and orange coon shrimp and spotted shrimp.

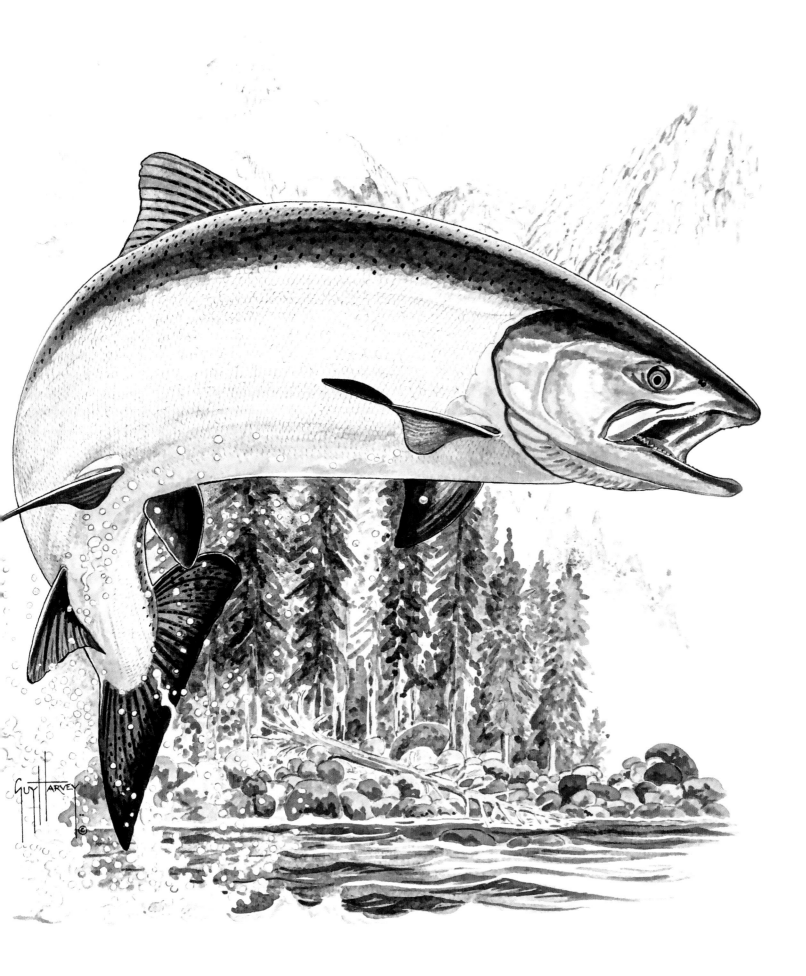

On this 8-by-4-foot canvas, salmon are feeding on herring and sand eels, and are too distracted to notice the approach of an orca. Acrylic on canvas.

For the rest of the week, Jessica and Alex caught numerous king salmon up to 41 pounds, as well as many cohos and a couple of chum. Jessica hooked a bigger fish and fought it on her own. With Jay driving the boat, Travis eventually netted the salmon, and we kept it whole on ice for weighing later because it was a potential junior angler world record. (The IGFA had just initiated the junior angler category.) When we got back, we weighed her salmon at Sitka Sound Seafoods and filled out the IGFA record application form. At 28 pounds, it happened to be the first record application submitted by a junior angler.

The art that resulted from this expedition was just the start. With all the anatomical details nailed down, including scale counts, fin ray counts, head and jaw structure, plus many photos and notes, I was more confident in tackling some major pieces of art. One of my favorite all-time paintings, the 8-foot *Northern Exposure,* resulted from this expedition.

Returning to Alaska in July 2003, we brought friends and a film crew. Upon arrival, we were met by Travis and Ricky. I introduced them to my good friend, fishing aficionado and photojournalist Bill Boyce, and our film crew, Ricky Westphal and James Petit, who were there to shoot an episode of *Portraits from the Deep.*

On Day One, we trolled around Krishka Island in light rain with three lines at 30, 60 and 90 feet down on the downriggers. There is a steep drop at the north end of this island where lots of salmon hang out. Travis doesn't use the big flashers anymore because he found the naked herring to be just as effective. Rick put a small camera on the downrigger to get the bite. I was surprised to see how clear the water was. We caught six cohos for every king salmon.

Shifting gears, we moved 7 miles offshore and anchored up in 400 feet of water to target halibut. It took 30 minutes

*This 340-pound halibut was a
boat record for* Adventurous.

for the "barn doors" to find the chum bag and our baits. Bill caught an 80-pounder that took him quite a long time to reel up. We caught and released a huge skate of about 175 pounds, which made for a lot of boatside excitement.

The next morning, we moved up the Port Banks on an incoming tide, making our way to a big waterfall. We could see salmon heading up the river in the clear water. Below the waterfall was a deep pool where we set up cameras on tripods and began fishing the salmon in the pool. They jumped up the falling water, tails beating frantically.

Using a pole camera (this is before the GoPro), Rick was able to capture great footage of salmon turning and accelerating up the falls. Big fish stacked up like bars of freshly minted silver lying on top of each other. It was an amazing sight. At anchor that evening, we had fresh halibut on the grill, as well as salmon and spotted shrimp, as eagles called from the forest. You could hear the coho salmon jumping all night long around the boat.

The next morning, Paco showed Jessica, Alex and me how to cast the "sockeye fly." Bill was an old hand at this. He cast across the water where the fish were jumping. He reeled vigorously. "They are biting!" he exclaimed, the rod bent. We released about 20 sockeye salmon on fly.

We finished up around 1 p.m. and then went to haul the crab and shrimp pots loaded with spotted shrimp and Dungeness crab. Back at Ricky's beautiful house at Thunder Bay we had a wonderful shrimp salad and, of course, salmon. We put some salmon parts out on the rocks, and soon a dozen bald eagles came swooping in to pick on the scraps, providing a incredible photo opportunity.

It was seven years before we returned to Sitka, in June 2010. Travis and his fiancee, Jennifer, were now running *Adventurous*. James Power was the mate, and Travis' beautiful black Labrador, Lucy, was second mate. In beautiful weather we fished our way south toward Whale Bay. The first stop was at Biorka Island. We trolled three downriggers, as usual. James taught Jessica and Alex how to rig the herring baits: two 4/0 hooks on 30-pound leader, rigged so the bait spun slowly like a wounded herring. We caught several coho and a king, then Jessica got a halibut and a fine chum salmon, giving her a grand slam.

Travis decided to head out to his halibut spot 7 miles out. In the distance, humpback whales breached and slapped their tails, staying in the same spot even as we got closer. He showed me on the depth finder a sudden drop to 400 feet where a rock ledge met the sand. He anchored up, and we dropped our jigs and baits. I used a 16-ounce leadhead soft-pink jig tipped with a piece of salmon belly. This was attached to an 80-pound braid line on a Shimano Tyrnos two-speed on a short rod. I was jigging—up, down, up, down—and watching the whales gallivanting nearby. Then—*kaboom!*—I got a bite.

"Big one! Did you hook a whale?" Travis asked, laughing. Jessica, Alex and James all brought in their lines. The whales no longer had our attention. Instead we watched the taut line cutting through the green water. I could have used a good harness; it was like fighting a big tuna.

The fish was spinning slowly in the current, and I was struggling to retrieve the last 20 feet of line. We were at a stalemate. Sweating in the cold air, I took off my jacket, put the drag up to full, then clamped my left hand on the side of the reel. Travis finally got the leader. It took three gaffs to bring the thrashing fish to the side door. Travis was hollering, "It's a boat record!" Using a tape, it measured 85 inches with an estimated weight of 340 pounds. Dinner that night was fresh halibut baked in mayonnaise and lemon juice covered in crushed potato chips. Absolutely fabulous!

Redfish Bay is a good place to spot brown bears in the evening. Upon arrival, it wasn't the bears that got my

BIG SALMON STACKED UP *like bars of freshly minted silver lying on top of each other. It was* **AN AMAZING SIGHT.**

Humpback whales were seen on a regular basis: some jumping, some feeding, some just tail slapping. Watercolor.

With a 48-inch length and a girth of 30 inches, the formula put the salmon at 54 pounds—a "Crown Royal" fish (over 50 pounds), according to Travis. This meant we would all have a shot of Crown Royal to cele-brate. Some of us had two shots. It was a chilly day!

attention, but rather the bald eagles. They came in close for the small rockfish we tossed in the boat's wake. Suddenly a peregrine falcon thumped onto the back of an adult bald eagle! Using her tremendous momentum, she rose sharply upward, and circled back over the eagle and swooped in again. The eagle ducked and changed direction, bobbing this way and that, looking clumsy compared with the agile falcon. I was lucky and caught it on camera. She must have had chicks in a nest in the rocky cliff above us nearby. This experience inspired a painting of a different kind: a watercolor of the falcon grabbing the back of the bald eagle.

A young adult brown bear appeared, cautiously surveying the landscape. It came toward us through the grass and over fallen trees toward the water's edge. It stopped and began to consume the bright green grass like it had not eaten for a week.

We quietly motored the skiff for a closer look. I was able to get decent images with my long lens. We could hear the bear's teeth cutting the grass like a grazing cow. I was amazed; I'd never heard about brown bears eating grass. It walked along the intertidal zone, snuffling through kelp fronds, turning over small rocks looking for clams and crabs, then disappeared back into the forest. Spectacular!

Overnight, the heavy rain drummed the deck above our heads. Under a very gray dawn, we made our way north again toward Whale Bay. We approached Port Banks and fished in the fjord in 150 feet of water. Everyone was staying out of the rain in the salon. I was the only one on deck when we had a bite.

Grabbing the rod and reeling quickly, I came tight and felt the weight of a big fish. There were some head shakes, but the fish just kept pulling deep. Suddenly it changed direction, came toward the surface, and then burned line off the reel in a long run. "Big salmon!" Travis said. The fish came up close to the boat, and we could now see the length. Oohs and aahs from everyone. It made two more short runs before James quickly netted it and lifted it with a grunt through the side door.

This was the biggest king salmon we had seen in three expeditions on *Adventurous*. The salmon was very fat, with a metallic green and purple back, pink and bronze on the upper flanks. Its sides were like polished silver in the gloomy light. Travis used the 50-pound hand scale to get a weight, but it was over 50 pounds.

With a 48-inch length and a girth of 30 inches, the formula put this salmon at 54 pounds—a "Crown Royal" fish (over 50 pounds), according to Travis. This meant we would all have a shot of Crown Royal to celebrate. Some of us had two shots. It was a chilly day!

Alaska remains one of the best fishing destinations on the planet because the recreational and commercial fisheries for different species are well-regulated.

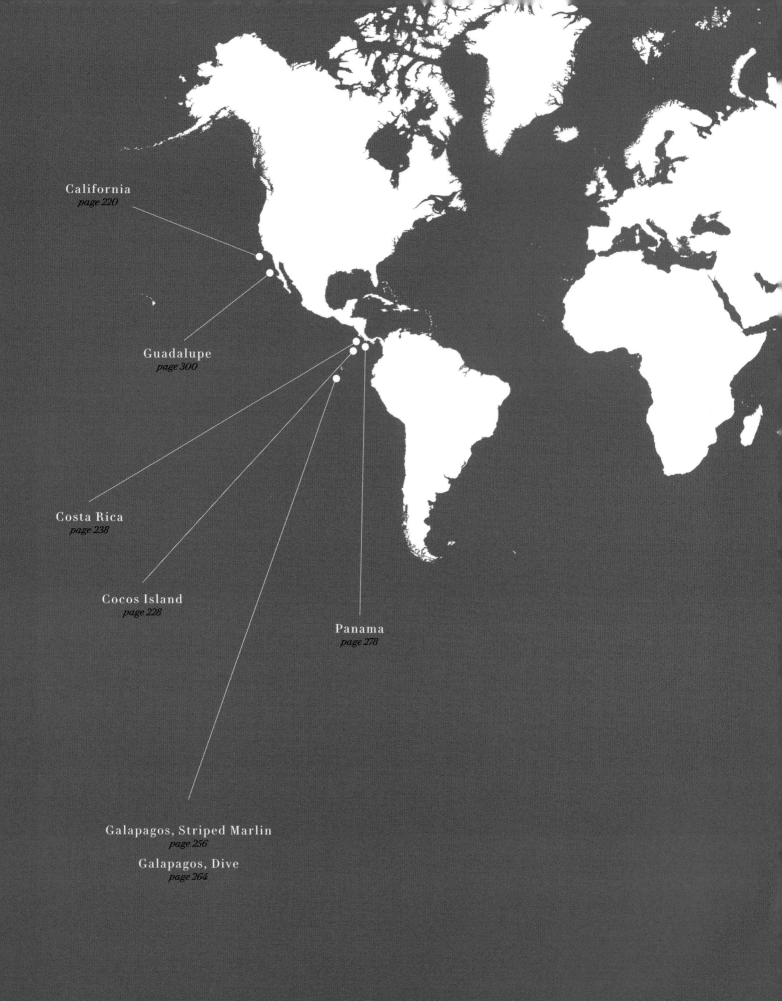

California
page 220

Guadalupe
page 300

Costa Rica
page 238

Cocos Island
page 228

Panama
page 278

Galapagos, Striped Marlin
page 256

Galapagos, Dive
page 264

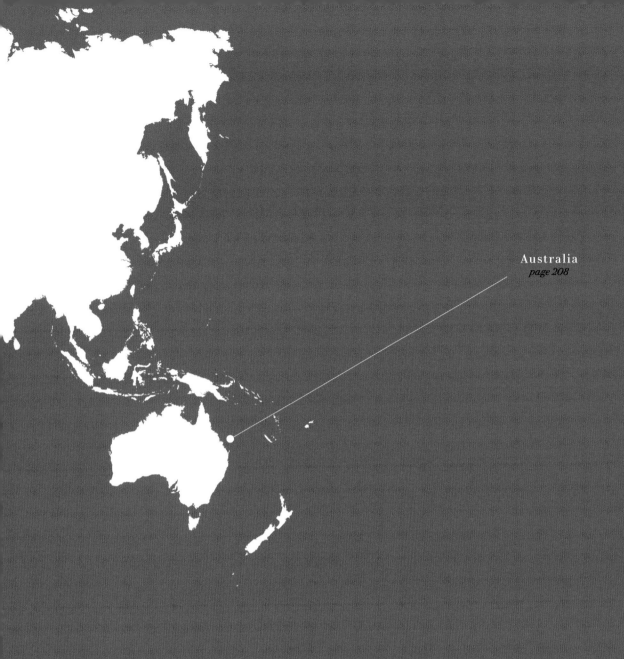

Australia
page 208

04

P A C I F I C   O C E A N

The ocean's name, which means "peaceful," was bestowed upon this body of water by Ferdinand Magellan for its calm nature. It is a massive sea that touches a wide variety of unique locations, from the third-largest state in the US to the world's smallest continent.

Big, gravid black marlin gather to spawn along the Great Barrier Reef from September to November. Often multiple males will escort the females, and spawning might occur several times in the spawning months. Mixed media on paper.

Australia

BLACK MARLIN AND BARRAMUNDI DOWN UNDER

AUSTRALIA'S GREAT Barrier Reef is the annual gathering area for spawning black marlin in the western Pacific. A lot of big female marlin are found all along this 1,200-mile stretch of water adjacent to the eastern side of the coral walls that form the base of the reef. The attendant males are numerous, as we found out back in 1991 and on several subsequent expeditions in the 1990s. We saw and hooked a lot of 150- to 300-pound rats, as they are called.

In early November 2003, we embarked on a family vacation to the reef, fishing with Capt. Laurie Wright and his mates, Jimbo Bladen and Adam Gailey. *Iona* was the game boat, and our mothership was *Kona*. Bill Boyce was along, as well as our cameraman, Rick Westphal, to document the action for our television series, *Portraits from the Deep,* and for a documentary called *Billfish: Nomads of the Ocean.* Dr. Julian Pepperell was our guest as the premier billfish biologist in Australia and the western Pacific. He had been a good friend over many years, and I took the opportunity of his availability to have his experience in the episode. My son, Alex, and daughter, Jessica,

were still junior anglers according to the new IGFA categories, so the aim was to have them both try to catch a black marlin record during the six-day expedition.

We headed out of Cairns on a rough day and started fishing at Linden Bank, heading north and going downsea to Opal Ridge, then past the five Agincourt Reefs and in behind St. Crispen's for the night; we fished without a billfish bite the whole way. My wife, Gillian, and Jessica had traveled aboard *Kona*, and so we joined them at St. Crispen's. There is a magical feeling about being on a reef at night, as the fish flit in and out of view in the lights and the occasional exclamation as one of the kids had a bite on the line.

We did two dives every morning before going fishing. Some were drift dives, others were leisurely swims on some of Laurie's favorite bommies, or large coral heads. Then we went bait-fishing for scad and scaly mackerel, important for our trolled baits. Alex and Jessica loved that action. The scaly

mackerel, some up to 15 pounds, made good skipping baits, and the scads, also a mackerel, were the perfect swimming bait. We were zero-for-3 on small fish the next day and did not get a hook in a marlin until 4:15 p.m. the following day off Escape Reef. The 400-pound black marlin ate a 20-pound live yellowfin tuna right on the drop-off. After some great jumps on the leader, which Bill and Rick needed for the show, the marlin was tagged with a pop-up satellite tag and released.

November 8 was another day with two early dives; the marlin still had lockjaw. Gillian, Jessica and Julian headed out the following morning from the helipad at Agincourt Reef. We planned to meet them in Christchurch, New Zealand, after this trip; it was a pity it had been so rough for the girls. We fished that day off Anderson Reef and pulled the hook on a small fish late in the afternoon, but we had two days remaining.

After a superb dive the next morning, we headed out fishing and trolled south against the weather toward Opal Ridge.

ABOVE

Dr. Michael Domeier about to tag a large bull shark with a PAT tag. The shark's incredibly tough, thick skin made it very difficult to insert the barb of the tag.

FACING PAGE

A PAT goes into a 300-pound black marlin, which pops off after a predetermined time, floats to the surface and transmits its information to a satellite. It is then downloaded and analyzed by scientists.

We had the splashing scaly mackerel on the left, a swimming scad on the right, and down the middle, a scad on an 80-pound outfit for Alex. At 5:50 p.m., the center bait was eaten by a marlin. Alex was in the chair quickly, did a short drop-back and came tight on the fish. Backing the boat into the sea had us all soaked, but the fish was jumping close by. We could also see that the wire leader was wrapped on its tail, which would make it tougher for Alex to get the fish up. He was soaked, cold and tired when he did finally get the leader in range for the mate to grab, thanks to some brilliant boathandling by Laurie. The marlin jumped close to the boat, orange sky behind us— beautiful. Then the marlin sounded and kept going down. The inevitable jerking on the line a few minutes later signified that sharks had gotten to the marlin—no junior record for Alex, but he did get a technical release on a fish we called 550 pounds.

November 11 was our last day out on the reef. We did one dive in the morning and then went to fish for the razor gang for some variety: dogtooth tuna, wahoo and big Spanish mackerel. Jimbo and Adam had rigged up a couple of scad with double hooks on short wire leaders, plus a couple of Rapala lures. We trolled out toward Opal Ridge, where Alex caught a big scaly mackerel and a Spaniard. I was watching the baits when a small black marlin came up and ate the scad on the left rigger, on a 6/0 Penn Senator reel and a bait rod. Alex fought the marlin standing up as the 150-pound fish jumped all over the place. It was stubborn and would not give up, plus it was on a short 2-foot leader intended for much smaller fish.

Bill and I were anxious to get some underwater footage of the fish with a PAT tag, so eventually we tagged it and let it swim back out. We jumped in and quickly swam down to the fish 50 feet below us in clear blue water. Laurie warned us as we went in, "Just be aware there is a reception committee down there waiting for you." Sure enough, it was as if the bottom came up to meet the marlin: brown shapes suddenly

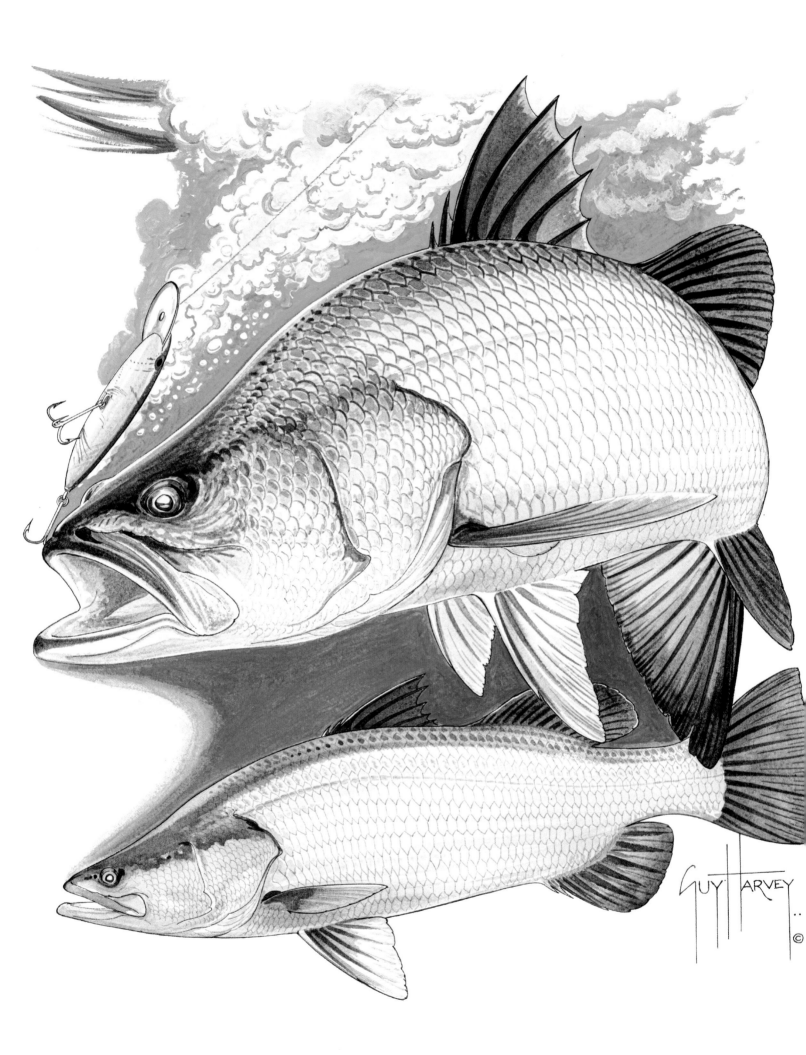

Guy Harvey

materialized all around the fish. Bill and I stayed 30 feet above as a dozen large bull sharks were tracking the marlin. I watched in amazement as a big bull shark put its face on the back of the marlin and took out a huge bite. As if a switch went on, the gang attacked—we could hear the crunch of teeth on bone as the marlin was engulfed in bodies. A big bull shark swam out of the red cloud with the marlin's entire head in its mouth, the bill sticking out. The sharks consumed the whole marlin in 20 seconds.

Bill and I were back at the surface by then and watched as the mob disbanded. On our October 1995 expedition here, we had a 1,000-pound marlin eaten by sharks not far from the boat. It was a sickening thing to happen, but in various places along the reef, the sharks have become conditioned to the sound of boat engines changing note—the vibrations of a thrashing fish are like the dinner bell ringing. A similar situation exists on the North Drop off St. Thomas in the US Virgin Islands, and at Cat Island in the Bahamas.

After spending the next day ashore taking in some of the many local attractions, we hooked up that evening with Graham Johnston, a legendary figure on the Cairns gamefishing scene, whose young son, also named Alex, was in the hunt for a junior angler world record black marlin. Alex Johnston had just caught a black of 864 pounds off Linden Bank, which was the pending record. At Graham's pub, the Cock and Bull, we were treated to some great Aussie hospitality involving lots of Victoria Bitter (aka "VB") beer. The next day we heading off to the bush to fish for barramundi for two days with none other than the legendary Dennis "Brazakka" Wallace.

Outside of the black marlin season, he had started a heli-fishing business, dropping in to remote spots to fish for barramundi with spinning gear or fly. Given the great distances and rugged terrain, this was the way to do it.

Naming the company Cape York Helicopters, Brazakka had turned this into a good business after retiring from 35 years fishing marlin on the reef. He had two yellow-and-black Robinson helicopters—he flew one, and his friend Paul was the other pilot.

Alex and I rode with Brazakka, while Rick and Bill went with Paul as we lifted off and headed north on a windy day. I am not a good flyer at the best of times, but after 10 minutes chatting with Brazakka, I soon left the fear of flying on the pad in Cairns. The banter was most amusing, with Brazakka flying the helicopter, his bare feet on the pedals, pointing out all the different landmarks and animals we flew past with his very colorful descriptions. We headed north following the coast over Port Douglas, took on fuel, and continued north. Brazakka flew low so we could clearly see dugongs, saltwater crocodiles, and different species of sharks, rays and turtles. After buzzing and therefore scaring off the sunbathing crocs, we dropped in on a nameless sandbar and began fishing.

We started out by catching a couple of juvenile giant trevally and mangrove jacks before we got a couple of the target species: barramundi. They are a beautiful fish, with a body like a snook and the scales of a tarpon. They are silvery with a dark green or brown back and a touch of copper on their flanks with subtle purple hues. The shallow water around us was full of life. We left after an hour and flew up past Cape Flattery to Queen Charlotte Bay. The trip was magical, flying 500 hundred miles up the Cape York Peninsula and surveying every conceivable river delta from the aerial perspective, not just for barramundi habitat, but more important, the presence of crocodiles that would eat more than a lure cast in their direction.

Our next stop was in the middle of nowhere. Really. Not even on the coast. We landed, and then I saw three 45-gallon drums out in the open near a rock with a hand pump. Brazakka

THEY ARE A BEAUTIFUL FISH...*silvery with a dark green or brown back and a touch of* COPPPER ON THEIR FLANKS *with subtle purple hues.*

LEFT

Mate Dave Cassar rigged this scaly mackerel so well, it's good enough to eat. Note the large circle hook, which helps ensure that the marlin is hooked in the corner of its jaw rather than deep in its throat.

FACING PAGE, TOP

All smiles: Bill Boyce, me, Dennis "Brazakka" Wallace and Rick Westphal celebrate the first of many barramundi of the trip. Heli-fishing is the ultimate way to explore these remote lands in search of great fishing action.

pumped fuel into both helicopters with a big smile and explained that this was the key part of the whole operation. The difficulty was in finding a truck driver to come this far out into the bush and drop off the drums of fuel. I could only imagine the logistics behind this operation.

In the late afternoon, we headed 25 miles due west inland toward Coen, a small cattle town. The journey over the mountains, covered in dense green rainforest, was memorable—it was like flying over the Darién Gap rainforest in Panama. We landed behind the small Exchange Hotel, operated by Brett and Ros Santowski, friends of Brazakka. The hotel had comfy rooms, a great bar and even better food in the little restaurant. The banter was loud as we shared fishing experiences. Brett showed us a large gold nugget he had found, impressive because of its size and that is was shaped just like the outline of the continent of Australia.

The next morning we had a quick walk around the small town, enjoyed a big breakfast cooked by Ros and Brett, and then said cheerio. It had been an interesting and educational experience staying in a small cattle town, meeting the local aboriginals, and sharing experiences. We lifted off and headed east back over the spectacular mountains and forest to the coast, dropping in at various rivermouths, some of which we had fished on the way up. We stopped in a couple more places to fish before landing at Walter Komsic's fishing camp, appropriately named Boomerang Sportfishing Holidays, located on a wide, brown river just in from Princess Charlotte Bay. The sign on his front door read in red and black letters: "This house guarded by shotgun three nights per week...you guess which three." In addition to fuel, we also picked up a cooler full of delicious mud crabs for lunch.

We continued south and stopped in a couple of new estuaries, catching some smaller barramundi and jacks. We still needed a big barra for the episode, and time was running out. We passed a sandbank in front of a rivermouth where a big croc was sunning. "Look at that big bastard, mate!" Brazakka said. "Want a closer look?" We wheeled around and went down 15 feet over the croc, where it reared up, mouth wide open, tail slashing from side to side, and ran into the river, leaving a wide

foamy wake. Waiting for the others to catch up, we landed and walked to edge of the water, keeping an eye on the small dragon that was in the shallows 50 yards to our left.

From the sandbar, Alex cast into the estuary. Immediately there was boil on his lure—Alex hooked up to a massive barramundi. It jumped like a tarpon, sending spray across the lagoon. I wound in my lure really fast so I could grab my Sony video camera from the helicopter while Alex was tight on this fish. *Kaboom*! Ten feet from the beach, my lure got inhaled by another big barra, and we were doubled up. My fish was jumping, going away into the deeper water, while Alex was working on his fish far out in the estuary. Eventually Brazakka waded out, grabbed the leader and slid my fish up the sandbank, holding the Sony video camera in his other hand. It was a beauty of 21 pounds. Alex worked his fish into the shallows; Brazakka handled this fish like it weighed 1,000 pounds and slid it up on the sand as well, a fine 25-pounder. We took photos and put both fish back in the water, where they quickly swam off. Double hookup converted. What a finish! It was truly the adventure of a lifetime, and it is a memory etched forever in my brain.

The 2006 expedition was planned to coincide with the 40th-anniversary celebrations of the first 1,000-pound black marlin landed off Cairns in 1966. There were several activities planned for the week, and we were offered the space to hold an art exhibition, where we set up along with several other artists, including Craig Smith and Bodo Muche. There was photographer David Granville and photojournalist John Mondora. The show went on all day, and that evening, there was the gala event at the convention center, where 800 people gathered to honor several key personalities in the Australian fishing community being inducted: IGFA trustee Jonno Johnston, Jack Erskine, Dennis "Brazakka" Wallace, Capt. George Bransford's daughter, Gale, who accepted the honor on her late father's behalf, and Richard Obach, the angler who caught that first black marlin over 1,000 pounds with Bransford off Cairns.

We had another shot at the exhibition the following day, then it was time to break down the show and meet the film

Brazakka lends a helping hand in the release of my first barramundi.

The Robinson helicopter takes off from a beach in Queen Charlotte Bay, Australia.

Alex's big barramundi, which he caught in the bottom of the ninth inning of this trip. This catch made it all worthwhile.

Alex hooked this big black marlin right at sunset, with the beautiful light serving as a backdrop for an incredible battle to follow.

Rendezvous on the Great Barrier Reef: Seven male black marlin jockey for position, spawning with a 1,000-pound female off Ribbon Reef No. 5. Acrylic on canvas.

crew; Rick Westphal and Dee Gele had arrived to shoot more for *Portraits from the Deep* and the billfish documentary *Nomads of the Ocean*. Bill, Dr. Michael Domeier and I were on the 47-foot O'Brien *Sir Reel*, captained by Laurie. The weather was typical—25 knots of wind as we fished Linden Bank. Michael brought a dozen satellite tags with him for black marlin. We did a wonderful drift dive on the incoming tide in the morning before breakfast, and then went bait-fishing for scad and scaly mackerel. We began marlin fishing at 11:30 a.m. and had a bite right away, where Bill caught an active 200-pound marlin, but it was foul-hooked and the hook pulled on the leader—not much luck so far with the tagging. We missed a window shopper, then I got a small one of 250 pounds, but again the hook pulled on the leader. Bill caught his third for the day, and we ended up 4-for-5 as we pulled in behind Ribbon Reef No. 5 for the night.

Our next day was good for bites but poor for conversions into catches. After a dive and catching bait, we were fishing by 11 a.m. We raised 12 marlin for the day, got bites from six and caught only one, a 200-pounder into which Michael finally got a tag. We spent the night behind Ribbon Reef No. 10, and the next morning we headed to one of my favorite dive sites, called Pixie Bommie. This massive tower of coral rises straight up to the surface from 80 feet down, festooned by living coral and smothered in fish of all shapes, sizes and colors. With less current here, we had a good dive, with Bill, Rick and Michael all filming away.

Fishing again, Bill caught a small marlin of 175 pounds, no tag. I caught the next fish, but we pulled the hook on the leader, so no tag. Then we dropped a shark bait and immediately hooked a massive bull shark about 400 to 500 pounds. With Dave wiring the big shark, Mike finally got a PAT tag in its thick skin. Mike caught the next marlin of about 250 pounds but pulled the hook again at the boat. No tag. We dropped the shark bait again, hooking a large silvertip, of which we got back only the head. Amazing. There were some big sharks around. We missed another small marlin later in the day and finished up 3-for-5.

We had a wonderful dive at Cod Hole the next morning. Cod is Australian for grouper, and the signature species here is the potato cod, named for its pale body and large dark chocolate spots on the body. They look cartoonish. They average 300 pounds and can be rather pushy. This is one of my favorite dive sites in the world.

We fished for a while that afternoon, where we jumped off another small marlin before switching to teasing in order to get some underwater footage of free-swimming black marlin. We sat on the covering boards for four hours in the hot sun pulling teasers with no hooks. Nothing. We switched back to hook baits later in the afternoon, raising two small marlin, and then we hooked up on something big. I was on the bridge with Laurie when a big dark shadow swam up and inhaled the scad. Michael fought the fish, but there were no jumps, and our initial excitement was quickly replaced by doubt. We had the big fish on the leader after 20 minutes, where it turned out to be a massive great hammerhead shark about 800 pounds. It broke the leader a minute later and kept swimming along at the surface behind the boat.

We did a drift dive before breakfast, followed by another dive at Pixie Bommie. These old reefs have amazing biodiversity compared with our Caribbean reefs. After loading up with fresh scad and a queenfish, we started by trolling no hooks and teasing again. At noon, a decent fish crashed the swimming queenfish, but it got spooked and started jumping right away before we even got in the water. It was a decent one of 600 pounds, and another lost opportunity. The next marlin also ate the queenfish; we all went in, but I lost my mask on the way, and Bill and Rick got only distant shots of the fish. This was not easy.

That evening I had the chance to talk with Julian about the new book he was writing called *Fishes of the Open Ocean*. I was being considered for the book's illustrations, and we reached an agreement there and then. In the coming months, I did 160 individual lateral fish portraits for the book. In addition, the publishers used several dozen existing pieces of art, many of them depictions of predator/prey interactions, to illustrate the text. This 266-page essential reference for divers, anglers, mariners and anyone with an interest in the ocean was published in 2010.

Black marlin are active predators of other medium oceanic species such as dolphins, tunas and jacks. Ink and watercolor.

Guy Harvey

California

THE SCIENCE OF SEABASS

THE WHITE SEABASS is one of the larger members of the croaker family of fishes, *Sciaenidae*, with the current world record at 93.12 pounds. The largest species in the family is the beleaguered totoava from the northern Sea of Cortez. They can attain 200 pounds. Seabass are located from Alaska to the southern tip of the Baja Peninsula, where they inhabit rocky bottoms and kelp beds in waters below 65 degrees. They are active inshore predators feeding on squid, small fishes and crustaceans.

One of the most interesting episodes we undertook during the early seasons of *Portraits from the Deep* was about the white seabass. This iconic West Coast species has been the basis of a commercial and recreational fishery for over a century. Commercial-overfishing activity, mostly using gill nets, was the main cause for the population collapse. For decades, inshore gill nets had been profoundly effective at catching white seabass, particularly when they gathered to spawn. By the early 1980s, the commercial catch was a mere 10 percent of historical levels.

Journalist Ron Ballanti explained in a *Sport Fishing* magazine article how the species was brought back from a near mythical status in the '70s and '80s to the robust recreational fishery it is today. "Several actions caused the transition, the most significant of which was California's passage of Proposition 132 in the early 1990s," Ballanti writes. "The regulations went into effect in 1994, banning commercial gill and trammel nets within 3 miles of the coast and 1 mile of the islands. Putting this issue on the ballot and pushing its passage became the driving force for the creation of the United Anglers of Southern California. Prop 132 remains one of the group's key achievements."

Nowadays, even with restrictions, white seabass commercial catches increased tenfold from 1996 to 2002. According to the California Department of Fish and Game's White Seabass Fishery Management Plan published in 2009, commercial landings reached nearly 300 metric tons from 2007 to 2008.

Like so many other species we've seen, the white seabass was close to extinction due to indiscriminate overfishing, but

The white seabass is an active predator in kelp beds and over rocky bottoms. Mixed media.

The white seabass is widely distributed along the coast of California and northern Mexico, but it is not easy to see a seabass in its natural surroundings underwater. And unless you are lucky enough to get close to one while diving, you will miss all the detail and variations in color and size. The next-best reference is to have a caught sample on hand to study. In the early and mid-1990s, when I was researching Pacific species for the West Coast market, the kelp bass (called the calico locally) was the primary species. People attending the Fred Hall Fishing Show in Long Beach would visit my booth and bring me fish to look at. I fired one up for T-shirts, then another. They both did well in the market. People started requesting other prominent species: California yellowtail, halibut, albacore tuna, mako shark, white shark, thresher, swordfish, striped marlin, salmon and white seabass. Living in the Caribbean, where was I going to get access to this species? In 2003, I went to the Hubbs-SeaWorld seabass hatchery in Carlsbad with Bill Shedd and Bill Boyce (as described in this chapter). Here, the adult brood stock in the hatchery could be viewed in their holding tanks through narrow ports in the tank walls. Good for a start. The best experience was had a couple of days later at the grow-out pen in Catalina, where there were more adults in holding pens. We could swim with them. The cold green water, the kelp, baitfish and squid all helped me create the authentic piece of art for which I was striving. We fed the seabass and they responded with rapid feeding strikes, fins up, bars showing up on their flanks, the sunlight catching their popped gills, eyes focused on the next morsel and the proximity of the competition. I added a calico in the background lurking in the barnacle-encrusted kelp.

This painting was used by the United Anglers of Southern California as limited-edition prints to raise funds for the white seabass hatchery program.

BELOW LEFT

Bill Shedd and Bill Boyce cast for seabass off Dreamer, *close to Catalina Island.*

BELOW RIGHT

The Tuna Club in Avalon, the birthplace of big-game sport fishing.

a fishery-management plan was developed in 1996. The goal was to reduce commercial fishing and activate an enhancement program focused on the culture and release of fish back into state waters. An additional part of the equation was meaningful size limits. There is a 28-inch minimum size limit and a three fish per angler per day limit for recreational anglers (and one fish per day during spawning season). A better limit would be to release all mature fish during spawning season between March 15 and June 15.

Bill Shedd, president and CEO of AFTCO, was at the forefront of the white seabass hatchery program based at the Hubbs-SeaWorld Research Institute in Carlsbad, California. Friend and photographer Bill Boyce and I visited Shedd at the hatchery on May 12, 2003. By then, the research and replenishment program was in full swing; this would be an integral part of our *PFTD* episode. The Hubbs-SeaWorld Research Institute works with the United Anglers of Southern California and hundreds of volunteers. Together they have raised over 2 million juvenile white seabass into state waters.

The facility contained a large adult brood stock in six different tanks with a climate-control system that managed water temperature and day length. As a result, egg production was year-round, not limited by seasonality.

At six months, the juveniles were transferred to outdoor grow-out pens located up and down the coast, managed by local angling and conservation clubs and members of the United Anglers of Southern California. The juveniles grow fast and are released at about 10 inches long. Each one carries a microscopic coded wire cheek tag. Recaptures of tagged fish have shown extensive coastal migrations as well as to banks 100 miles offshore of San Diego.

The film crew and I grabbed some dive gear and headed out to meet Capt. Alan Wilson and mate Cindy on *Dreamer* at the Pier Point Landing at Long Beach. On the way to Catalina, Alan secured plenty of bait—live squid—from a local purse seiner.

Alan showed me how to rig the live squid and use a light sinker to keep the bait close to the bottom and free of rocks and kelp. The cold, gray morning was unproductive, resulting in some bycatch—calico bass, guitarfish, triggerfish—so we moved south to a large kelp bed.

Here I caught my first seabass of about 20 pounds. Soon after, Alan hooked a keeper, and we had a mixed bag of

sheephead, calicos and a California halibut. Cindy caught an undersize seabass, and Bill Shedd checked for a PIT tag in the cheek. It in fact had a tag—a hatchery fish! A second juvenile was caught, also with a tag. This brought the story full-circle. The fish was quickly measured and put back into the water.

The next morning we moved to Two Harbours, where there is a seabass grow-out facility. We tied up *Dreamer* to the big floating pen with a boardwalk all the way around, moored off in deeper water. The facility was managed by Scott "Skooch" Aalbers, who greeted us by feeding a mackerel to a bald eagle that swooped in to pick it up right in front of us. An impressive move that made for great TV.

We put on dive gear to go into the pens, and enjoyed swimming with adult seabass and wild yellowtail. We fed the seabass. They sucked down the sardine right in front of the camera, which made for a great action shot in the clear, green water.

I absorbed their anatomy in detail, their metallic-silver

gill covers as they popped open to inhale the prey, jaws half open. Their faces also had a touch of pink and bronze, while their heads and backs were a dark green with a metallic-purple sheen.

The final act was to film the release of the juveniles. Skooch and volunteers untied an outer panel of the pen and lowered down the mesh. The fish milled around for quite a while until they began to swim for the exit. They poured out, venturing into the next stage of their lives to face all the challenges nature would throw at them. How many would grow to a reproductive age?

That's a wrap! Thrilled with the shoot, we headed to Avalon, the birthplace of saltwater big-game sport fishing.

We checked in at the Tuna Club. Having read all of Zane Grey's fishing books and met so many members of this legendary club, it was an honor to stay there. The walls were decorated with IGFA-record certificates, fishing tackle and black-and-white photos of the great catches from the dawn of the sport.

It is likely that the reduction of commercial-fishing pressure, combined with large-scale replenishment of the white seabass, will turn this species around.

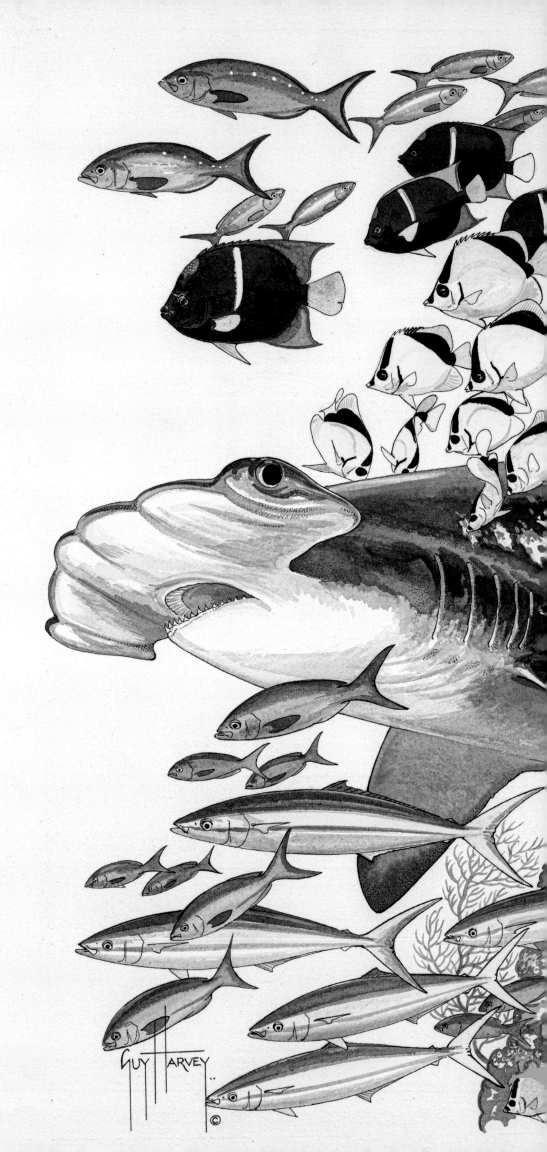

The signature species of Cocos Island is the scalloped hammerhead shark. When not gathering in large schools surrounding the seamount, these sharks swim in close to the rocks at various cleaning stations to be cleaned by king angelfish and barberfish. Watercolor.

Guy Harvey

BEYOND HALCYON

IT HAD BEEN A DECADE since we'd visited Cocos Island, so when my friends—brothers Jim and Steve Valletta—organized an expedition in 2012, we were eager to return. There had been stories about all the changes there, particularly following the arrival of tiger sharks to the area. When people ask me my favorite place to dive, I always answer: Cocos Island. The trip with the Valletta brothers would mark my seventh expedition.

Cocos is about 300 miles off the Pacific west coast of Costa Rica. The only residents are a number of rangers who try to protect the island and marine park from the constant barrage of illegal fishing vessels, mostly from Costa Rica. Currently the no-take zone extends 15 miles out from the island. The main billfish species are striped marlin, which average 200 pounds. There are also lots of blue marlin and sailfish, plus a few black marlin. Every day provides a shot at a grand slam.

Our previous dive expedition to Cocos was aboard the Aggressor Fleet's *Okeanos Aggressor* in 2002 with our friend and managing director of the fleet, Wayne Hasson, and my then-12-year-old daughter, Jessica. We had a great time, even catching a 250-pound blue marlin on the way home off the stern of *Okeanos*. Cocos is like a mini Galapagos: All the same species are present, except for sea lions and penguins.

For the 2012 expedition, Jim and Steve booked us on the Undersea Hunter flagship, *Argo,* a comfortable 130-foot vessel that also carried the *DeepSee* submarine, operated by Undersea Hunter. My daughter, Jessica, and son, Alex, were on board, along with Guy Harvey Ocean Foundation executive director Greg Jacoski and film producer George Schellenger. Jessica was going to host the TV production. For the first time in my 11 years shooting TV fishing shows and documentaries, I was passing the baton to my very capable daughter.

It took 30 hours to get from Puntarenas to Cocos Island. The beauty of the open ocean was on full display as turtles, dolphins and a pseudo orca passed by. Red-footed, brown and nasca boobies dived on the flying fish. Master divers Manuel

and Pius briefed their teams. We planned to do four dives per day on 32 percent nitrox. We were cautioned about currents, air consumption and diving responsibly.

We tied up on a mooring next to the islet of Manuelita in Chatham Bay. The first couple of days' diving were mediocre due to rough weather and low visibility. However, with the powerful Mangrove lights we were using, we could turn the place into daylight even on a rainy day down at 90 feet. I was still using the heavy Gates housing back then. It was quite a large piece of metal to push around in the current.

The major change from previous 10 years was that there were now tiger sharks. In all the hundreds of dives we'd done here in the '90s, no one ever saw a tiger shark. We'd never even met someone who'd seen a tiger shark. Now there were

ABOVE

A trio of scalloped hammer-heads. Stippled ink.

ABOVE RIGHT

The Undersea Hunter flagship, Argo, *at anchor in Chatham Bay, Isla del Coco.*

several that cruised the channel between Manuelita and the main island. I suspected they were hunting marbled rays and green turtles. There were still lots of marbled rays, but I saw only one turtle during this expedition. The tiger sharks had clearly taken their toll.

Back at *Argo*, we heard a story from one of our friends, Zander Villagomez, who had become separated from his group at 80 feet. He was taking photos of a 9-foot tiger shark when it suddenly turned on him. He defended himself, losing a fin and his camera in the process, by striking the shark with a diver's knife. His buddies came to the rescue, and they all ascended. Zander was back in the water for the next dive. Since then, there have been several unprovoked attacks on divers at Cocos Island, possibly by the same shark.

To capture footage, George had the brilliant idea to leave GoPro cameras on the bottom at various dive sites and recover them on the following dive. A couple of species, particularly big blacktip sharks and Galapagos sharks, showed up on the bottom soon after we surfaced. The GoPros got them all. The divemasters on *Argo* were bemused at this discovery. Thanks to George's initiative, we acquired some of our best shark footage.

At the iconic dive site Halcyon, a massive school of mullet snapper was hanging high in the water column above the seamount. We would conduct our safety stops among this school. The vast number of fish, the swirling motion—it was mesmerizing. There were often rainbow runners and bigeye jacks in the mix. On one dive, a humpback whale made a cameo appearance.

At Dirty Rock, there was a huge resident school of bigeye jacks

During one dive near Viking Rock, we saw a massive female marble ray that was clearly pregnant and close to term. In fact, Jessica was able to locate and catch this newborn ray a few minutes later. It was a perfect miniature of its parents, which she then released into the tumble of rocks nearby, where it disappeared, taking cover from potential predators between the boulders.

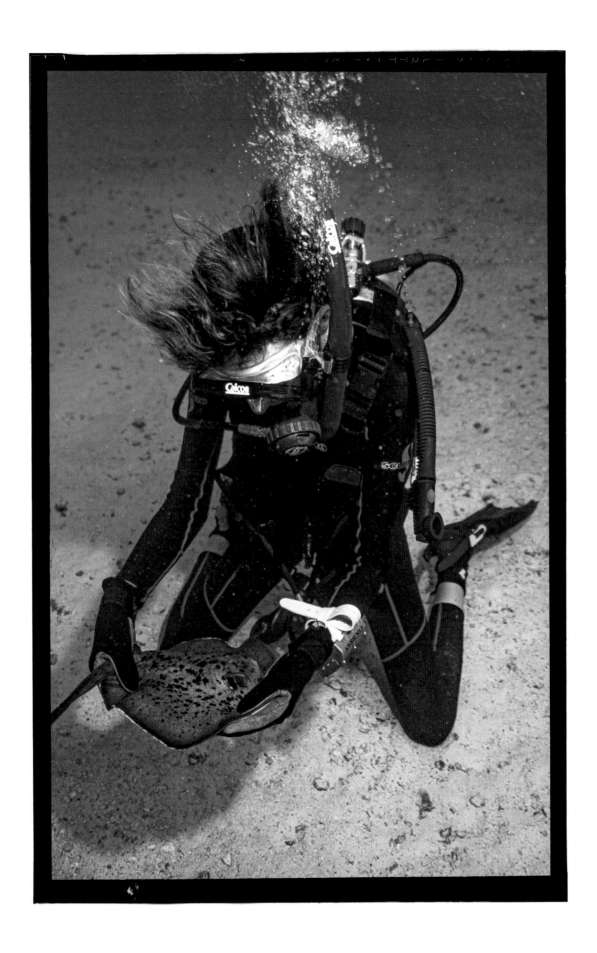

The magnificent silky shark is the most numerous pelagic shark around Cocos and often participates in baitballs with feeding yellowfin tuna and dolphins. Usually they are accompanied by schools of rainbow runners, which use the skin of the shark to rid themselves of ectoparasites. Acrylic on canvas.

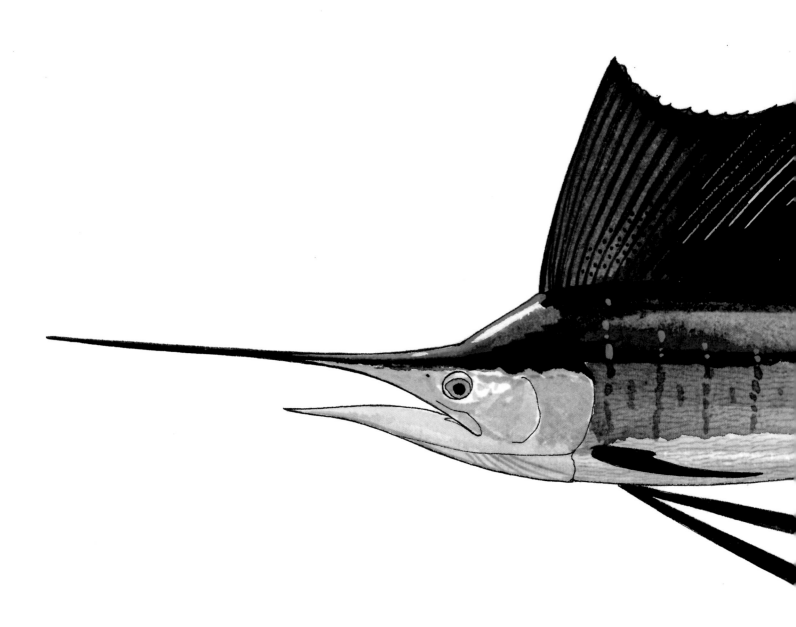

hovering above the deep reef, often near the surface. Another great way to spend a safety stop. The large blue jacks prowled the reef, occasionally taking a shot at the creolefish. A school of rare cottonmouth jacks also showed up. We saw big aggregations of scalloped hammerheads just on the edge of visibility.

Before diving on our third day, I spotted a young, 18-foot whale shark doing circles around *Argo*. We all snorkeled and dived with the beautiful shark before it headed back to the deep. Amazing!

Night dives in Chatham Bay were always exciting. Having the new Mangrove lights on my Gates housing was like having car headlights. They lit up the reef. The dozens of resident whitetip reef sharks were noticeably active, as usual. Manuel said the tiger sharks had been harassing the whitetips at night.

Another change from previous years was seeing large black jacks become such active predators during the night dive. One monster black jack followed us for the entire dive, feeding voraciously in our lights.

One of our best dives was on the northwest side of Punta Maria, where a cleaning station catered largely to Galapagos sharks—or so we thought. These were a larger version of the reef shark: bronze and gray, big dorsal fin and tail, a large animal capable of great speed. We also found a huge female marbled ray being escorted by several dozen ardent males, all atop of each other like a pile of spotted pancakes tossed from a basket. For this moment, the big dive lights were worth their weight in gold.

The highlight of the expedition for Jessica was diving in the

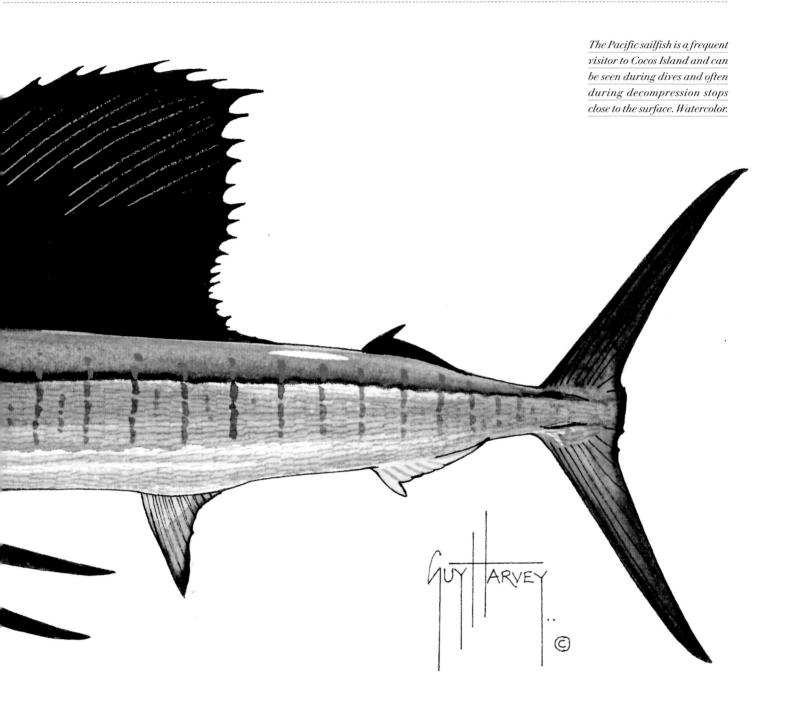

DeepSee submarine to 400 meters, a chance to see the geology and creatures of the deep ocean. The sub took several minutes to reach the target depth. On the way down, they saw mobula rays and deepwater sharks; at the bottom, grouper, spider crabs and scorpionfish. So much life, and so deep.

Nearing the end of the expedition, we encountered a humpback whale while diving at Halcyon. They are Southern Hemisphere whales that oscillate from Antarctica to have their calves in the warmth of Cocos Island's protection before continuing their migrations.

The reef life here is incredible. Most of the substrate at Cocos is volcanic rock covered in sharp barnacles. In certain places such as Chatham Bay, there was a fair amount of healthy coral. At Isla Pajara, just around the corner from Chatham, there was a large expanse on Montastrea-like coral holding schools of creolefish, yellow-tailed goatfish, blue-and-gold snapper, Moorish idols, cabrillas, soldierfish, Mexican hogfish, trumpetfish, wrasses, damselfish, parrotfish, guinea fowl puffers and boxfish. Frogfish were numerous. Several peacock flounders were courting females in amusing displays.

On our last day, the resident Costa Rican Coast Guard vessel finally stuck its nose outside and apprehended a Costa Rican commercial-fishing boat that was fishing inside the 15-mile no-take zone. We wondered what would become of the crew, vessel and fish they surely had on board.

The crossing back to Puntarenas was smooth. I made use of the time and calm conditions to complete an acrylic painting of a Galapagos shark at a cleaning station. We will return.

Costa Rica

BLUE MARLIN ON THE SEAMOUNTS

OUR EARLY VISITS TO COSTA RICA were in the late 1980s, fishing primarily for sailfish along the Pacific coast. Paul Hirschman had set up a charter operation in Flamingo Bay and invited us to fish on *Gamefisher II* with Capt. Richard Chellemi in July 1988. We went with John and Jenny Greaves from Jamaica, as well as my friend Capt. Bob Dehart, who has since passed away. We returned to Flamingo Bay several times over the next few years, catching sails on light tackle and fishing with such legends as Laurie Wright, Skip Smith, Jerry Dunaway and Raleigh Werking. The charter fleet grew steadily over the next decade, and the number of sailfish being caught was spectacular.

Things changed when fish aggregating devices, also known as FADs, were deployed on the offshore seamounts in the eastern Pacific, anywhere from 60 to 150 miles from the mainland. My first seamount trip was in 2016, several years after the FADs were first deployed. Jim and Connie Elek bought the chance to fish these waters at one of our Guy Harvey Ocean Foundation fundraisers, which was kindly donated by Will Cocke from Texas. We fished on Will's beautiful 61-foot Viking, *Suzy Q*, with Capt. Eric Carr. It rained a lot, but we went 5-for-6 on blue marlin the first day. The next day, Connie Elek caught a fine 350-pound fish at a FAD called Imperial. My appetite was whetted—this was pretty good fishing by Caribbean standards.

Near the end of June 2017, we went back to Costa Rica and stayed in Quepos at the beautiful Parador Hotel. Armed with six pop-up satellite tags, dive gear, cameras and tanks, we set off from Marina Pez Vela aboard the 48-foot G&S *The Hooker*, captained by Frank "Skip" Smith. Skip was the captain of Jerry Dunaway's *The Madam* and *The Hooker* operation for a decade, and later acquired *The Hooker* from John Richardson in May 2016, after which the boat underwent a complete overhaul.

On this expedition, we planned to fish for blue marlin and tag them with satellite tags, filming every release and diving to document the underwater life on the FADs. The expedition team consisted of my daughter, Jessica, and son, Alex, as well as Andi Marcher and George Schellenger. Once we started fishing, Jessica maintained a log of all the billfish we raised, hooked, caught and tagged. It was a good thing to do because there were a lot of bites every day. George and I were filming and taking photos, so the angling was done by Andi and the kids.

Our first tag went out on the fourth marlin of the trip, a 250-pounder that Alex caught. It goes to show that tagging billfish is not as easy as just catching and releasing them. Anything that can go wrong will go wrong, even with the finest crew in the world. There was a bit of a lull, followed by a doubleheader—Jessica on one and Alex on the other. I was really enjoying the action, and having both my kids fighting a doubleheader of blue marlin with Skip Smith at the helm was incredibly exciting. We got Alex's fish tagged first and then

Jessica's tagged, so a family caught, tagged and released the double. Not two minutes later we had a tripleheader on, shook off one, and the other two were caught by Andi and Alex, then we tagged both fish before it got dark. So we tagged four blues in 30 minutes, and were 8-for-9 with five PAT tags deployed on our first day.

We stayed out drifting in the calm weather attached to a sea anchor for the night. The big advantage about staying offshore is that we start fishing before the sun even comes up. The next day, we had bites in the gray of dawn: Alex broke one off on 30-pound-test tackle, and then Andi caught a good fish of 250 pounds, and we got the last tag deployed on this fish. The pressure was off. George had yet to catch his first marlin, so he caught the next two. In beautiful weather, we caught several

more with Andi, Alex and Jessica all adding to the score.

The FADs here were constructed of two 4-foot-diameter steel balls joined by a heavy stainless-steel swivel shackle. Below this was a long length of chain and some large tarpaulins that hung out like flags in the strong current. The visibility dropped at around 50 feet; the water was green and much colder, with more current than the top layer of blue water. Around the FAD, schools of juvenile yellowfin tuna and black skipjacks were swimming in and out of view. There were lots of rainbow runners, some rainbow chubs and juvenile mahi, along with triggerfish, green jacks, wahoo and many small silky sharks. On the depth finder, we had seen lots of larger marks down deep, probably more sharks.

Resuming fishing, we caught two more blue marlin late, the last one in almost pitch-darkness. We had enjoyed 13 hours of trolling and diving. By comparison, on most charters one has an average of eight hours of fishing. We raised eight and caught six blue marlin for the day before we quit fishing and chugged back to Quepos overnight.

We arranged to return in August of the following year, and were joined by Pete Foster-Smith. We departed Quepos on

The Hooker and started fishing the following morning, with the first bite coming at 6:32 a.m., then another at 6:39 a.m., but the first tag went out a few hours later on a 150-pound blue. Soon after, Pete caught a 300-pounder, but we pulled hook at the boat, so no tag.

After lunchtime, we had a double that Pete and Alex caught; Alex's fish was well over 300 pounds and one of the bigger ones we had seen. The average size of the fish we were seeing was 175 to 225 pounds. We were teaching Jessica to tag marlin with the PAT tags, about the mate getting the fish in the right position, with the tagger coming in behind the mate and putting the point of the tag stick against the skin before pressing it in rather than jabbing at the fish. At $4,500 per tag, it was vital that the tag go deep in the muscle, preferably between the pterygiophores—the bones that support the fish's dorsal fin—to provide a solid anchor. Unfortunately, far too many PATs come off prematurely, particularly from blue marlin. These fish live very exciting lives: They can make sudden turns and accelerate rapidly, putting a lot of drag on the tag anchor. Our results show more tag shedding from blue marlin that other billfish species, and it is frustrating when you hear of a tag coming unbuttoned from a marlin that was tagged in the perfect spot.

Our second day was very slow, going 2-for-3 out at the 150-mile seamount. The captains were all frantically texting each other on their satellite phones; apparently, there was an earthquake in Golfito that morning, which may have shut down the fishing. We still had several tags to deploy.

On our last day, the first marlin was at 5.35 a.m., a small 125-pounder that jumped like crazy. Pete was the angler and caught it quickly, but the hook pulled on the leader before we could tag it. A few minutes later, Jessica caught a 150-pounder on a lure, but the hook was lodged in the bony socket just above the eyeball, so I decided not to tag the fish. We finally got a tag in a marlin at 8:15 a.m.

As a large rain squall bore down on us, we hooked a big blue marlin, with Alex on the rod. Skip had *The Hooker* going full speed in reverse down-sea, and it could really move. Our deckhand, Cholo Chaves, had the marlin on the leader several times, jumping around the boat, and Jessica finally got the last tag in. We had a good day, going 7-for-12, with a total of

Skip had The Hooker *going* **FULL SPEED IN REVERSE DOWN-SEA,** *and it could really move.*

30 marlin raised in three days.

We booked Skip for a couple more days in September before he moved the boat south to Panama so we could spend more time diving on the seamounts. Pete returned, along with GHOF staffer Louisa Gibson (Sax), her first time in Costa Rica. We left Quepos on September 1 and traveled overnight to a seamount 80 miles offshore. We lost the first fish of the day, then Jessica caught the next marlin. Then we switched to hookless live baits so we could dive with the marlin. When a marlin appeared in the spread, the mates, brothers Cholo and Keller Chaves, had to be ready to yank the baits out of the water. The advantage was that there was no wake and no foam to interfere with the filming of the marlin. As soon as the marlin came into the spread, we would jump in.

At 7:30 a.m., a marlin crashed the right rigger bait. Cholo had it out of the water, shouting "Olé!" with the marlin wondering where it went. Three of us jumped in as the marlin raced right past us to eat the left rigger bait. The fish was completely black with a bright iridescent blue tail; its eye was bright blue against the dark face. It was about to eat the live bait when it too suddenly disappeared out of sight as Keller pulled it out of the water. Cholo dropped the right rigger bait back in, and the marlin came back through the spread, still black with a bright blue tail. This is their feeding color, which I had seen many times before in the Cape Verde islands, the Azores, Madeira, Venezuela, St. Thomas and elsewhere. When a marlin gets really close to you, in good light, you can see that its back is a dark green/blue and its flank is a dark bronze color. The combination seen from 10 feet away in ambient blue light is a velvety black. This 200-pound fish had its fins out for turning

ability, and its blue eye was looking, looking, looking—as soon as the bait hit the water, it turned within its own body length, and with a flick of the tail swooped in on the fish.

After a minute of frantic back and forth, it started to change color with more pastel hues. The fish's stripes appeared, and it went away 30 yards or so. The crew also had a strip bait rigged with a pink skirt on a spinning rod. This was our prime switch bait when we teased billfish while trolling. Skip cast this out far, and the action of the lure at the surface got the marlin moving in again, attacking the strip, which was easily pulled from the fish's mouth. Drop in a live bait and the action started again. This marlin seemed to lose interest and went out to the edge of our visibility, fins down, all pastel ocean colors now.

Skip put the boat in gear with two teasers out—something different for the marlin to look at—when it came racing in and crushed the big green and yellow softhead teaser. The boat stopped, out went the live baits, and once again the fish grabbed the bait. We were all enjoying this prolonged experience. By the time the marlin left, we had been filming it for nine minutes. Back in the boat, everyone was high fiving; this was the way to tease these fish.

The next fish was a big sailfish, which stayed for ages, all black, dorsal fin up and pelvic fins lowered as it repeatedly hit the live baits. The crew let the fish grab the bait several times and then pulled it out of the water. Then the sail had the leader wrapped around its bill; it felt tension and started to head-shake trying to free itself. The swimming bait was keeping the leader tight on the bill, but finally the leader slipped off and the sail went back chasing the bait, not spooked at all by the experience. Eventually it folded down its massive dorsal

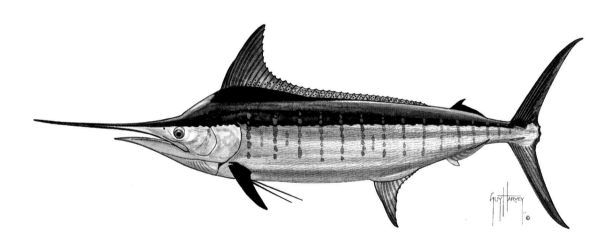

FACING PAGE

Blue marlin abstract: Capable of sizzling speed and jaw-dropping acrobatics, it's no wonder these are a favorite gamefish around the world. Acrylic on canvas.

ABOVE

Blue marlin portrait: the distinguished gentleman in the blue suit. Watercolor.

ABOVE

The Hooker *mates Cholo and Keller gaff a 180-pound yellow-fin tuna for Andi Marcher, caught on 30-pound-test line.*

FACING PAGE, TOP LEFT

There are many juvenile dorado (dolphinfish) around the FADs. We released them all. A fish this size is about three months old. They grow to 40 pounds in one year.

FACING PAGE, TOP RIGHT

Connie Elek fights a 350-pound blue marlin on Suzy Q. *She elected to use the fighting chair on this fish, although most of the smaller marlin we catch using a harness while standing up.*

fin, turned a beautiful pastel blue and silver, and decided to go elsewhere.

The color changes exhibited by the marlin and sailfish were amazing to behold. These are obvious to see in the footage we shot, but from an artistic perspective, do you paint the marlin completely black? Does a paint exist that is bright enough to show the florescent tail?

That afternoon, we went for a dive on the FAD. There were tons of bait everywhere. Mixed in was a good number of silky sharks. They were all juveniles, making one wonder where their parents were, the big 8-footers that used to be so common in the Eastern Tropical Pacific until the incessant commercial longlining for the shark-fin trade annihilated this species.

Back to teasing. Skip said he was missing out on the action, so he put a big live bonito on his left bridge teaser. Ten minutes later, a 300-pound blue marlin crashed it in a flurry of spray, and we all dived in. The marlin made two more passes, then left as quickly as it arrived.

We moved over to another FAD 2 miles away, and on the way found a school of bottlenose dolphins slowly moving along. We asked Skip to drop us in front of the oncoming school because the two girls wanted to swim with them; Pete went in with a tank as well. It was flat-calm and sunny. Skip then said to me, "Look at the depth sounder—we are marking a big group of something down at 200 feet." Pete was nowhere to be seen, not even his bubbles.

About fifty yards away, a pilot whale popped up, then another, then several whales—all were moving slowly toward us. I wondered when Jessica would see them. Sure enough, there was screech of excitement and much chattering in snorkels as the pilot whales swam into view and stayed lolling at the surface. Pete popped up in the middle of them, and they just remained in position, about two dozen whales in all. He was surrounded. I went in with a GoPro and got footage of Jessica filming them from below, with the big bull out front just hanging 20 feet down, barely moving. This was as good an encounter as I have ever had with this species. The bottlenose dolphins that started the interaction had already moved on.

After a gentle night's drift, we started fishing at 5:15 a.m. on a dark morning with heavy rain around us. Jessica caught the first marlin of the day, a 175-pounder, with lots of jumps. We switched to teasing with live bait at 9:45 and soon had an aggressive fish come in, but it did not stick around. One wonders what turned it off when there were three live baits there to be eaten? The next marlin was small but very persistent, and we got great action, with the mates working hard to keep this fish in the spread.

After diving on the FAD, we went back to teasing at 1 p.m., and soon after, a marlin came up to the right bait but did not stay long. Some are like that: just stopping by to check it out, not at all hungry. About an hour and a half later, another bigger marlin swooped in. I got some great overhead passes just feet above me as the fish ate the bait a couple of times, and the mates got it away from the marlin, blood clouding the water. What drama!

Ten minutes later, a 350-pound fish came in—jet-black—and

FACING PAGE

Bottlenose dolphins are sometimes seen far offshore, and often accompany vast schools of yellowfin tuna. Watercolor.

ABOVE

Blue marlin are the main predator of dorado (dolphinfish, or mahimahi) in the world's tropical oceans. Acrylic on canvas.

Diving with teased billfish is one of the greatest thrills one can have in the open ocean. When sailfish and blue marlin first appear in the spread swimming rapidly, they are completely black, with no counter-shading. As the encounter continues, they might slow down and change color, becoming more pastel and with stripes appearing on the blue marlin. Some encounters lasted up to 10 minutes.

crashed Skip's big bonito right behind the transom. We all went in, and the marlin had to swerve aside to pass us. The mates shouted "Olé!" each time the fish charged the live baits, according to Louisa, who was up top getting all the action. I put my head out of the water and told the mates let the fish eat one of the baits because it was getting frustrated. The fish went down 30 feet, then came up on the bait, crashing it from underneath. The marlin crushed the bait in a puff of blood and swallowed it in half a second, and feeling the tension, started jumping right above me; the light leader then broke, and the marlin departed. Incredible. Those last two days had been worth the price of admission—why buy the whole seat when you only need the edge?

Back in the boat, there was a buzz. Skip said the big marlin nearly tore the outrigger off the boat. He told me: "I have learned a new way to fish light tackle and tease in marlin using hookless live baits, then pitch a hooked bait to the fish. It is much more visual than trolling for them, and you can clearly see the size of the fish because there is no wake from the boat." The key is to have a good source of live bait.

In 2019, we did two back-to-back expeditions on *The Hooker* with Jessica, Alex, Andi and George to film marlin. We were going to push the underwater stuff at every opportunity. As we started fishing for bait, a marlin popped up and ate one off Alex's bait rod—the first marlin we had seen all day. Later, a striped marlin swam in and teased as well. Three divers went in and had a great time with this very interactive marlin. It was black with bright blue stripes, tail and pectoral fins, lit up like a Christmas tree, the most beautiful of all the billfish species. After 15 minutes of filming, Cholo threw out a small bonito and Alex hooked it, catching his first striped marlin.

We stayed in the area overnight, though it was more than lumpy. We began fishing at 5:15 a.m. and missed the first two bites. It was gloomy and choppy, and rain was all around us. When we switched to filming, a small blue marlin came in and stayed with the divers for 10 minutes—not really feeding, just checking everyone out.

The weather continued to deteriorate, so we went back to fishing with hooks at noon. Alex caught an active fish of 225 pounds, and right afterward, Andi hooked up a small blue of 125 pounds—Skip pushed *The Hooker* hard, backing down-sea at full speed. We got the leader for a quick release, turned around and hooked up again—the bite was on! Andi was up again and caught a 200-pound marlin. In 65 minutes we caught three blues. With such a good bite, we went back to teasing, raising one quickly, which stayed around for a couple of minutes, but it was now quite rough. We trolled down-sea for 20 miles to get around a massive squall and set up for a bumpy night on the sea anchor.

We started again early the next morning, happy to be moving forward again after a rough evening. A blue marlin crashed the right teaser—no one else was up yet, so I pitched it a bait and caught the small blue, the only one for me for the week. Later that morning, we moved to a different seamount that looked very fishy, but there were no marlin bites. We trolled to a no-name FAD just a few miles away and had another double on live bait, then a third as we were clearing the lines, losing one in the fight and releasing two. It was really happening now. On a choppy, gray afternoon, we raised 11 blue marlin, had some great bites, and caught four before starting the long chug home. It was a successful trip though, with 21 fish in the spread over three days in spite of the rough, rainy conditions.

Back in Quepos, Carl Treyz—one of our GHOF volunteers, freediver and ace photographer—joined us on August 9 as we were preparing to head back out. We started fishing at the drop-off in the late afternoon and were enjoying the magnificent sunset when the left long got a bite. Carl was up and fought his first marlin in the burning orange-and-crimson light. We released the 250-pound blue marlin and continued on, chugging offshore through the night.

Then the rain came, really hard, throughout the night and into the next morning. We were surrounded by lightning strikes. Using the radar, Skip went around the worst of the storm for a couple of hours, and we ended up near the 67 FAD once it cleared again. We caught three more marlin in the afternoon, one a good one of 250 pounds by Carl. He was having a blast; we raised seven blues, caught five and dived on one marlin in some serious conditions. We chugged over

FACING PAGE

A jumping Pacific sailfish. Ink.

Using hookless teasers is one of the most exciting ways to billfish: The marlin or sailfish is teased in by the crew and then is switched over to a hook bait right behind the boat. Mixed media.

Jessica caught **BACK-TO-BACK BLUE MARLIN** *of 150 and 175 pounds, the second one just as the sun came out and there was* **A BEAUTIFUL RAINBOW BEHIND HER.**

toward a different FAD (Cholo's FAD) and then drifted on the sea anchor for the night.

The next morning, in preparing to swim with marlin, I asked Keller to rig up a dead *oioi*—a frigate mackerel—and have it flopping far back on the center rigger, out of sight really, but as a backup for any fish we missed up close. Carl was rigging a trolled camera off the transom to cover the short baits; I was ready to swim with him, and Jessica and Andi would be in the cockpit. Then there was an explosion on the right teaser just behind the boat. I did not see a fin or a fish—what was that? No one saw anything, just a huge boil. Just then, the stinger line went off, and Andi was tight on a fish. Nothing happened for a while—the line just kept going steadily off the reel and down. We all said this is not a billfish, a shark perhaps, or maybe a big tuna. Andi fought the fish expertly for an hour on 30-pound-test. The spirals began as Andi put the heat on the fish. Soon we saw it was a giant yellowfin tuna. Keller and Cholo were able to get the gaffs in and swing it over the covering board, a beautiful fish of 180 pounds. Wow!

After photos with Andi and his fish, we cleaned it and found

eight fresh oioi in its stomach. It was jammed full. The ninth was just one too many. With all those juvenile yellowfin tuna and bonito mixed in around the FAD, the tuna was obviously cherry-picking the oioi. Were they slower, tastier or just a little dumber?

We teased five blue marlin between 11:50 a.m. and 1:45 p.m. Carl was really enjoying the interactions and color changes in spite of the poor light. Jessica was in her element, showing everyone the great footage she was getting. We teased in two more marlin that afternoon, then switched back to fishing with hooks in the water. Jessica caught back-to-back marlin of 150 and 175 pounds, the second one just as the sun came out and there was a beautiful rainbow behind her. It was a good day at the Cholo FAD: We raised 13 blues and one striped marlin, caught four and swam with seven, as well as catching that beautiful 180-pound yellowfin tuna.

That night on the sea anchor was no joke, and it was good to be moving forward again at 5 a.m. We missed an early bite, then went to fishing live baits, with rain all around. A sailfish came up and ate the right rigger bait, which Andi caught. We

raised a bigger marlin that sat in the spread for a while and faded. Soon after, although we were teasing, a blue marlin ate the stinger bait (a dead oioi again), and Carl was on a much bigger fish. Skip powered down-sea, and we were able to release the largest blue marlin for the week at 375 pounds. Skip said that was probably the fish we raised earlier that did not bite. We raised nine blue marlin, one striped marlin and one sailfish for the day, and not one came up on a teaser or close bait. What was causing the change in behavior?

We did one more dive on the FAD, then headed toward Quepos. We enjoyed the down-sea course toward home and had fresh tuna steaks on the grill. For the six days of fishing, we raised 55 blue marlin, swam with 17, caught 21 blue marlin, one sailfish and a striped marlin, plus a bonus yellowfin tuna. We also caught and tagged 30 silky sharks. Happy with all the footage we had accumulated, it had been a great expedition.

Back in to Marina Pez Vela, we saved some bait to feed Pancho, the massive roosterfish that frequents the docks. Indeed he was fully grown, aggressively beating out the snapper and jack crevalle to the food, with its comb raised. It ate Jessica's GoPro twice.

A review of the tracks we developed from the blue marlin we tagged in 2017 and 2018 showed there was no conclusive evidence to suggest that blue marlin stayed in the general area of the FADs for protracted periods. Migrations were haphazard, as they are at the best of times with this species. But there is a difference in the average size of the marlin in Costa Rica. Apart from a few 300-pounders, most of the FAD blue marlin were in the 150- to 225-pound range. In Panama, just 400 miles to the southeast, the blue marlin are generally bigger, averaging 275 to 400 pounds. With more PAT tags being deployed in Panama, we will know more in the next couple of years. What is apparent is the lack of a cyclical pattern in blue marlin movements compared with the tracks seen in our research projects made by tiger sharks, mako sharks, whale sharks and oceanic whitetip sharks in the northwestern Atlantic.

An interesting comparison will be to compare habitat use and depth profiles in the ETP, which is affected by low oxygen content below 150 feet, with blue marlin tagged in the Cayman Islands, where oxygen levels are much higher at those depths.

The striped marlin is the most abundant marlin species in the Eastern Tropical Pacific. They usually hunt in small packs, often working with marine mammals such as sea lions and dolphins in their search for prey. Acrylic on canvas.

Galapagos Islands

LAND OF THE STRIPED MARLIN

AS PART OF MY DEDICATED series on billfish for *Portraits from the Deep,* our intrepid team of producer Ken Kavanaugh and two amazing cameramen, Rick Westphal and Dee Gele, flew to Guayaquil, Equador, on January 30, 2006, and stayed the night before, getting a flight out to the Galapagos Islands the next morning. The word about striped marlin in the Galapagos was that they were numerous and all big fish. We flew out to San Cristobal to spend a few days fishing with Tim Choate, who was trying to set up a charter-fishing operation. Not as easy as it sounds, but Tim had successfully pioneered offshore fishing in Mexico, Brazil, Costa Rica and then Guatemala. Now he turned his attention to the Galapagos.

Kathy Espinel, owner of the Miconia Hotel, met us at the airport. San Cristobal was a small, quaint town, with an inviting waterfront and sea lions lounging all over the place. We wandered around the municipal dock and watched as the crew of a local snapper fishing boat unloaded a catch of Pacific cubera snapper and smaller yellow snapper. Hundreds of them. I wondered where these fish were heading—probably back to the mainland.

EVERY FIVE MINUTES, *we had a school of striped marlin in the baits, and caught* **DOUBLES AND TRIPLES ALL DAY.**

After a wonderful lunch, we all went up the volcanic slopes to see a local attraction: a massive kapok tree with a trunk about 30 feet wide. A third of the way up was a treehouse with a great view down the forested slopes of the volcano. Soon we reached the crater lake at the top of the volcano at 2,000 feet of elevation. We took up positions and watched as frigate birds came in from the ocean far below and did an amazing thing: They got down on the water and bathed, holding themselves aloft with their wings as they dunked their heads and bodies in the fresh water. Frigate birds do not dive like boobies and terns, so this is how they bathed.

Back at the hotel, Tim had just come in from fishing. His infectious smile said they had a good day and recounted the action, going 7-for-20 on striped marlin for the day. Tim explained that the harbormaster had asked us to leave and return in the dark because our permits for sport fishing were still pending. No problem. Tim, the film team and I were on the 40-foot *Intensity*; our friends Jim and Steve Valletta, Roger Manes and Bill Watts were fishing on *Millennium*, a 35-foot Bertram also owned by Tim. We all got going at 4 a.m. and loaded our fishing and dive gear aboard *Intensity*. Both boats cruised for two hours out to Banco Rosa, 40 miles southeast of San Cristobal. It was worth the long run.

We arrived at the western end of the 10-mile-long bank and put out the spread of two bridge teasers and two lures with hooks on the riggers. A minute later, a group of striped marlin attacked our spread—there were marlin dorsal fins everywhere! I wanted to take photos of jumping striped marlin, so we handed off the rods to the crew. One marlin came off, and we ended up tagging two striped marlin. I took fin clips from these fish because Dr. John Graves of Virginia Institute for Marine Science was conducting a genetic study on striped marlin from the eastern Pacific. Rick, of course, was filming everything, and we dived on every marlin as we released them.

The sky and water were alive with bait and birds— blue-footed boobies and brown boobies, as well as frigate birds. There were bottlenose dolphins and sea lions mixed in with the marlin. It was unbelievable. Every five minutes, we had a school of striped marlin in the baits, and caught doubles and triples all day. After we had caught 10 marlin, we switched to pulling teasers only so Rick and I could jump in and get action shots of striped marlin, all lit up. Where we raised two or three in the spread, there were eight or 10 below in the clear water; the visibility was maybe 60 feet.

We finished up at 5 p.m. What an amazing day. We were 14-for-35, easily raising 80 marlin for the day. *Millennium*'s numbers were 10-for-29, and they estimated they raised 55. As we had dived on many groups, we knew there were more fish under those that could be seen at the surface. We ran back in for nearly two hours before *Millennium* ran out of fuel, so we towed them the last few miles, finally getting in around 7:30 p.m. Nothing was easy.

The presence of many booby birds as well as frigates shows the way to the action. Pacific sardines are corralled together by predators below and hemmed in at the surface, making the prey available to diving birds. Dorsal fins of attacking marlin cut the surface. Watercolor.

We retreated to the bar, where Tim explained that the crews had to refuel the boats off the dock by purchasing diesel fuel 5 gallons at a time from the gas station up the road and taking it by car to the game boats. So that is why the other boat ran out of fuel—it needed just 5 more gallons.

We got going very early and left in the dark again, and now knowing what to expect, we were ready when we arrived at Banco Rosa by 7:30 a.m. Each time we found the packs of marlin, everything in the spread had a marlin on it. The mates had snagged a few fresh local ballyhoo for pitch baits, which worked like a charm, until we ran out and went back to pitching with small lures. The teaser bites were just amazing, sometimes two or three marlin after the same bait: dorsal fins up, bright blue pectoral fins lit up, stripes on their bodies clearly visible— they are the most beautiful of all marlin when feeding.

We decided to head in because the bite had slowed down, and got back to the harbor just after dark and without running out of fuel this time. The other group was leaving the next day, so we would be on *Millennium* for two days; there was another charter coming in for *Intensity*.

The following day, we arrived at Banco Rosa at 7:30 a.m. on a much calmer morning. Dolphins, sea lions and birds were everywhere, and it took all of 30 seconds to get a bite. The big striped marlin were like blue marlin—very aggressive and responding well to lures. Tim caught a striped marlin whose bill was angled up sharply. I had seen fish like this at Cocos Island—maybe half of the striped marlin there had this shaped bill—and I wondered if this was a subspecies of striped marlin.

We switched over to all teasers; Rick and I went into the water on several groups of marlin. The water was green compared with the previous day, but the marlin were just as accommodating. After a bit we went back to fishing, and soon after jumped off a blue marlin about 300 pounds, the first one we had raised. Tim said blue marlin and black marlin were more common in the northern part of the archipelago around

TOP LEFT

With the Three Amigos, Bill Watts, Steve and Jimmy Valetta, and the late Roger Manes, at the Miconia hotel.

Wolf and Darwin islands, where we had dived many times. When we finished, our numbers were better: 16 striped marlin released from 35 bites and over 50 raised, not including all the marlin we dived on, perhaps another 30 or 40. They were long, action-filled exciting days.

For our last day, we were out on *Millennium.* Sometimes we saw one or two marlin, and then on the next circle there were three or five more in the spread coming past us. A big 250-pound striped marlin grabbed a teaser right in front of me in an explosion of foam and bubbles, all lit up, pectoral fins so bright, their stripes glaring blue against the dark bodies and dark water, and bright blue eyes all-seeing, fins erect, turning in their own body length at speed.

Happy with all the footage, we went back to fishing and released some more striped marlin, all over 200 pounds. The bite shut off at 3:30, and according to Tim's unwritten rule, if you don't get a bite in the next half-hour after the last bite, then it is time for the run home. Our numbers were 10-for-25 marlin bites, and we had raised another 20 or 30 while teasing. The only comparable location to see this many striped marlin is Magdalena Bay, Mexico, in October and November.

In the 1940s and 1950s, pioneering US anglers such as Michael Lerner, Kip Farrington, Alfred Glassell and others were catching striped marlin that averaged 300 pounds off Ecuador, Peru and Chile. Many of the world-record fish they caught were in the 400- to 450-pound range. Striped marlin that size can be found consistently only around New Zealand nowadays.

Today, in 2020, the marlin fishing around the Galapagos continues to be spectacular, with several sport-fishing operations doing good charter business out of San Cristobal. The conservation of the resource is of paramount importance, and artisanal exploitation of billfish and sharks has to be better regulated to ensure sustainable use. The passing of the Billfish Conservation Act in 2018 in the United States now prevents the importation of billfish into the US, effectively closing a legal loophole through which much of the striped marlin from the Galapagos and mainland Ecuador, as well as sailfish from Costa Rica, were reaching American markets.

The message to the fishery managers and politicians in Ecuador is still the same: The billfish catch-and-release sport fishery is worth 100 times more to the Galapagos economy than killing the fish and selling them. Federal and local governments should support sport-fishing efforts, and training programs need to be organized to facilitate the change from commercial operations to catch-and-release fishing.

FACING PAGE, TOP RIGHT

Intensity *trolling, with divers ready on the covering board to jump in.*

FACING PAGE, BOTTOM LEFT

Many bottlenose dolphins live on Banco Rosa, which is south-east of San Cristobal.

FACING PAGE, BOTTOM RIGHT

On board Intensity *with owner Tim Choate and our film crew, cameraman Dee Gele, Ken Kavanaugh (producer in white visor), and underwater cameraman Rick Westphal.*

ABOVE

The striped marlin is the most beautiful of all billfish, with fluorescent fins and stripes.

Galapagos Islands

A DEEP DIVE INTO A REMOTE PARADISE

IN THE PAST 18 YEARS, we have been on six different liveaboard expeditions to the Galapagos archipelago, which is located in the Pacific off the coast of Ecuador. You cannot be in a rush to get there because all of these remote locations are, well, remote. We have also seen the number of visitors there increase significantly, resulting in adjustments to the accessibility of the wildlife so as to not to overexpose various species and their habitats to people. What was so attractive about the Galapagos expeditions was the opportunity to dive three or four times per day and do a land tour daily on different islands—there was no scientific-research component here, just seeking inspiration for new art and seeing some new species.

Each expedition has been aboard *Galapagos Aggressor I*, a two-vessel franchise owned by Herbert Frei, an entrepreneur from Guayaquil, Ecuador, and a good friend of Wayne Hasson, managing director of the Aggressor Dive Fleet. Wayne kindly invited my daughter, Jessica, and me on a familiarization trip in July 2002. Making our way from the Cayman Islands to Guayaquil, then on to Baltra, we were met by divemaster

BELOW, LEFT

The team heading north to explore the waters around Darwin Island aboard Galapagos Aggressor II.

BELOW, RIGHT

A common sight throughout these islands, a big land iguana poses for a photo on North Seymour.

FACING PAGE

Shimmering in silver: This massive school of black striped salemas provides a unique backdrop on one of our many Galapagos dives.

Chris Merz and ferried to *Galapagos Aggressor I*, which was at anchor in the harbor.

Because some of the clients had not yet arrived, we waited in port for another day, although we did get our briefings from Chris and then had a checkout dive nearby. Safety is a top priority in the Galapagos because of the strong currents; each diver was equipped with a collapsible flag, loud whistle and a personal locator device. At 12, Jessica had not dived in cooler water before and was getting used to wearing a thicker wetsuit.

The following day, we went diving not far away at North Seymour, on a steep rocky ledge with great visibility and the current pushing north at a good 1.5 knots. The view was filled with creolefish, as is every dive in the eastern tropical Pacific. Along the barnacle-covered rock walls were blue chin parrotfish, a school of bumphead parrotfish, hogfish, bacalao, cabrillas and bigeye jacks in large numbers, while yellowtail surgeonfish pecked at the rocks looking for algae. Sea lions whipped in and out of view. Where the rocks met the sand, yellowtail goatfish patrolled the edges. It was an incredible profusion of life.

Then we came to a large cave beneath a basalt cliff, and could see the white-tipped tails of several sharks sticking out of the entrance. There were 15 or 20 whitetip reef sharks piled atop each other like freshly fallen logs, completely undisturbed by our noisy presence. We took in the view for several minutes before the tugging current hurried us farther along the wall. In the middle distance, a hammerhead went by, then another.

We returned to same spot after a short surface interval and spent more time with the big marbled rays and the whitetips in the caves and pockets, one of which was filled with colorful sponges. Big schools of shiny Peruvian grunts kept close to the wall, opening up suddenly to allow a sea lion through

without incident. That afternoon, we did a land tour on North Seymour, where we encountered lots of sea lions warming in the sun, then blue-footed boobies with nests on the ground, plus frigate birds in nests at eye level, and noddy terns, gulls and delicate longtailed tropic birds. We departed later that evening with the additional divers and made the crossing to Wolf Island in 16 hours.

Wolf and Darwin islands are farther north of the main group of islands and are in warmer blue water for the most part. In the early morning, we were joined by a school of dolphins and lots of red-footed booby birds; frigates could be seen working the surface waters. *There must be lots of yellowfin tuna here too,* I thought.

The prevailing current this time of year moves to the north. It hits the south side of Wolf and Darwin, splitting and going around the sides of each island. Where the current actually hits the island, there is a calm area. Our first dive was at the Point, where the current becomes a factor, and we had to get down the wall quickly to find a place to hang out among the steep boulder field—not so easy when you have a camera in hand. We sat there and watched the world go by, smothered in the usual plethora of plankton-eating creolefish that filled the water column. A big Galapagos shark, then a second, followed by a group of massive spotted eagle rays, then nothing for a while.

In the early morning, we were joined by **A SCHOOL OF DOLPHIN** *and lots of red-footed booby birds; frigates could be seen working the surface waters.* **THERE MUST BE LOTS OF YELLOWFIN TUNA HERE TOO,** *I thought.*

There are more green turtles in the Galapagos islands than in any other destination we have visited. Acrylic on canvas.

We scooted into the calm waters of the bay during our mandatory surface interval and went snorkeling with a group of inquisitive fur seals. Jessica loved their antics. Back into the bay for lunch, a large school of bottlenose dolphins were there and not moving much, so Jessica and I went for a quick snorkel. Swimming toward the group and looking down in the blue water, a school of big yellowfin tuna swept by not 10 feet below us, long yellow fins streaming out behind, wide, large eyes and spread pectoral fins. Each of these fish was over 200 pounds—wow!

In the afternoon, we went back to a site called Landslide, appropriately named for the tumbling slope of rocks sprawling from the surface to 100 feet down. We went with the current until we found the school of jacks; Jessica quickly got lost within the large mass of quicksilver, around which a loose group of Galapagos sharks persisted. Spectacular. We stayed there for the remainder of the dive and then blew around the corner, whisking past hammerheads and silky sharks during the three-minute safety stop. It had been a fabulous day. Lots to see, and Jessica had done well.

The next morning, we arrived at the unique arch at Darwin Island. The image of the isolated, jutting rock arch whose base is constantly pounded by the Pacific surge is as iconic as any famous lighthouse. It is a waypoint for the nomads of the ocean. In my mind, it conjured up images of schools of hammerheads, silky sharks, dolphin, sailfish, marlin, wahoo and tuna marching past the steep walls seeking their prey during their timeless migrations. Above us, there were thousands of seabirds that nest on the island. They depend on these predators to drive food to the surface where they can reach it. The level of anticipation was electric.

Our first dive was at the arch, and it was quite a moment to be rolling into the water in the shallows at its base. It was flat-calm with good visibility. We went to the wall at 60 feet and hung out on the wide ledge that faced the current. There was a large school of barberfish, bright yellow with a black line through their eyes, standing by to clean sharks. Creolefish filled the blue. Black jacks and blue jacks patrolled the steep walls, and a few green turtles swam higher up the wall. Our patience paid off as a 40-foot whale shark swam silently overhead, going to the right with the current. We all abandoned our positions and went up to get a closer look. With pectoral fins spread like wings, it looked like a jet airplane sweeping past, as big as a bus. The current carried the shark out of range very quickly, so we returned to the rock wall.

Back on board for a surface interval, we decided to check out

BELOW

A small school of rare Risso's dolphins swam around our mothership. Below them were lots of big yellowfin tuna. Watercolor.

a school of Risso's dolphins near the mothership. I had never seen this species before: These were pale gray all over, with lots of scratch marks on their heads and bodies. Yellowfin tuna could be seen deeper below the dolphin as well.

The late dive of the day was a ripper. Sitting and waiting on the 60-foot ledge, we saw bigeye jacks, barberfish and a large bacalao before half the team quickly swam off to the right and down. In the distance, I saw the receding spots of a whale shark. Dammit! Nearby, our divemaster, Richard, was shaking his rattle hard and pointing up. A bigger whale shark was just 20 feet above us, but I had missed it completely. How is that possible? It was huge! We swam up and went with it in the current. This was another large shark, clearly 40 feet or longer. It was barely swimming, but we could not keep up,

finally heading back in to the wall, exhilarated. Everyone on the boat had seen whale sharks this day.

We spent the night at Darwin and got an early start the next day. The weather was good, visibility was awesome, and as we went in at the arch, there was drama: A big Galapagos shark was chasing a fur seal close to the rocks. They both moved with great agility, the shark not far behind the seal, before they both went up into the breakers and out of sight. So the Galapagos shark is the white shark of the tropics.

We stopped at Wolf Island on our way back south. We did a dive at Landslide again, and the current was ripping. Not to worry because we had plenty of sharks. A group of bottlenose dolphins went by before we surfaced. Then we were on our way south to Cousin's Island. Here the small island sticks up

BELOW LEFT

A juvenile whale shark spent several dives with us at Darwin's Arch.

BELOW RIGHT

Herbert Frei, the owner of the Galapagos Aggressor fleet, is a keen diver and conservationist.

BOTTOM LEFT

A wonderful view of the iconic Pinnacle Rock, one of the many scenic landmarks in the Galapagos.

BOTTOM RIGHT

These Sally Lightfoot crabs add a bright pop of color to the black volcanic shorelines.

out of the sea. The layers of rock continue underwater and are covered in bushy antipatharian corals. A sea lion swam rapidly through the green gloom. Green turtles were resting here and there on ledges. A hammerhead passed close by. We swam to the point where great clumps of corals hang over the rocks in which thousands of copper sweepers, creole-fish, sergeant majors, wrasses, cardinalfish and other small brightly colored fish were feeding. The wall began again, with lots of king angelfish, sea lions zinging by, yellow striped snapper, Peruvian grunts with their serious look, and a couple of eagle rays passing by on undulating spotted wings. At the end of the dive, a couple of sea lion pups caught Jessica's attention, splashing in and out of a rock pool. It was a magical spot, with so much life and a great variety of species.

That afternoon we went to Bartolome Island, famous for the iconic Pinnacle Rock. After a briefing from Chris, we went ashore, dodging Sally Lightfoot crabs, and hiked up 500 feet to the lookout post. It was windy and cool, but we could see over to Santa Cruz and Bartolome Island. Grabbing a wetsuit each, we went in search of the Galapagos penguins near Pinnacle Rock. We found a group of four penguins busy chasing a school of small fish—they had created a baitball and were too busy catching fish to worry about Jessica in among them.

The last day was reserved for a land tour at Santa Cruz. After another briefing from Chris, we went ashore. Sea lion pups were all around, some lying on the shore, disinterested parents sleeping nearby. We walked farther along the marked pathway and found land iguanas and marine iguanas in the

The weather was good, the visibility was awesome and as we went in at the arch, there was drama: A big Galapagos shark was chasing a fur seal close to the rocks. They both moved with great agility, the shark not far behind the seal, before they both went up into the breakers and out of sight. So the Galapagos shark is the white shark of the tropics.

same place. Along a cliff edge there were swallowtail gulls nesting, plus warblers and Galapagos finches working among the weathered branches of windblown trees. In the middle distance, a big school of bonito was foaming up the surface of the ocean, chasing bait.

Our last dive was at Gordon's Crater. It is a collapsed parasitic volcano crater with four bits of rock sticking out above the surface, with the crater in the center. The crater walls were steep, dropping straight down to 100 feet. At the surface, we were surrounded by steel pompano. At 50 feet we found several turtles, and swimming was easy, with little current. We could see hammerheads below and far away over the sand. We hit the sand, where the Galapagos garden eels were plentiful. Over in a rock pile there were big cubera snapper lurking and marble rays resting. This really was a cool spot with lots going on, and in the good conditions we could see both sides of the crater. Groups of shy hammerheads passed by. On the outside of the crater, the walls fell steeply; there were many more hammerheads deeper down.

After lunch, we went into Puerto Ayaro and anchored up. Chris and Herbert gave us a tour of the tortoise national reserve at the Charles Darwin Research Station, which was fascinating. The replenishment program for the giant land tortoises was working well. There were hundreds of juvenile tortoises in pens with numbers painted on their shells, which are released back onto their respective islands.

We spent the rest of the afternoon walking around the quaint capital of these islands. There were some good little restaurants and shops with beautiful local arts and crafts in curbside kiosks, but I was more fascinated by the public fish market. Here a fisherman was cleaning some wahoo and yellowfin tuna on a concrete workbench. On one side, there was a small line of people waiting to buy fresh fish; on the other was a sea lion escorted by four brown pelicans, waiting patiently for scraps.

We returned for another expedition to the Galapagos in 2005, which was memorable. A group of friends chartered *Galapagos Aggressor I* and headed out to San Cristobal on July 7. My wife, Gillian, and our children, Jessica and Alex, were on board, along with family friends from England: Vince and Jan Snell, with their two daughters, Georgie and Katie. The professional divers were Steve Valletta, his brother Jimmy Valletta, Bill and Beverly Watts, and cameraman Rick Westphal—the A team for sure.

In San Cristobal we were again met by Chris and his fellow divemaster Walter Torres. The boat moved around to the north side of the island to Stephen's Bay, where Alex and I buddied up for the checkout dive. The water was a cool

Spotted eagle rays are large and plentiful in the Galapagos. The great hammerhead shark keeps the eagle ray population under control. Acrylic on canvas.

BELOW

A dainty Galapagos penguin warms up in the sun.

FACING PAGE, TOP

Jessica relaxes in the dive boat after a dive below the Darwin Arch.

FACING PAGE

Wayne Hasson introduced Jessica and me to the Galapagos islands and its inhabitants.

FACING PAGE

Our home away from home for the expedition, Galapagos Aggressor I, *off Wolf Island.*

72 degrees and clear, with lots of creolefish and a few bonito zipping in and out of the massive schools of fish. There were a lot of sea lions, making it an exciting checkout dive for everyone. We did a land tour and then departed later that evening for North Seymour Island, north of Baltra.

Friday, July 8, was Jessica's 15th birthday. The two morning dives were as good as always, going with the current through clouds of Peruvian grunts, snapper, surgeonfish and creolefish, as well as sea lions blasting through curtains of fish. We sought out the big stuff: diamond rays, marbled rays and quintessential whitetip reef sharks, and even the odd blacktip or hammerhead. There were loads of Moorish idols on some parts of the reef. Alex had not seen eastern Pacific species before, so after each dive, we would go to the fish-ID book and write down the details. Good discipline. The Moorish idol is one of the few reef species that is widely distributed all across the Pacific and Indian oceans.

We had to get fuel from Baltra, so we also had lunch, then we went to the north side of the island to do a land tour. Gillian, not being a diver, was really enjoying the land tours and getting into the nature part, aside from the iguanas. It was a magical tour with swallow-tailed gulls nesting, blue-footed boobies and their chicks, sea lions resting up, and my favorites,

the frigate birds. In the Caribbean it is hard to get close to nesting frigate birds. Here they were in every low tree. Some males had their chest sacs puffed out and were drumming at the females circling high above. Two species were present: the magnificent frigate and the great frigate bird, one having blue eye rings and the other pink eye rings.

We made the transit to Wolf Island through the night and did three dives there, with the usual big Galapagos sharks, hammerheads in the distance, and lots of big spotted eagle rays hanging in the current as if it did not affect them. Holding on to the rocks, if you turned your head sideways, the current was strong enough to rip the mask off your face.

The third dive was a ripper; we saw barberfish cleaning numerous hammerheads, plus the added bonus of having a hawksbill turtle join us for a while. There are lots of green turtles around the islands, but that was the first hawksbill for us. We were starting to use the current to pull us around the corner when Alex tugged my fin sharply; I looked up, and there was a 40-foot whale shark passing just overhead. It felt like we were waiting at a bus stop and a spotted bus just pulled up beside us. As with most encounters with these amazing creatures, it was short with a lot of hard swimming involved.

July 11 saw us arrive on the northeast side of Isabella Island, where we had not stopped on previous expeditions, and we had our first dive at Cabo Marshall. It was quite different from anywhere else we had been so far, with a surface layer of warm green water and cool clear water below, as we swam north along a vertical wall with lots of green turtles. In fact, I have never seen more green turtles than in the Galapagos. Chris was then going to take us farther east to the island of Santiago for a land tour. Here was the perfect spot to get Gillian in the shot as she came around the corner, having not seen the iguanas yet. Here she comes, and with a little distraction from Alex—bingo!

It's a long way to go for a week, so we all decided to return for two back-to-back expeditions in July 2008. Our diving friends from Cayman were Brynley Davis, Justin Uzell, and Dr. Larry Caven, plus Bill Watts, Andy Daniels, Zander Villagomez from Florida, Michael Domeier, Jimmy and Steve Valletta, their business partners, Dean Formanek, Steve Jackson, Chuck Buss,

BOTTOM

*Portrait of a young female
sea lion.*

Tod Miller, Alison Shea and Bobby Thrasher. We followed the same cruise itinerary for the first week, as usual. Outstanding encounters were had at Wolf and Darwin, as before. Dean had a kiss with the biggest whale shark we had ever seen, a 50-footer at Wolf Island.

During the second week, we went to the northwestern side of Isabella to see the flightless cormorants in the shallows at Banks Bay, inside the dramatic scenery of Punta Vincente Roca. On the deeper side, we encountered several large mola mola in the cold, deep water. Higher up were enormous schools of black striped salemas, a species endemic to the Galapagos. With such an abundance of small fish, I expected to see loads of attentive predators, such as sierra mackerel and almaco jacks, and some sharks as well. But they were unmolested. I wonder what happens at night?

Snorkeling in the protected bay, we saw more Galapagos penguins feeding in the shallows and in the surf. Then we found what we came to see, the rare flightless cormorant searching for fish among the rocks. They hold their breath for a long time and are very nimble underwater.

It was a three-hour run to our next stop, an island called Roca Redonda. Our guides, Patricio and Richard, took us to another site nearby where there are streams of gas bubbles pouring out of the gravel substrate from warm vents beneath. Very surreal. There was no life around this site; I imagine the water would be very acidic from the sulfurous gas emissions. We had a long swim from this site to a big rock pinnacle, where we rested and watched lots of hammerheads come and go, plus some full-grown Galapagos sharks. Then there were *lots* of Galapagos sharks! One was at least 11 feet long. This site is seldom visited by the liveaboard dive fleet and is the best-kept secret in the Galapagos—we should have done more dives there.

For the expedition, we logged 36 dives each. We enjoyed some amazing encounters and all had wonderful experiences. Thanks to its isolation, the Galapagos archipelago is like nowhere else on the planet. In spite of modern human influence, each island has its own unique fauna and character. There are land animals and birds that are found nowhere else on the planet. Linking these islands are the currents that bring cold water and nutrients, warm water and migrating predators, and seabirds that come and go.

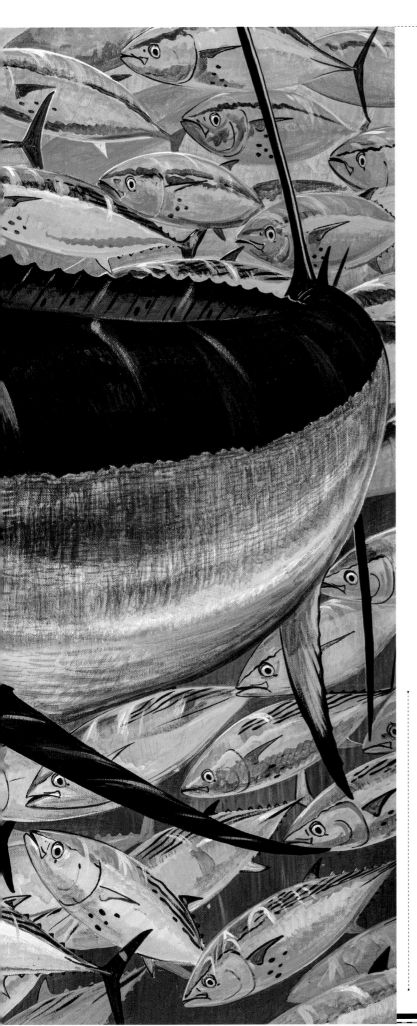

A big black marlin crowding a school of bonito on the Piñas Reef off Tropic Star Lodge in Panama. Acrylic on canvas.

Panama

HOME AWAY FROM HOME

WE HAVE BEEN FISHING at Tropic Star Lodge since the early 1990s. Many people ask why I go there so often. The answer is simple: The fishing is excellent and always consistent. In addition, for people who like a remote destination, being close to nature, and who enjoy five-star hospitality, this is the right spot. Nestled on the edge of the mountainous Darien Jungle and the Pacific Ocean, the lodge is situated in the upper arm of Piñas Bay, sheltered from the Pacific surge.

What you fish for in Panama changes by the season, and the available species have changed considerably over the past 30 years. The biomass has certainly gone down since TSL founder Ray Smith declared that you could walk on the marlin there more than a half-century ago.

Black marlin are typically available in respectable numbers from November to March, ranging in size from 250 to 500 pounds, but they can be caught in any month as well, just like blue marlin. There was a reasonable population of striped marlin off Piñas Bay up to the late 1990s, but they have largely disappeared, with only one or two caught now by lodge boats

A 300-pound black marlin jumps toward the boat off Tropic Star. When the mate has the leader at hand, get the camera ready for some explosive jumps.

each year. The Billfish Conservation Act of 2018 in the United States, which banned the importation of billfish for food, can only improve the situation.

Sailfish season used to be in April, May and June, but sails have not been seen in large numbers for a decade. We used to see many sharks on the Piñas Reef—mostly scalloped hammerheads and large blacktips. Nowadays there are scant few sharks; they have been decimated by the shark-fin trade. Conversely, after several decades of catching only a few, dorado have recently made a remarkable comeback.

Another negative influence are the bait-stealing bottlenose dolphins that have invaded the Piñas Reef. The TSL crews call the dolphins *chupacabra*, or "blood sucker." Sometimes

they refer to them as *malo*, meaning bad. Nevertheless, these intelligent mammals work together to get the job done. One dolphin grabs the bait by the head, avoiding the hook, while its partner twists off the body, leaving a hook bridled to an empty skull.

So many questions remain unanswered about these aforementioned species. Their behavior, migration patterns, post-release survival rate—among other mysteries. Unfortunately, there has been very little research conducted in the region. Until now.

Since 1991, I have kept all the details in my journal. It includes every single day of fishing and diving in all the countries we've visited. Every detail about the boats, captains, mates, weather, water color, lures, bait, and people we fished with. These details are important. If you write down what you see, the memory is captured forever. I have kept my Mum's diaries from her early fishing days in Jamaica during the '50s and '60s, where they struggled with boats, primitive reels and early technology. It's amazing they caught anything, but then again, there were more fish to catch.

With so many Tropic Star memories in my journal, I'm going to choose a few highlights that largely fall into two categories: tournaments and research.

TOURNAMENTS

TSL's annual billfish tournament, known as the *torneo* to those familiar with it, takes place every year in late November. The lodge closes at the end of September (the middle of the rainy season) for two months, allowing time for staff vacations and refurbishments on the boats, guest rooms, and public spaces.

The torneo is an important event for the lodge because it not only marks the opening of the season, but it's also a qualifying event for the prestigious Offshore World Championship, the Super Bowl of big-game fishing, held in Quepos, Costa Rica. To enter the OWC, a team has to win a sanctioned fishing tournament happening anywhere in the world, which includes Tropic Star's offseason event. In revisiting my journal for this book, a few of the torneos over the past 10 years truly stand out.

A mother and calf humpback whale off Punta Carolita in August. Humpbacks from the southern hemisphere visit the Panama coast up to the Perlas Islands to have their calves. Mixed media.

Being on a boat with the beloved Dr. Neil Burnie was always fun, action-packed and filled with music. Neil had never caught black marlin, so in late November 2010, we fished for a few days before the annual torneo. Two friends from Cayman—Andi Marcher and Tony Berkman—joined us. As we waited at the gate in the Miami International Airport, a loud blast of music filled the concourse. It was a saxophone being played by Neil to the startled amusement of hundreds of travelers. It inspired a rousing roar of applause, followed by an encore. Neil had entered the building.

Our first couple of days, November 19 and 20, were on *Miss Australia*. Fishing was slow, with only some big dorado and one sailfish. One sunny, calm morning we were up top staying cool out of the sun, and suddenly blaringly loud music blasted out of the cabin. The sax again! Unfortunately, it didn't bring any marlin into the spread.

Multiple days of rain and no billfish bites followed until November 23, when our captain, Candelo, finally found the marlin for us. We were at the reef at 7:30 a.m. on a gloomy morning. The clouds rolled low off the mountains, casting a gray chill on the ocean. It's always hard to get good action shots in low light. At 7:45, the bonito on the right rigger suddenly took off. Once it could not go any farther, it started jumping out of the water. Right behind it came the unmistakable purple fin of a black marlin. Tony was hooked up, and the marlin jumped all over the place, the white water standing in

stark contrast to the dark blue-gray backdrop of mountains and clouds. I was struggling to get the proper shutter speed to freeze the marlin. I did just in time for the beautiful 300-pound fish's release.

The bite cooled off, so we went outside the reef and found a big school of young yellowfin tuna. We caught a few and bridled them up for bait. Big black marlin love this size yellowfin. I've seen a few take the bait off the rod as you are winding them in. In this case though, the chupacabras stole them all.

Back to the reef. It turns out we should not have left. As Neil was putting the line in the outrigger clip, a black marlin ate it. Neil was properly hooked up and overjoyed. He even broke out the harmonica as he was fighting the marlin. The marlin was allergic to water and stayed in the air most of the time. When the faintest glimmer of light peaked out of the clouds, I could see that beautiful bronze sheen on its flanks. Neil was ecstatic about catching his first black marlin. It was a good day, and the torneo hadn't even started yet.

We had a good boat draw, but we lost Tony to his team, Cayman No. 2, with Troy Burke and Andrew McCartney from Cayman. On Team Cayman No. 3 were Alistair Walters, Sebastien Guilbard and Marcos Montana. We set out with Capt. Armando on *Miss Puerto Rico*, and caught a sailfish and several large dorado but did not see a marlin in our spread. Very frustrating. Cayman No. 2 did well, catching three blue marlin with Capt. Libardo, putting them in first place.

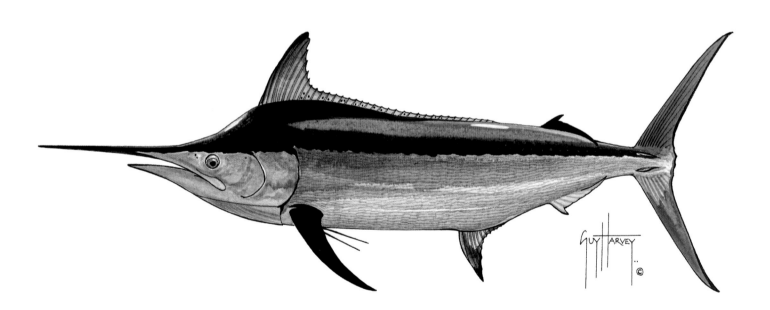

ABOVE

A black marlin in the green waters of Panama shows a dark green back and bronze flanks compared with those from clearer ocean waters. Watercolor.

FACING PAGE

The mate wires a 400-pound black marlin for angler John Gill. Tim Choate (on right) watches the action.

On Day Two, we fished offshore with Capt. Dagoberto on *Miss Panama*. The ocean was alive with spotted dolphins, small tunas, and skipjacks. We stayed in the zone for a long time before a blue marlin raced in to terrorize our three baits. It was so calm, you could see through the surface and behold the marlin in its feeding colors: jet-black with a neon blue tail. It ate the bait closest to the boat, then Neil settled in for a fight that featured a long series of jumps that took it farther and farther into the distance. He landed his first Pacific blue, around 450 pounds.

We fished with Capt. Gilberto on *Miss South Africa* on the last day. We needed two marlin to get into first place. After catching bait, we started to fish right away. A marlin came in and window-shopped all three baits. The black fish with a bright blue tail darted from bait to bait, like a butterfly moving from flower to flower. It drove us crazy! All of a sudden Andi was hooked up, fighting the 450-pound fish for 30 minutes, but lost it when it dropped the bait.

We had an hour to go and desperately needed a marlin.

The short bait disappeared in a boil of foam, and a big blue marlin started leaping right away. The hook was nowhere near the fish; the leader and line were wrapped around the marlin's face and head. There was so much white water that I could not see the fish. It was a Jet Ski on steroids. A lassoed fish is much harder to wind in than one hooked in the mouth. As the mate pulled the fish closer, the mess of tangled leader and line slipped off. The perfect release. We were lucky on that one.

We ended up in fourth place. A great end to a great week.

On Thanksgiving Day 2013, we arrived once again in Piñas Bay, and promptly headed out for a half-day on *Miss Texas* with Capt. Gavilan. At 3:45 p.m., Gavilan called me up to the bridge and showed me an area of commotion a few hundred yards ahead. "Tuna?" I asked. He didn't think so. As we got closer, I was on the bridge with my camera and couldn't believe what I was seeing: 200 blacktip sharks and thousands of jack crevalle feeding on an unseen school of bait below. What was amazing was how these two species had teamed up to feed on a common food source, similar to the yellowfin tuna/spotted dolphin association. Is one species taking advantage of the other? Or is it mutually beneficial? I wished so much that I'd had my mask, fins and camera to put below the surface. Never get on a boat without them.

On November 29, we got bonito at the reef and ran offshore finding the spotted dolphins. We were so focused on a story being told by our friend Michael Kelly that we didn't see the boil on the right rigger bait. The fish screamed out several hundred yards of line with no jumps. In a flat-calm sea, Gavilan backed down fast on the fish, and we caught up with it 17 minutes later, a big blue approaching 600 pounds.

November 30 arrived. We were on *Miss Spain* with Capt. Masso, the legendary captain on the 1,200-pound black marlin we filmed on January 25, 2005, which was tagged and released.

As she turned sideways, I could see the full length of the fish. Her **HIGH DORSAL AND TAIL** *were far apart.* **THIS MARLIN WAS OVER 700 POUNDS.** *Her face was iridescent blue, purple and bronze.*

But our high expectations were not met. The radio was quiet all day. Only four marlin were caught by the entire TSL fleet.

It was a Bimini start on Sunday, December 1. All the Bertram 31s in the TSL fleet and private boats raced down the bay and out to the reef. We rounded up some bonito before running offshore. With no bites, we ran west to the 35/35, a small canyonlike cleft in the edge that holds tuna and billfish. Our Capt. Candelo recommended that we use lures because *Miss Canada* had just released a marlin caught on a lure. He had a batch of his own homemade hard-head rigs, so I put out three. It worked. A blue marlin ate the right rigger lure, was hooked by angler John Crimmins and made some lofty jumps before speeding off to the horizon. I reached for my camera. Candelo chased the marlin, and 25 minutes later, mate Elio got the leader and made a quick release. We were on the scoreboard. Finally! Time to make up some ground.

We promptly put out the same lures again and two big teasers. I was having a celebratory Panama beer when a big color spot appeared under the right teaser. There she was! From the size of the color spot, I could see it was a big fish as I pitched a small bonito to the marlin. When the dorsal fin and thick bill came up, I thought 600-plus pounds. "A big fish, señor," Elio quietly said to me. I wanted to say, "This is not my first rodeo," but my Spanish wasn't good enough. Then the marlin pushed the bait out of the way with its bow wave, its head was so big.

The marlin turned bright blue and spun around to crush the bait in a puff of blood. I came tight, and nothing happened at first as the marlin swam off to the right, then pushed out its massive head and started shaking. Elio said, "*Grande, grande!*" She sounded, but we were on top of her. She did very little, *muy tranquilo,* just cruising along. After 15 minutes, I moved to the fighting chair to put more pressure on her. She suddenly woke up and started jumping, her body halfway out of the water for a hundred yards. The foam she left behind looked like a 40-foot boat had gone by.

We caught up with her again, and Elio got a good hold on the leader. As she turned sideways, I could see the full length of the fish. Her high dorsal and tail were far apart; this marlin was over 700 pounds. Her face was iridescent blue, purple and bronze. Elio leaned down and cut the leader, and off she went, jumping and pushing water at the surface for some 200 yards. In 45 minutes, we had gone from the outhouse to the penthouse.

RESEARCH

In August 2014, I invited President George Hanbury of Nova Southeastern University and his longtime friend and lawyer, Tom Panza, to fish with me. The mission was to show him the research opportunities that exist for species that are facing resource issues and are being overharvested. After a successful six days during which time George caught a wide variety of species—several blue marlin, sailfish, sharks, tuna and dorado—he liked the concept a lot. With Dean Richard Dodge and Prof. Mahmood Shivji providing supervision, the proposed project would be a three-way collaboration. The Guy Harvey Ocean Foundation would provide a grant for all tags, gear and related expenses. NSU would provide the students, supervision and expenses. TSL would cover accommodations and logistical support (boat and crew) over a five-year period.

George was a patient and attentive student and angler without much experience in big-game fishing. We soon fixed that. On our second day, we were live-baiting around a big log, and

Hunting mullet in the surf, the iconic roosterfish is the ultimate inshore gamefish on light tackle. Mixed media.

George caught a sailfish plus a couple of dorado. As I pulled in a bait that looked tired, the leader was yanked from my hand as a blue marlin took the bait, kicking curtains of white water to the left and right. George was stoked; he had never caught a blue marlin before. We got to the fish quickly and released the 350-pounder.

Toward the end of the week, after more blue marlin, several large dorado, sailfish, yellowfin tuna and some tough blacktip sharks, I saw an unusual thing. We were pulling live baits, and a big bottlenose dolphin swam up near the boat. It had a big brown remora on its side. The dolphin was not interested in the baits. It was interested in rubbing the remora off its head on the forefoot of the keel.

I grabbed my camera. As the remora moved from the right side of the head to the left, I saw that the remora's powerful suction had dug out a shallow pit in the dolphin's head. It must be very irritating and painful for the dolphin. It was incredible to witness the dolphin use its intelligence to remove the annoying hitchhiker.

Thanks to TSL's CEO and general manager, Ursula Marais, and Richard and Mallory White, the current fishing director and manager (respectively), the lodge welcomed the first two NSA postgraduates, Ryan Logan and Tyler Plum, in May 2018. Their first charge was to begin research and data collection on inshore species of sharks and roosterfish.

Roosterfish have become the most coveted inshore species. Little is known about their migration, growth rate and life history. They look and behave like a big jack and have the face and jaw arrangement similar to an almaco jack, with a large mouth and rubber lips to grab and suck down their prey. Their coloration is striking: dark green or purple and bronze back, silver flanks that have four dark curving bands along the head and body, and elongated fin rays resembling a rooster's comb. An underwater zebra. Aesthetically they are a beautiful fish to paint.

The lodge holds an annual torneo for roosterfish in May,

ABOVE LEFT

Jessica's biggest yellowfin tuna of 230 pounds. Jay Perez and mate Vicente help hold the fish.

ABOVE RIGHT

Capt. Jose Mosquera put his client on this 400-pound black marlin on Miss Canada.

when they are most abundant. This provides a tagging opportunity for anglers to deploy conventional streamer tags in fish they catch and then measure before releasing.

Another species we are studying is the dolphinfish, or mahimahi, which are called dorado in Central America. During the 2018 torneo, we invited Wessley Merten of the Dolphin Research Program, based in Maryland, to initiate a dorado-tagging project. It seemed to be a natural addition to the study on pelagic species. We were focused on billfish and sharks, but dorado is the most commonly caught fish in Atlantic and Pacific bluewater recreational fisheries. It was dorado season, and there would be a lot of fish.

At the outset of the tournament, Ryan and Wessley gave comprehensive presentations to all the anglers about the research project and how important data collection is for these species. Wessley explained that it was a numbers game with low returns expected, so it was dependent on a lot of effort. We had no idea where these dorados go after they pass Panama, but we would find out.

Wessley handed out tagging equipment to every boat, and the anglers were enthusiastic about tagging them—citizen scientists at work. During the torneo, 250 dorado were tagged and released.

In January 2019, Jessica and I returned to tag black marlin at the height of the season. We had Gavilan as captain, and our mate, Manuel, was superb. Working with the other boats, most of the black marlin were being caught in an area 3 to 5 miles out in front of Punta Piñas, and farther north toward the reef. The reef itself did not have much bait, and when we did catch bait, the chupacabras got us every time.

The other captains were tremendously cooperative. They would call us as soon as they hooked up. We would take in our lines and run to their location. Going down-sea was fine. Going north was like getting a baptism.

One of the advantages of this strategy was good boat-to-boat action photos. The black marlin often have a lot of energy as

TOP LEFT

Team Canada, the indomitable trio of Greg Steers, Michael Kelly and David McBain, after a successful day on the water. They have fished every tournament for the past two decades.

TOP RIGHT

Team Cayman Islands, with John Crimmins and Sebastien Guilbard, placed second with two blue marlin that they caught on the last day.

ABOVE LEFT

Looking southeast over Bahia de Piñas at dawn. Needless to say, sunrises at Tropic Star Lodge are quite spectacular, and this one was no exception.

ABOVE RIGHT

Common dolphins like these are not common off Panama. Pacific spotted dolphins and bottlenose dolphins are frequent visitors to the reef and are called chupacabras, aka bait thieves.

Panama

Painted on location at Tropic Star Lodge, a black marlin and sailfish crowding bonito, one of the primary prey species in these prolific waters. Acrylic on canvas.

they near the boat and do some awesome jumps. Tropic Star's full-time photographer/videographer Keishmer Hermoso rode along with us and was able to capture a lot of action. Jessica would often hop into the water and follow the marlin to get underwater footage with her GoPro.

In his weekly presentations to clients at the lodge, Ryan would explain the reason for tagging billfish. He would discuss how the miniature pop-off archival transmitters (mini PATs) are used to track the long-term movements of these highly mobile species. The transmitters record depth, temperature and light data that are relayed to satellites when the tag detaches from the fish after predetermined lengths of time (eight months to one year). The archived data is used to reconstruct migration and diving behavior, which can then be used to predict where they might be in the future as ocean conditions change. This data will also provide critical information to local government officials, including potential hotspots where there's the greatest potential for billfish to be caught and killed in commercial fisheries.

How billfish behave right after catch-and-release is unknown, including how long it takes them to resume normal behavior. In September 2019, with the generosity and assistance of GHOF board member Rich Andrews and the crew of his yacht, *Compass Rose*, Ryan and team began their study of the movement behavior and recovery of billfish after release from recreational-fishing capture. To get this information, the team deploys a biologging tag that includes an accelerometer (to examine tail-beat information), compass, depth sensor, temperature probe and speed sensor. Developed and built over the course of a year, this custom-made tag is designed to detach from the fish after three days. The tag is made of a buoyant material so that when it detaches, it floats to the surface and begins to transmit its location via satellite. Once we have a general idea of where the tag is, the team can run out to that location and use a handheld receiver to home in on its exact location.

Once we have an idea of how long it takes these fish to physically recover from the fight with the angler, we can then

begin to look closely at their fine-scale behavior and habitat use that mini PAT tags are unable to capture. Because the tag measures individual tail beats, it's a measure of relative activity. A marlin on the hunt has a burst of rapid, strong tail beats, which isn't the case when it's cruising near the surface. This data, in combination with the geographic location of the fish, can provide insight into what behaviors are being exhibited where and at what depths. This type of information has previously been impossible to obtain. These recent advances in technology allow us to look into the secret lives of billfish like never before.

Knowledge of a region's biodiversity is an essential first step in an effective conservation strategy. In a research project being led by Tyler Plum, the team is using underwater video to provide the first view of the diversity and relative abundance of large-bodied vertebrates off Tropic Star Lodge. During a two-month stay at the lodge, they deployed newly developed, custom-made video cameras (baited remote underwater video stations, or BRUVS) at 25 locations within a 20-mile radius of the lodge, at depths of 10 and 40 meters. Thus far, the BRUVS have captured 300 hours of video documenting the underwater life around TSL. A lot of video remains to be reviewed, but so far, a great diversity of life has been observed, including silky sharks, scalloped hammerheads, blue marlin, sailfish, manta rays, jacks, dolphinfish, Ridley sea turtles and Pacific spotted dolphins. Our next step is to repeat this sampling effort in the dry season to better understand how seasons,

depth, and distance from shore affect the pelagic vertebrate abundance and diversity in the area.

We flew in to Piñas Bay on August 24, 2019, to join Ryan on a research and tagging expedition. We jumped on *Island Star* with Gavilan, mate Hermel, Keishmer, and my CEO, Steve Roden, from Fort Lauderdale. It was a cloudy day, with wind from the southwest. No chupacabras to be seen. At 2:30 p.m., the left rigger bait went crazy as a black marlin ate the right rigger bait that was jumping at the surface. Steve was on, and we chased the marlin as it jumped high and far, the cloud-covered mountains serving as the backdrop.

Unfortunately the marlin became tail-wrapped while jumping and went into the mud at 300 feet. We took it in, and Ryan was glad for the opportunity to show how his accelerometer is attached to a billfish. Autopsy and bio samples are a valuable part of his research, and all the meat is used to feed the staff, so the fish is well-utilized.

We were later joined on the expedition by NSU president George Hanbury and Tom Panza, as well as Steve Hudson, Bill Gallo, Rob Kornahrens, Ed Davis, Gene Fall, Ray Young and Gordon James III. We fished on *Island Star* for the next two days. After a morning of torrential rainstorms and blazing pink lightning, we were just surviving. The rain eased a bit as we arrived at the 35/35. I asked Hermel to rig up the small sierra mackerel we'd caught earlier.

Keeping the dorados off the fresh, dainty sierra was not easy. Hermel had rigged it up on a 12/0 circle hook and lighter leader, so I put it out on a 50 on the far-back center rigger. At 10:40 a.m., a dorado was on the sierra, so I reeled it in closer to the boat while Hermel sent back a belly strip for the dorado. Just then a 400-pound blue marlin came head and shoulders out of the water and rolled on the mackerel, Steve Hudson was hooked up with the marlin jumping in crazy circles.

This marlin turned out to be an unusually tough fish. It would come within 40 feet of the boat, then do a wide circle like a big tuna. It repeated this maneuver again and again for two hours. Steve is a pretty good angler and was putting a lot of heat on the marlin, but we could not get it up. Gavilan did all sorts of maneuvering. After 2 hours, 45 minutes, Hermel

FACING PAGE

A huge remora attached to the head of the bottlenose dolphin. The remora will detach itself and nibble at the small scraps when the dolphin consumes a larger prey species.

BELOW

A blue marlin at the boat about to be released. Note the hook is outside-in, in front of the eye. The lure is homemade by Capt. Candelo, but clearly it does produce bites.

got the leader. The circle hook was in the left corner (where it was supposed to be), but the leader went under the throat, around the head, behind the dorsal fin and under the base of the left pectoral fin, then went back on the hook before going to the swivel. I tagged the blue marlin with a PAT provided by the Smithsonian Institute, which was studying post-release mortality on gamefish in Panama.

Our last day was cloudless, sunny and flat-calm. Rob Kornahrens, Gene Fall and Ed Davis were with me, and Keishmer was on board to film. Out at the 35/35, several commercial boats were working over a 5-square-mile area, fishing just beyond the 20-mile boundary. There were birds and spotted dolphin everywhere. Conditions were awesome.

Several yellowfin over 200 pounds were jumping close by. We caught fresh bonito next to the commercial boats, set them out, dropped back 100 yards and waited. At 1:05 p.m., a blue marlin hit one of our big bonito, and Gene was hooked up. It did nothing for a while and then started jumping at the boat, going past on the starboard side. Hermel got the leader. A five-minute fight for a 350-pound fish. I tagged it with another PAT tag provided by the Smithsonian.

As the commercial boats hauled in their lines, we pulled alongside and I took some shots of them gaffing tuna that came up on the line. There were three tuna for every four hooks hauled back, most between 40 and 60 pounds. There were no sharks or billfish among the catch.

We went back the following year, on January 25, 2020, with our great friend Martin Lancaster and his son, Sam. Martin is a big supporter of the GHOF and has been to the lodge a few times, but he was still waiting to catch his first black marlin.

Ryan had already been there for a week and was tagging lots of billfish. The black marlin season was not what it had been in 2019, but blue marlin were out in full force. Shortly after arrival, we hopped aboard *Miss Canada* with Capt. Lorenzo and mate Inut. It was a rough sea with a stiff north wind. As I was trying to hold on, I spotted a big "breezer" of bonitos ruffling a calm area in the choppy surface. There were no birds on it. We put out baits and fished for a while but lost the school in the waves. Trolling back up-sea, we found the school again, this time thanks to the birds. We put out live bait and quickly had a bite. The marlin had been tracking it and lazily came up to swallow the bait. Sam was on. It started jumping down-sea, covering a lot of ground. I was enjoying getting the sequences; the light was good as long as the fish didn't turn west into the sun.

The leader was going over the fish's shoulder and behind its dorsal fin. Ryan was ready with the tag pole. The 350-pounder was *right there*. Inut had the leader, but the fish shook its head and out came the bait. The hook was never in its mouth. It had swallowed the bait, but when the mate put on the added pressure, the marlin regurgitated the fish and the hook along with it. This has happened so many times.

Back at the dock, a small crowd had gathered. They were carving up a massive blue marlin caught on a private boat. It

FACING PAGE

A blue marlin displaying its glowing neon pectoral fins and tail about to be released. Sometimes when they attack a teaser right behind the boat, they show these vivid colors.

"SIX HUNDRED POUNDS," *the captain announced to all within earshot.* JESSICA WAS SUPER-STOKED: *her first black marlin after all these years.*

had died after a two-hour fight on 50-pound line. The TSL weigh station made it official: 852 pounds. It was the biggest blue marlin I had seen there. The marlin provided great data for Ryan, who collected all sorts of tissue samples.

The following day, we were running across the sea on *Island Star* when the call came that Jessica was hooked up to a black marlin on *Miss Canada*, with Ryan right next to her. We got there as mate Inut grabbed the leader, and Ryan tagged it perfectly. "Six hundred pounds," the captain announced to all within earshot. Jessica was super-stoked: her first black marlin after all these years.

My journal entry from January 28 noted a flat-calm sea. We found a large inverted stump, with roots above the surface, the trunk going down 60 feet, with lots of bonito and juvenile yellowfin tuna hanging around. Jessica and I dived on it, getting good footage of myriad types of bait. Closer to the trunk were rainbow chubs, triggerfish, jacks, tripletail and sergeant majors. This was fantastic inspiration for a large painting! There was also a long fishing line wrapped around it, and a little farther down was a dead tuna on a hook. There had to be blue or black marlin in the vicinity. We switched to fishing teasers and lures. A blue marlin demolished the right teaser as I bent down to pick up the pitch bait. The marlin spooked and jumped completely out of the water, broke the heavy swivel on Gavilan's teaser line and departed with it. All I saw was the foam.

But another opportunity soon presented itself, this time with Martin on the rod. It was an active blue marlin that became tail-wrapped and sounded. Martin eventually got it up to the surface, after which we spent 20 minutes reviving the fish before Jessica and Sam swam the marlin off successfully.

The blue marlin bite that day was excellent: seven marlin caught, all on lures. Before that action started, there was an early bite from big yellowfin tuna mixed in with spotted dolphins on several baitballs. We found a baitball of green jacks, went in closer trying to get a bite, and got a big tuna on but lost it. The next baitball was dense with small baitfish. Booby birds were diving. Frigate birds plucked fish from the surface. Tuna busting left and right. I grabbed my snorkeling gear and a GoPro and jumped in.

I have dived on several tuna/dolphin baitballs here in the past, but this was different. The bait was lanternfish: 4 inches long, pink and brown. It is a species that's part of the deep scattering layer that lives in the mesopelagic zone during the day and migrates to the epipelagic zone at night. Sometimes these fish get trapped near the surface by predators before they can dive down early in the morning. That phenomenon was currently in progress.

I was surrounded by big yellowfins rushing through the water, their gold flanks reflecting the bright sunlight, finlets glowing, mouths open like buckets to scoop up the morsels. I got some footage in the middle of the bait school, then moved to the fringe to find some clear water. There were some big tuna in the school, upwards of 300 pounds.

A blacktip shark swam past, interested only in finding a weak link or two, but the bait was too small for it to enjoy. I imagined a time 20 years ago when there would have been dozens of sharks in a situation like this. The shark-fin trade had removed them.

The spotted dolphins stayed on the fringe. Again it seemed that this prey species was too small for them to grasp. Meanwhile, the yellowfin sucked in the lanternfish several at a time. The conveyor belt of tuna was coming up from underneath, taking the bait in the densest aggregation. Jessica joined me with a tank on and got down below the school. Gradually the bait was consumed, and all that remained was a cloud of gradually sinking scales.

Life and death in the open ocean.

Guadalupe

DECODING THE APEX PREDATOR

A frequent occurrence off the California coast: A white shark makes a pass at a few yellowtail as they seek shelter in the kelp. Acrylic on canvas.

ANY YEAR WHEN you get hit by a major hurricane in the Caribbean is a bad year. Living in Grand Cayman, we absorbed the shock of the Category 5 Hurricane Ivan in September 2004. The island was devastated. The recovery was slow, long and hot. No water, ice, fans or cold beer. Electricity was slowly restored, and we gradually came off a series of curfews. Life was somewhat back to normal by late November. Then I got a call from Michael Domeier of the Pfleger Institute of Environmental Research in Oceanside, California. He invited me on a white shark tagging expedition in a couple of weeks to Guadalupe Island. Michael had been studying white sharks in Guadalupe and the Farallon Islands off San Francisco since 2002. Having never seen a white shark, I was eager to go.

At Fisherman's Landing in Point Loma, under the watchful eye of our captain, Tom "Riddles" Rotherie, we loaded the long-range fishing boat *Polaris Supreme* with shark cages and 250 scoops of live bait from the large bait pens in the harbor. The many sea lions and seabirds hanging around the pens made for good photographic opportunities. For offshore big-game fishing, live bait is the key to catching big yellowfin tuna, wahoo and billfish.

Riddles typically fishes faraway locations such as Hurricane Bank and Revillagigedos Islands on 16-day expeditions. By comparison, the jog down to Guadalupe was short—just nine hours. On board were Chugey Sepulveda and Nicole Nasby-Lucas from PIER, plus Michael and several friends. Rick Westphal was on hand to capture footage for an episode of *Portraits from the Deep*. Paxson "Packy" Offield from the

Guadalupe

Offield Center for Billfish Studies ran ahead of us on his new 78-foot Garlington-Landeweer, *Kelsey Lee*. Tom Pfleger from PIER arrived on his boat, *Hana Pa'a*, having caught some albacore on the way. It was a gray morning, with low clouds concealing the bulk of the 25-mile-long volcanic island. The east side is somewhat protected from the prevailing northwesterly winds that we had experienced on the way. There was too much surge, so we couldn't deploy the cages. We went fishing instead, catching a couple of fine yellowtails. While looking for tuna and yellowtail, we spotted a white shark at the surface cruising a scum line, checking out a piece of flotsam.

We anchored up in front of the old lighthouse and prison compound. Just then a small panga came by with four Mexican divers who were using a hookah rig to dive for abalone. There was no mothership in sight. They came to offer some abalone for sale. We said no thanks, but Chugey engaged in a conversation, translating for us.

"Do you see white sharks while you are diving?"

"Yes, we see them all the time."

"And you are not afraid of them?"

"Why would we be afraid? There are so many the sea lions around here. Why would they want to eat us?"

We started chumming, and very quickly a fat, 14-foot white shark swam around the boat. I was amazed at the size of the fish: stout body with a pointed head and face, wide pectoral fins, and caudal keel on the caudal peduncle like a tuna. Mike got the PAT tag poles ready. On the next pass, the white shark was tagged in the muscle at the base of the dorsal fin. No catching, no fighting, no tying up to the boat required. Just chum into range and tag.

A much bigger shark came by, an 18-footer. The *Jaws* music was playing in my head. It circled below before coming up to

"Do you see white sharks while you are diving?"
"Yes, we see them all the time."
"And you are not afraid of them?"
"Why would we be afraid? There are so many sea lions around. Why would they want to eat us?"

take a bait. Tom tagged her minutes later. The big sharks did not react to being tagged. In fact, they didn't even flinch; they just turned back around toward the bait. They had such a graceful, lazy swimming action. I could not wait to get in the water tomorrow.

Once *Kelsey Lee* was secured, a cage was deployed behind each boat. There was enough space for four divers in each cage. With the correct weight packs for shoulders and ankles, dressed in 7 mm suits with boots on, we were ready. The first shark did not appear for a couple of hours, but when it did, it spent a lot of time next to the cages. It was so close, so majestic, and so...big. Working from the skiff just off the stern, Michael tagged the shark and took a biopsy.

As the morning went by, the water cleared. The visibility was tremendous. This is what Guadalupe is known for: blue water. More white sharks came in. One had scars all over her face and gills. The scars could be from fur seals and elephant seals, the white shark's favorite foods. They are vicious when fighting back. Or it could have been from a mating encounter. As in all sharks and rays, white sharks bite each other when mating. The male holds on to the female's dorsal fin, pectoral fins or

gill area with his jaws, which carves deep scars. Michael was able to tag four more sharks that day without a single shark being caught. Some of the sharks had a transducer on their back from a different research organization.

The next day, the cage-diving action started around 11 a.m. Although it was overcast, the water was crystal-clear. The shark's white face, black eyes, menacing grin, and great tail sweeping from side to side could be seen from as far away as 200 feet.

Many of them were aggressive on the baits, coming close to the cages, affording us good shots and footage. I was shooting slide film in my Nikonos RS and got out of the water only to change the film. The action was so compelling, I stayed in the cage until 4 p.m. There was one shark called Stumpy because its dorsal fin was just a nub. It became one of the featured sharks in the episode Rick was shooting.

It was easy to see how the sharks surprise their prey. In one instance, I was looking straight back out of the cage for 10 seconds, then turned around to face a 15-footer right next to the cage. The shark had used the protection of the hull to get up close without being seen. Crafty and deadly.

ABOVE

The clear blue water of Guadalupe and the presence of numerous white sharks make it a perfect destination for the ultimate big-shark cage-diving experience.

FACING PAGE, TOP LEFT

Tom Pfleger's boat, Hana Pa'a, *at anchor off Guadalupe in front of the island's old prison complex and lighthouse.*

FACING PAGE, TOP RIGHT

Paxson "Packy" Offield on the 78-foot Garlington Kelsey Lee. *He was an outstanding conservationist as well as an excellent angler and photographer.*

FACING PAGE, MIDDLE LEFT

All smiles with Packy after a day of diving with white sharks. It's hard to beat spending time with friends on the water.

BOTTOM LEFT

Bill Boyce and Alex with a couple of nice stringers of tasty calico bass.

BOTTOM RIGHT

Guadalupe elephant seals rest on the beach. These seals and fur seals are what white sharks are hunting around this oceanic island.

Pacific Ocean / Guadalupe **307**

The weather had picked up again on our last day. The surge was banging the cages against the stern, but we still dived. There were fewer sharks now, but they were huge. One enormous female hung 30 to 50 feet below the cages most of the morning and would not come up higher. Another big female arrived. She had scars all over her left side and gill area, so bad that I could see the red gill filaments underneath.

Rick and I interviewed Michael and Nicole, mostly about the shark-photo database, a cooperative effort between researchers, dive boats, and other marine operations that stores and organizes photos of sharks that have come to the island. Twelve white sharks had been tagged during the week, and Michael was hopeful they would leave the island soon to migrate to other areas of essential habitat, and perhaps even reveal where they mate and give birth.

An expedition on *Solmar V* in September 2005 marked our return to Guadalupe. The crew was a large group of friends that included documentary producer Diana Udel, Dr. Ellen Pikitch, Dr. Mahmood Shivji, director of the GHRI, Wayne Hasson, CEO and president of the Aggressor Dive Fleet, photographer Bill Boyce, Steve McCulloch from the Harbor Branch Oceanographic Institute, and my 12-year-old son, Alex.

We took a bus from San Diego to Ensenada to join our guide, friend and shark expert Lawrence Groth, who had a great deal of experience with white shark filming expeditions in the Farallon Islands and Guadalupe. We boarded *Solmar V* and headed south through choppy seas. The group gathered in the salon to introduce ourselves. What an experienced group we

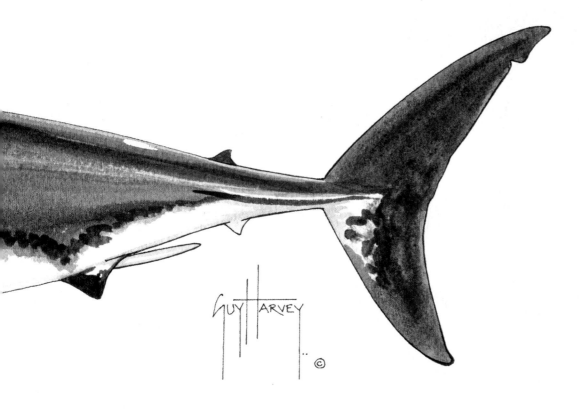

were: decades of diving, and every ocean covered. Then it was Alex's turn: "My name is Alex Harvey. I am 12 years old, and I have been diving for 14 years."

It was an overcast morning when we arrived. The island's craggy peaks were covered in clouds. Michael was already there with his team on the PIER research vessel *Palolo*.

Lawrence gave us a briefing about cage etiquette: Don't reach out to touch the sharks, one-hour rotations, and other safety procedures. It was a constant stream of sharks all day, and the visibility was exceptional. The bait was half of a 50-pound bluefin tuna on a hemp rope.

Along with the two cages attached to the stern, Lawrence had a third cage that was lowered amidships. It could go 30 feet down under the vessel and provide two divers on tanks a different viewpoint. The action was continuous; there was always two or three white sharks in view at any time. We just stayed in as long as we wanted, coming out only to change film.

No one can describe the feeling you get with your first pass of an apex predator the caliber of a white shark. Nineteen feet of muscle mass, with that big grin just a meter from your face isn't a feeling with which you'll ever feel comfortable.

After four days of filming and fishing, we headed home with exceptional life memories, images that will be with us forever. Going on an expedition with our best friends, in the best conditions, and with the best charter made for an epic adventure.

But the research must continue. Michael and his team currently conduct the world's longest-running white shark research project centered on Guadalupe and the Farallon Islands. These sharks visit Guadalupe in fall and winter months, and then make annual migrations to an area between Mexico and Hawaii that Michael has termed the Shared Offshore Foraging Area. The researchers photographed 142 white sharks between 2001 and 2009, of which 113 went into the photo database. To date, more than 350 sharks have been identified.

GHRI is also contributing to white shark research. In 2019, Shivji and his team at GHRI were able to successfully decode the entire genome of the white shark. The goal was to better understand what makes this animal such an evolutionarily finely tuned predator at the most basic and fundamental level: its DNA blueprint.

BUSINESS RELATIONS

ALL THE STORIES THAT are told in this book are the result of a lot of work over a long period of time by staff, licensing partners and business associates. Without a successful licensing and art business, there would be no fishing, diving, research or education, and less conservation.

After my first art shows in Jamaica in 1985 and Florida in 1986, the apparel license began in 1987 with Raleigh Werking and Barry Shulman at T-Shirts of Florida. Raleigh was a visionary who saw the potential of my art on apparel. Being a very keen fisherman, avid light-tackle angler and world-record holder, Raleigh knew that my art in four-color process printing would be new to fishing-industry apparel.

The trade shows, consumer shows, fishing tournaments, boat shows and seafood festivals all became must-attend activities. My support for the licensees was critical. Building good relationships with owners of independent accounts was paramount. They were the backbone of the business. It started in Florida, and then spread to other coastal states.

Over the years, we built relationships that turned into long-term business associations. Larger accounts such as Beall's, Bass Pro Shops and Academy Sports got on board early. Good partnerships with Dillard's, Macy's and Belk helped expand the footprint.

But after many years, the line was still heavily dependent on white cotton T-shirts. Customers suggested colored shirts. Keeping ahead of the innovation curve proved difficult. Sales were flattening out.

In March 1999, I was exhibiting at the Fred Hall Fishing Show in Long Beach, California. Milt Shedd, owner of AFTCO, approached me about doing a line of men's woven shirts with repeat designs. Given current contractual commitments, this was a difficult decision, but we eventually made an agreement in 2004. We expanded our offerings through AFTCO's ability to source and print the Hawaiian-style shirts in Asia.

Supplying a primarily East and Gulf Coast business through a West Coast supplier was a challenge. Nevertheless, the refreshing approach by AFTCO increased sales by 700 percent over the first four years. We added new big-box accounts such as Dick's Sporting Goods, West Marine, Hibbert's and many independent stores outside Florida. The AFTCO reputation for quality product and good service meant a great deal to our accounts. This growth fed the research, education and conservation efforts.

As time went by, it became apparent that our cause-marketing efforts based on relevant research work was making a difference in how we fish and where we fish. Catch-and-release had not yet taken root. Responsible fishing and conserving marine resources were mission-critical. Everyone in the boating and marine industry knew our collective success depended on healthy marine resources. In short, conservation was good for business.

AFTCO CEO Bill Shedd and I were aligned on this. There's no doubt his understanding of the politics of fishing made a very positive impact on the brand. We could see this in the people who came to the public appearances; school-age kids, families and university students all embraced the brand. It was gratifying and inspiring to see how many of them brought their own art to show me.

The majority of customers were more appreciative of the conservation efforts than the product offerings. The next challenge was to bring my ocean experiences to people's lives and homes through a fishing television series. In 2002, we hired Sea Lion Productions, which had successfully filmed and produced legendary angler Flip Pallot's series *The Walker's Cay Chronicles*. We worked with Sea Lion for one season, then shifted to Bonnier Corporation and the *Sport Fishing Television* production crew headed by Ken Kavanaugh. The series *Portraits from the Deep* aired on Outdoor Life Network and Versus from 2002 to 2007.

Many of the stories I tell in this book are from that era. From Panama to Venezuela to Australia, stories are told with a focus on the species, their natural history and the conservation issues they face. My love for diving in the open ocean also came to the fore. Marlin, sailfish, swordfish, tuna, tiger sharks: None of these species can be kept in captivity, so the only way people could be exposed to a free-swimming fish was through underwater videography. We would go on to produce a 13-episode series entirely on billfish, the first one-hour documentary about billfish ever made, and a documentary about Emma, the famous tiger shark, and the diabolical shark-fin trade taking place in the Bahamian archipelago.

The art and apparel business continued to do well. With apparel, there was increasing competition, and retail sales were moving into e-commerce. One of the big moral questions was: Do you compete with your store accounts by offering merchandise for sale on your own? The accounts responded by setting up their own online-sales capabilities.

At Guy Harvey Incorporated, we embraced the internet and used it to sell art online. We opened the Gallery and Shoppe in Grand Cayman in 2006, the brand's flagship store. All of our licensed merchandise and art were available in one place.

Other business opportunities arose with SeaWorld through both research collaboration (on mako sharks, for example) and merchandising opportunities. I visited their locations around the country on a regular basis. The connection between fishing, diving, research and conservation with the SeaWorld passholder was strong. We had considerable overlap with our membership base.

In 2014, Norwegian Cruise Lines asked me to become the hull artist for their new ship, *Norwegian Escape*. As the vessel was being built in Pappenberg, Germany, in July 2015, I went to see it for myself, taking photos from a scaffold. It was breathtaking to see the sailfish mural come to life along the hull of a 1,200-foot ship. It would be a moving symbol of awareness and conservation for the marine environment. NCL is like-minded in its conservation efforts, including effective strategies to recycle plastic, aluminum, glass and cardboard, plus a no-plastic-straws policy.

The association with NCL opened up a new relationship with Park West, the largest art dealer in the world. It had the onboard concession with several cruise companies to sell art through an auction-based system. The main benefit would be to expand the reach of the brand. In the years that followed, I went on several VIP art cruises each year, and the Guy Harvey Ocean Foundation hosted one Conservation Cruise per year.

We continued to face increasing competition from similar brands that had better sourcing, product and price options, particularly in performance fabrics. We were slow to respond to the customer's preference for these materials rather than cotton and rapidly lost market share. It was clear: The brand had outgrown AFTCO. The search went far and wide, and we would eventually join up with Intradeco in July 2019.

Intradeco is a family-owned company led by CEO Felix Siman. While the company has offices in Miami, New York, South Carolina and Arkansas, the manufacturing takes place in El Salvador. Here, all the apparel is made from scratch. Felix assured me that their processes are very sustainable.

On invitation from Felix, the GHI team visited Intradeco's state-of-the-art facility in El Salvador. While I had fished in neighboring countries, this was my first visit to El Salvador. I was not prepared for the scale of the operation.

We toured the large warehouses where incoming bales of traceable cotton, sustainably grown and harvested in the U.S., are stored. The bales are broken out, cleaned and stretched into long, rope-like forms that become yarn. The yard is spun and blended with man-made fibers, much of which is made from recycled plastic waste. The material is woven into fabric by vast machines built in Germany and Switzerland, then dyed and cut. Hundreds of people sew and assemble the garments in large, air-conditioned buildings.

The roof of every building is covered in solar panels (Intradeco currently produces 45 percent of its electricity). In addition, bio-waste such as coconut husks are burned to produce energy. All the water used for dying is recycled and reused. The staff is very well-accommodated with all the benefits one expects in a developed nation.

Another advantage is that we are less dependent on Asian manufacturing capabilities, shipping times and trade disputes. Product made in El Salvador is shipped to the US from Honduras. It takes only two days for shipments to arrive in Miami.

The experienced design team at Intradeco is led by Kathy McConville, who has 35 years of experience in this field. Her team of six graphic artists quickly immersed itself in our extensive library of art, designing new product with everyone in mind: men and women, kids and toddlers.

Like Felix and Intradeco, my business is a family affair too. My son, Alex, is on the business side of GHI, and my daughter, Jessica, handles much of the GHOF responsibilities. We are poised for a merchandising renaissance, powered by a 35-year track record of creating the unique marine-wildlife artwork that is the backbone of this brand.

ABOUT MY ORGANIZATIONS

THE GUY HARVEY RESEARCH Institute was formed in 1999 with the assistance of Charlie Forman, his father, Dr. Charles Forman, Dean Richard Dodge at the Nova Southeastern University Oceanographic Center, and NSU President Ray Ferraro.

Having started licensing my art in 1986, it took about 12 years to achieve sufficient royalty income to be able to provide a portion of the proceeds to fund marine research and conservation projects. This was the start of the return to academia. Under the direction of Dr. Mahmood Shivji and his team, we have conducted research on sharks and bony fish around the world. Dr. Brad Wetherbee from the University of Rhode Island has worked with the GHRI team for 20 years. Nowadays most of this effort has been spent close to home around the continental United States, the Caribbean and Central America.

As you will read in this book, the GHRI has collaborated with other leading researchers, conservation organizations, trusts, foundations, colleges, and universities around the world to achieve these aims and goals.

GHRI ACHIEVEMENTS:

Identified new species of billfish (roundscale spearfish).

Discovered that sharks can give virgin birth (parthenogenesis).

Identified new species of scalloped hammerhead shark.

Identified new species of spotted eagle ray.

Provided first quantitative estimate of the number of sharks killed to supply global shark-fin trade.

Invented DNA forensics tool to find illegal shark and billfish body parts in international trade.

Pioneered DNA-forensics investigations to identify seafood fraud.

Identified predictable seasonal migrations of Atlantic tiger sharks.

Provided the first detailed understanding of migration patterns of endangered shortfin mako sharks in the Atlantic Ocean.

Identified overfishing of shortfin mako sharks in the western North Atlantic.

Identified seasonal migrations of oceanic whitetip sharks in the Caribbean.

Identified the season range of whale sharks in the Caribbean and western Atlantic.

Decoded the entire white shark genome, making pioneering discoveries of the genetic adaptations in this species for efficient wound healing and genome stability.

Working on decoding genomes of the mako shark and great hammerhead shark.

GHRI RESEARCH USED TO HELP ESTABLISH/ ENACT:

Bahamas National Shark Sanctuary.

Cayman Islands National Conservation Law, protection of sharks and rays.

US shortfin mako shark protection.

Shortfin mako shark added to CITES Appendix II.

World's longest running WIZ survey at Stingray City, Grand Cayman.

Bermuda Shark Sanctuary.

ABOUT THE GHRI LEADERSHIP TEAM:

Dr. Mahmood Shivji has been the director of the GHRI since 1999. He is a professor of conservation biology at NSU's Halmos College of Natural Sciences and Oceanography in Florida. He's also director of NSU's GHRI and Save Our Seas Shark Research Center. Shivji received his undergraduate degree at Simon Fraser University in Canada, master's degree from the University of California at Santa Barbara, and doctorate from the University of Washington. A faculty member at NSU since 1993, Shivji received the NSU Student Life Achievement (STUEY) Professor of the Year Award in 2006, the Broward Business Alliance World Class Faculty Award in 2007, the NSU President's Distinguished Professor Award in 2012, and the NSU Provost's Research and Scholarship Award in 2017.

Shivji's work through the GHRI and Save Our Seas Shark Research Center integrates high-tech genomics research with fieldwork to study and solve problems pertaining to the management and conservation of sharks, billfishes and

Brad Wetherbee (on left)

Dr. Mahmood Shivji

Bill Boyce (on right)

coral-reef ecosystems, and explore the biodiversity and population dynamics of deep-sea fishes.

His research has appeared in *Time, Newsweek, The Economist, The New York Times, The Washington Post, USA Today, Forbes, National Geographic,* the *Today* show on NBC, *ABC World News,* National Public Radio and the BBC.

Dr. Brad Weatherbee obtained his Bachelor of Science in biology and environmental science at Willamette University in Oregon, followed by graduate school at the University of Miami, undertaking research work on lemon sharks in Bimini.

Weatherbee received his doctorate from the University of Hawaii, where he completed a dissertation on the biochemical and physical adaptations of deep-sea sharks. With acoustic telemetry as his focus, Weatherbee would go on to study sandbar sharks in Delaware Bay, tiger sharks and Galapagos sharks in French Frigate Shoals in the Northwest Hawaiian Islands, and lemon sharks at Atol Roca in Brazil. He has been teaching at the University of Rhode Island since 2001, where he continued his work with the GHRI on the shortfin mako shark, silky shark, and oceanic whitetip shark research projects in Mexico, the United States, and the Caribbean.

The Guy Harvey Ocean Foundation was formed in 2008 to administer fundraising and outreach to support research, education, and conservation of marine resources. The board members of the GHOF have played an important role in helping fund and logistically assist many of these research projects.

The GHOF film team, under the guidance and leadership of George Schellenger, would accompany many field expeditions to document the work, deploy tracking devices, and film marine wildlife for educational documentaries.

GHOF ACHIEVEMENTS:

Funded over $7 million to hundreds of schools, research groups, education programs and conservation groups around the world.

Funded over $700,000 in scholarships for 82 marine biology students.

Produced 19 award-winning long-form documentaries, plus short-form documentaries.

Supported the successful passage of the Billfish Conservation Act.

Supported the successful passage of the Modern Fish Act.

Supported the successful passage of the Kristen Jacobs Ocean Conservation Act (banning shark-fin trade in Florida).

In 2020, GHOF collaborated with Discovery Education, C Palms, Florida Virtual School, Ocean First Foundation, Mission Resolve and Florida's Department of Education to create a marine education curriculum for Florida schools.

In addition to funding these projects, the GHOF has established long-term relationships with several business that now support our research, education and conservation efforts. These include SeaWorld, Norwegian Cruise Line, the Florida Lottery, and the Florida Department of Highway Safety and Motor Vehicles. In the Cayman Islands, our major supporters include the Cayman Islands Brewery, TAG Heuer, the Kenneth B. Dart Foundation, KPMG International, HSBC Holdings, as well as many generous residents, individuals and volunteers.

AWARDS

GUY HARVEY HAS received many awards throughout his career for his contributions to the art, science, fishing, diving and conservation communities. Some notable awards include:

International Game Fish Association
IGFA Lifetime Achievement—1998
Hall of Fame Inductee—2010
In 1998, Guy Harvey was awarded the first-ever IGFA Lifetime Achievement Award from the World Fishing Awards Committee. In 2010, he was officially inducted to the IGFA Fishing Hall of Fame for his contributions to the sport-fishing community.

Society of Animal Artists
Signature Member—1999
The Society of Animal Artists is devoted to promoting excellence in the artistic portrayal of the creatures sharing our planet and to the education of the public through informative art seminars, lectures and teaching demonstrations.

Academy of Underwater Arts & Sciences
NOGI Award—2004
Wyland ICON Award—2009
The NOGI is the oldest and most prestigious award in the diving industry, given to artists, scientists, educators and other distinguished individuals. Guy earned his in the field of art for bringing the majesty of the underwater world to people everywhere.

The Wyland ICON Award recognizes achievements of individuals who exemplify the adventurous spirit of the ocean and inspire others to do the same through their art, research or diving.

Artists for Conservation
Signature Member 2005
Artists for Conservation aims to lead a global artistic movement that inspires individuals and organizations to preserve and sustain our natural heritage by uniting the talent and passion of the world's most gifted nature artists.

International Swimming Hall of Fame
Gold Medallion Award—2010
The International Swimming Hall of Fame Gold Medallion Award is presented each year to a former competitive swimmer for his or her national or international significant achievements in the field of science, entertainment, art, business, education or government.

The Jamaica Committee
Award of Excellence—2010
The Jamaica Committee presented Guy the Award of Excellence for his hands-on commitment to marine sciences, his inspired promotion of the protection of the marine environment and his philanthropy.

Country of Panama
Vasco Nunez de Balboa Grand Officer Order—2010
The Vasco Nunez de Balboa Grand Cross is the highest honor the country of Panama bestows on a non-Panamanian. Guy was presented this award for his work to preserve and publicize Panama's marine resources.

Artists for Conservation
Simon Combes Conservation Award—2011
AFC's Simon Combes Conservation Award is the most prestigious award and highest honor AFC presents to a member artist who has shown artistic excellence and extraordinary contributions to the conservation cause. Guy received this award for his lifetime of dedication to art and conservation.

Newport Beach Film Festival
Special Achievement Award in Environmental Filmmaking —2011
This Is Your Ocean: Sharks, the first in a series of educational documentary films produced by Guy, won the prestigious award from MacGillivray Freeman Films at the 2011 Newport Beach Film Festival in Newport Beach, California. *This Is Your Ocean: Sharks* featured the unique marine environment and spoke about the value of a living shark for ecotourism in the Bahamas.

Nova Southeastern University

President's Award for Excellence in Community Service—2013
H. Wayne Huizenga School of Business and Entrepreneurship Entrepreneur Hall of Fame—2014

The President's Excellence in Community Service Award recognizes superior professional engagement activities in the community by alumni, students, faculty, staff and a member of the South Florida community.

The NSU Entrepreneur Hall of Fame honors the lifetime achievements of outstanding businesspeople in the South Florida community. Guy was presented this award for his success as an entrepreneur and his contributions to educational, social, and other philanthropic organizations.

Florida House on Capitol Hill

Distinguished Artist—2013

The Florida House on Capitol Hill presented the Distinguished Artist Award to Guy for his prolific works of art reflecting Florida's culture and environment.

International Scuba Diving Hall of Fame

Hall of Fame Inductee—2013

ISDHF exists to recognize those who have contributed to the success and growth of recreational scuba diving in the areas of dive travel, entertainment, art, equipment design and development, education, exploration, and adventure.

Caribbean American Heritage Awards

Luminary Award—2013

The Caribbean American Heritage Award is presented by the Institute of Caribbean Studies. The institute works to recognize the outstanding contributions of Caribbean immigrants to the United States.

Elon University

Elon University Medal of Entrepreneurial Leadership—2015
The Elon University Medal for Entrepreneurial Leadership is given to recognize an entrepreneur who is a leader in his or her industry and who exemplifies the values of Elon University, including integrity, innovation and creativity,

passion for lifelong learning, and a commitment to building a dynamic community.

Seafarers' House

Golden Compass Award—2016

The Seafarers' House International Golden Compass Award is awarded annually to individuals who have made significant impacts on the maritime world and the lives of seafarers the world over.

Sea of Change Foundation

Lifetime Explorer Award—2017

The Sea of Change Lifetime Explorer Award honors individuals to celebrate a lifetime of excellence in ocean awareness and exploration.

Florida Southern College

Honorary Chancellor—2018

The honorary chancellor investiture is presented to nationally and internationally recognized artists, scientists, and leaders whose character and careers epitomize the founding mission of Florida Southern College to prepare students to make a positive and consequential impact on the world. Guy was awarded an honorary Doctorate of Humane Letters.

American Friends of Jamaica

International Humanitarian Award—2019

The American Friends of Jamaica honors individuals and organizations that have distinguished themselves by demonstrating leadership in their service to Jamaica, particularly through exemplary contributions in the fields of economic development, philanthropy and strengthening the bonds of friendship between the US and Jamaica.

Broward County (Florida) Sports Hall of Fame

Hall of Fame Inductee—2019

The Broward County Sports Hall of Fame honors and recognizes Broward County residents who have set the standard of excellence and positively affected the county through sports and athletic involvement.

The bull dolphin is the lord of the weed line as well as any flotsam in the open ocean. Many species of fish seek shelter from oceanic predators during their early stages in life, hiding under floating objects while seeking to avoid the attention of voracious dolphin. Under big logs and trees, mini ecosystems thrive in the blue oasis. Mixed media on paper.

INDEX/CREDITS

PHOTO CREDITS

Courtesy Jim Abernethy, 3, 13, 15, 19, 33

Courtesy Aggressor Fleet, 71, 76

Courtesy Neil Hammerschlag, 19

Courtesy International Game Fish Association, 208, 214

Courtesy International Tuna Cup, 182

Jason Washington, 99, 100

Courtesy Bill Watts, 259

EPILOGUE

AS THESE WORDS ARE being written, the final pages of *Guy Harvey's Underwater World* are being shipped to the printer. This is the last of the 340 pages to complete, marking the end of my six-month journey with Guy, who is marking the end of a 20-year journey with this beautiful tome.

Guy has often made cameo appearances in my professional life as the editorial director of *Salt Water Sportsman, Sport Fishing* and *Marlin,* and writer and director of *Sport Fishing Television.* Whether it's serving as an expert source for a feature story, showcasing his images in our magazines, watching episodes of *Portraits from the Deep,* or seeing his large-scale painting in our corporate headquarters every day, Guy has always been somewhere in the mix. This book finally removed those degrees of separation and put us shoulder to shoulder.

This project began like many others in 2020: in a video meeting. Then the rough chapters arrived in bulk—voluminous volumes of moments and memories, detailed down to exact times of day. Browsing through his digital library of artwork revealed the scope of his prolificacy. It turned out that as the world closed down due to COVID-19, the world opened up through Guy's words and images.

Guy could not have been kinder or more enjoyable to work with. We chatted plenty about the book, but we also shared photos from family get-togethers and checked in after Hurricane Eta. On one occasion, we were waiting (perhaps a bit impatiently) for his approval on a layout, only to discover that he was out fishing. But that's Guy—dedicated to the underwater world this book captures so vividly.

I'm grateful for this project, and proud of the final product. And with these last words of *Guy Harvey's Underwater World,* my journey is now complete. However, something tells me that Guy's next journey is already underway.

Shawn Bean
Editor